W9-APM-290

# ANNE LINDSAY'S

# Smart Cooking

# ANNE LINDSAY'S

# Smart Cooking

## Quick and Tasty Recipes for Healthy Living

PUBLISHED IN COOPERATION WITH

Canadian Société
Cancer canadienne
Society du cancer

wiley.com

Copyright © Anne Lindsay and Associates Inc., 1986, 1996, 2002

All rights reserved. The use of any part of this publication reproduced, transmitted in any form or by any means, electronic, mechanical, recording or otherwise, or stored in a retrieval system, without the prior consent of the publisher is an infringement of the copyright law. In the case of photocopying or other reprographic copying of the material, a licence must be obtained from the Canadian Copyright Licensing Agency (CANCOPY) before proceeding.

Canadian Cataloguing in Publication Data

Lindsay, Anne, date.
  Smart cooking : quick and tasty recipes for healthy living

Published in cooperation with the Canadian Cancer Society.
Includes index.

ISBN 0-7715-7389-8

1. Cookery.   2. Cancer – Nutritional aspects.   I. Canadian Cancer Society.   II. Title

TX714.L6748  1996      641.5'63      C96-931518-X

5  6  7  TG  06  05  04  03  02

Cover photograph by Vince Noguchi Photography

Cover photo: Tex-Mex Chili, page 100

Interior photos Italian Vegetable Soup, Thai Honey Chicken, Plum Tart, and Lemon and Fresh Blueberry Tart by Doug Bradshaw/Bradshaw Photography Inc.; interior photos Crudites with Creamy Fresh Dill Dip, Scallops and Shrimp in Wine Bouillon, Pumpkin Raisin Muffins, and Navarin of Lamb by Fred Bird.

Author and Publisher have used their best efforts in preparing this book. Wiley Publishing, Inc., the sponsor, and the author makes no representations or warranties with respect to the accuracy or completeness of the contents of this book and specifically disclaim any implied warranties of merchantability or fitness for a particular purpose. There are no warranties that extend beyond the descriptions contained in this paragraph. No warranty may be created or extended by sales representatives or written sales materials. The accuracy and completeness of the information provided herein and the opinions stated herein are not guaranteed or warranted to produce any specific results, and the advice and strategies contained herein may not be suitable for every individual. Neither Wiley Publishing, Inc., the sponsor, nor the author shall be liable for any loss of profit or any other commercial damages including but not limited to special, incidental, consequential or other damages.

This book is available at special discounts for bulk purchases by your group or organization for sales promotions, premiums, fundraising, and seminars. For details, contact 416-646-7992.

Macmillan Canada
An imprint of Wiley Publishing, Inc.
Toronto, Ontario, Canada

Printed in Canada

# Contents

In memory of my mother,
Marion Grant Elliott
who died of cancer two months before this book
was first published

# Preface and Acknowledgements

S*mart Cooking* was my first cookbook and it's a treasury of my all-time favorite recipes, such as Tex-Mex Chili, Marinated Flank Steak, Chicken Dijon and Salmon Mousse with Dill. So much has happened since the book was published in 1986 that I wanted to write an updated edition in 1996. I wanted to develop some new recipes with the food products available, respond to a taste swing among Canadians, and make the most of a much-improved database for the nutritional analysis of recipes. In this edition I've kept my family treasures and added about 20 recipes. Try the Thai Honey Chicken and Plum Tart— they're the new favorites in our home. All the recipes still meet my criteria of being easy to prepare, tasting great and scoring high in nutrients (vitamins, minerals and fiber), yet being lower in fat.

Over the last fifteen years Canadians have embraced ethnic cuisine. Now our taste buds want stronger flavors and we eat a broader spectrum of foods. We want more pastas, rice and other grain dishes. We want beans and legumes. We continue to want food preparation simplified and dinner on the table in half the time it used to take. To reflect these demands, in 1996 I re-tested many of the recipes and made them even tastier and faster to prepare. And look for Make Ahead information, a feature of each recipe.

When *Smart Cooking* first came out, the amount of fat and fiber in many Canadian food products had not been measured so we had to rely on American data. Now we have a database for nutritional analysis of Canadian foods that shows our beef is much leaner than its American counterpart, and we have lower-fat products such as light mayonnaise and low-fat sour cream available for ingredients. All recipes, charts and tables incorporate the latest information.

The Canadian Cancer Society and Denise Beatty have written an excellent new introduction for 2002, which gives you the latest information on reducing your cancer risk through a healthy diet. It also answers concerns Canadians may have about possible cancer risks in our food. I would like to thank Alison Davis, Colleen Logue, and Cheryl Moyer at the Cancer Society for their dedicated support for this book and for being terrific to work with. I'm pleased to have the opportunity to work with the Cancer Society and delighted that a royalty from the sale of each book will go to that organization.

I'm eternally grateful to Karen Hanley, the Cancer Society volunteer who asked me to write the first cookbook and who worked hard to make it a success. She launched me on a marvelous career of cookbook writing!

I can't begin to tell you how much I appreciate the help from my friend and colleague Shannon Graham. We tested the recipes together for the first edition, and as we measured and stirred we wondered if Canadians would like the bubbly casseroles and spicy cakes we were pulling from the oven as much as we did. We stood back in awe as over 350,000 people have bought the first two editions so far, told their friends about it and ensured its success. Shannon is still hard at work testing recipes with me—thanks, Shannon! Thanks also to recipe testers Dana McCauley and Susan Pacaud. And a huge thanks to Nancy Williams for all the days and nights she worked to take the recipes from my kitchen to manuscript form.

I'm grateful to my publisher, Macmillan Canada, for the success of the first edition and for seeing the necessity of keeping the information current. A special thanks to Bev Renahan and Susan Girvan for their expert editing and to Carol Dombrow for managing the process in 2002. Thanks also to Barbara Selley and Sharyn Joliat for the nutritional analysis and for being such a pleasure to work with. Thanks to Doug Bradshaw, Olga Truchan and Janet Walkenshaw for the beautiful photographs. Thanks to Vince Noguchi for the new cover photo. Thanks to Elizabeth Baird and Daphna Rabinovitch at *Canadian Living* magazine for their help and support.

Above all, thanks to my husband, Bob, for his love, support and for always being there, and to my best critics—Jeff, John and Susie.

Anne Lindsay, 1996, 2002

# Introduction

## *Smart Cooking* in the New Millennium

When *Smart Cooking* was first published, it was a groundbreaking book in several ways. It was the first cookbook aimed at reducing the risk of cancer by encouraging healthy eating and it set the stage for what has now become a thriving market for cookbooks that promote healthy eating. Since its release, more than 350,000 copies of *Smart Cooking* have been sold.

When *Smart Cooking* first appeared in 1986, the idea that diet and cancer may be linked was relatively new. Since then, thousands of studies have concluded that what you eat can have an impact on the risks of developing cancer as well as on other diseases and conditions, including heart disease, stroke, being overweight and obesity.

It's well accepted that the risk of developing some types of cancer can be substantially reduced by adopting healthy eating habits, being physically active, maintaining a healthy weight and not smoking.

The Canadian Cancer Society is committed to promoting healthy eating in a number of ways, including support for publications such as this cookbook. In this edition of *Smart Cooking*, you'll find up-to-date information on the links between diet and cancer risk. Of course, you'll also find Anne Lindsay's delicious and nutritious recipes that use everyday ingredients and are easy to prepare, as well as tips for preparing meals that contribute to healthy eating and healthy living. Read on and enjoy!

## Food, Nutrition and the Prevention of Cancer

Much of what we know about food, nutrition and the prevention of cancer is summarized in a major international report, *Food, Nutrition and the Prevention of Cancer: a global perspective.*[1] Hailed by scientists around the world, this report reviewed more than 4,500 studies and offered new insights into the links between diet and cancer. One of its most important conclusions was that we now know more than enough to dramatically reduce and curb cancer rates.

This report highlights the potential of food-related choices for the prevention of cancer as being:

- eating right, staying physically active and maintaining a healthy weight to reduce cancer risk by 30%-40%;
- combining recommended dietary choices and not smoking to reduce cancer risk by 60%-70%;
- eating the recommended 5 servings of vegetables and fruit each day on its own may reduce cancer rates by 20%.

Wow! These are very significant risk-reduction rates, requiring relatively simple lifestyle choices. In fact, all of the diet-related recommendations included in this report are discussed in these introductory pages, and most of them are covered by the advice given in *Canada's Guidelines for Healthy Eating.*

[1]World Cancer Research Fund. *Food, Nutrition and the Prevention of Cancer: a global perspective.* American Institute for Cancer Research, Washington, 1997. To access a summary of the document go to: *www.aicr.org/report2.htm.*

## CANCER IN CANADA

In Canada, cancer is the second-leading cause of death in men and women. The top three types of cancer resulting in death are:

| For Men | For Women |
|---|---|
| Lung | Lung |
| Prostate | Breast |
| Colorectal | Colorectal |

The Canadian Cancer Society takes the position that as much as 70% of all cancers may be prevented by not smoking, eating a healthy diet and being more physically active. Looking at diet-related factors only, the Canadian Cancer Society estimates that 35% of cancers and 20% of cancer deaths may be related to a combination of poor diet, lack of physical activity and being overweight.

For more specific information about cancer, contact the Canadian Cancer Society's information service toll-free at 1 888 939-3333 or visit its web site: www.cancer.ca.

## THE HEALTHY EATING ADVANTAGE

Although there is widespread agreement that there are links between diet and cancer, some of the suggested relationships between individual dietary factors are controversial. For instance, the role of dietary fat as a major risk factor in breast cancer has not been confirmed by recent studies. Overall, the link between dietary fat and cancer still requires more study.

However there is very strong evidence and widespread support for the findings that a diet high in vegetables and fruit is associated with a lower risk of almost all cancers, and the evidence linking alcohol consumption with cancers of the throat, liver, colon and breast is convincing.

Continuing research needs to be done to sort out the role of individual dietary factors, but until such discoveries are made, the Canadian Cancer Society believes that a healthy eating pattern, being physically active and maintaining a healthy weight are important defenses against cancer.

As part of a healthy eating pattern, emphasis is given to:

- eating more plant-based foods, including vegetables, fruit, legumes and whole grain products;
- consuming less alcohol and salt-preserved and real-smoked foods;
- lowering overall fat intake.

This pattern of eating combined with increased daily physical activity will assist people in achieving and maintaining a healthy weight.

How do you bring these changes about? With a few exceptions, almost all of the cancer-reducing dietary strategies are encompassed in *Canada's Guidelines for Healthy Eating*. These five guidelines are the foundation for establishing a healthy eating pattern and are intended to promote good health overall and to help reduce your risk of cancer and other diseases such as heart disease and stroke.

# Canada's Guidelines For Healthy Eating

- Enjoy a VARIETY of foods.
- Emphasize cereals, breads, other grain products, vegetables and fruits.
- Choose lower-fat dairy products, leaner meats and foods prepared with little or no fat.
- Achieve and maintain a healthy body weight by enjoying regular physical activity and healthy eating.
- Limit salt, alcohol and caffeine.

There is nothing difficult about healthy eating. It's simply a common-sense approach to food and eating. With *Anne Lindsay's Smart Cooking* in hand, you'll have all the help you need to adopt the healthier habits recommended by the Canadian Cancer Society.

Before getting to the recipes, take some time to understand each of *Canada's Guidelines for Healthy Eating* and what each guideline means to reducing cancer risk.

## GUIDELINE # 1: ENJOY A VARIETY OF FOODS

This first guideline urges you to include different kinds of foods in your diet, to prepare them in different ways and to avoid eating the same combinations, week in and week out.

By including a variety of foods in your diet, chances are you'll get all of the nutrients needed for good health, in the right amounts. Eating a varied diet also gives you a better chance of keeping fat, salt and caffeine to moderate levels.

What's more, variety increases the likelihood that your diet will contain the anti-oxidant vitamins and minerals and natural plant chemicals (phytochemicals) that play a role in reducing cancer risk.

### Eating a Variety of Foods is Simple!

- The easiest way to eat a variety of foods is to plan your day's meals around the four major food groups recommended by *Canada's Food Guide to Healthy Eating*: grain products; vegetables and fruits; milk products; meat and alternatives.[2]
- Take advantage of the marvelous range of foods available in Canada. When fruits and vegetables are in season, buy locally grown foods. When winter sets in, enjoy frozen or canned vegetables and fruit, 100% vegetable or fruit juice or choose from the wide range of imported fresh produce.
- Put something other than apples and bananas in your fruit bowl. What about fresh pears, plums, kiwifruit or mango? Make a fruit salad starting with canned pineapple, adding whatever fresh fruit you have on hand. Add new vegetables to your list of favorites. Have vegetables such as broccoli, cauliflower, red cabbage, yams or sweet potatoes more often.
- Grains are great for variety. Buy different kinds of breads. Replace plain rice with brown rice, bulgur, cracked wheat, barley, couscous or a rice and lentil mixture. Enjoy enriched pasta of different shapes and colors.
- Try new recipes. Experiment with new foods or new combinations. Try foods and the cooking methods from different cultures. Set a goal to add one new food or dish to your menu each week.

[2]*Canada's Food Guide to Healthy Eating* builds on *Canada's Guidelines for Healthy Eating* by providing information on what and how much to eat from each of the food groups. For a copy of *Canada's Food Guide to Healthy Eating*, contact your Canadian Cancer Society office or your local public health unit (listed in the blue pages of your phone book) or download it from Health Canada's web site at *www.hc-sc.gc.ca*.

### To Supplement or Not

As our knowledge of the potential health benefits from vitamins, minerals and phytochemicals grows, it begs the question whether daily supplements should be taken. Although studies are often designed to analyse one component of food such as fiber, when you study food it is difficult to isolate one specific component from other factors in the food. So are the benefits being studied solely from the fiber? Or did some other vitamin, mineral or phytochemical play a part? Maybe it was an interaction that produced the end result.

The point is we just don't know for sure at this time. More research is needed. What we do know from over 4,500 studies is that plant foods contain a myriad of substances that are good for health in general and are powerful agents in reducing cancer risk. That's why food sources, not supplements, are promoted. Besides, there's no supplement in the world that can give you the thousands of phytochemicals (estimated to be around 4,000) that are found in vegetables, fruit and whole grains!

## GUIDELINE # 2: EMPHASIZE CEREALS, BREADS, OTHER GRAIN PRODUCTS, VEGETABLES AND FRUITS

The underlying message in this guideline is to shift the focus of your eating habits away from a traditional diet that favors protein-rich, higher-fat foods, to one that contains more plant foods—vegetables, fruit, grain products and legumes.

### The Power of Vegetables and Fruit in Cancer Prevention

The report by the American Institute for Cancer Research, *Food, Nutrition and the Prevention of Cancer: a global perspective*, concluded that simply eating the recommended 5 servings a day of vegetables and fruit could, by itself, reduce cancer rates more than 20%. This recommendation stems from the fact that plant foods contain vitamins, minerals, phytochemicals and fiber that have anti-cancer effects. As well, diets high in vegetables, fruit, grains and legumes tend to be lower in calories and fat, which may help people achieve and maintain a healthy body weight, reducing another risk factor for cancer.

---

**THE POWER OF PLANT FOODS**

Here are just a few of the components of plant foods that may have anti-cancer effects:

- **Carotenoids** such as beta-carotene found in orange vegetables, **lycopene** found in red and pink vegetables and fruit and **vitamin C** in citrus fruit are all antioxidant compounds that protect cells from the damaging effects of oxygen-containing molecules called free radicals. Free radicals are unstable molecules that try to oxidize other molecules and in doing so, damage or destroy cells. If left unchecked by antioxidants, more cells get damaged, which is thought to be one of the beginning stages of cancer growth.
- **Selenium**, a mineral found in small amounts in many vegetables, functions in combination with an enzyme to prevent oxygen damage of cells.
- **Lutein** in green leafy vegetables functions as an antioxidant that blocks damage caused by free radicals.
- **Flavonoids** such as **quercetin** and **kaempferol** in vegetables, fruit, tea and wine function as antioxidants; quercetin may reduce cell growth.
- **Isothiocyanates** and **dithiolthiones** in broccoli, cauliflower, Brussels sprouts and cabbage detoxify cancer-causing compounds.
- **Isoflavones** in soybean-based foods are weak phytoestrogens that compete with estrogen for binding-to-estrogen receptors and in doing so may reduce risk of estrogen-promoted breast cancer.
- **Fiber**, which is in all vegetables, fruit, whole grain products and legumes, is thought to reduce the time and opportunity that cancer-causing compounds have to react with colorectal tissues by keeping bowels regular.

---

### *5 to 10 A Day—Are You Getting Enough?*

The compelling evidence linking higher intakes of vegetables and fruit to a reduced risk of almost all cancers as well as of heart disease has given rise to a national health campaign, 5 to 10 A Day—Are You Getting Enough? As one of the partners in the campaign, the Canadian Cancer Society is aiming to raise awareness and encourage people to eat more vegetables and fruit daily.

#### TEN TIPS TO GO BY

With a little planning, it's easy to get your daily quota of 5 to 10 servings of vegetables and fruit. If you have any doubts, try any five of these ten tips!

1. Aim for two servings of fruits and vegetables at each meal.
2. Make at least one of your snacks a vegetable or fruit snack. Try baby carrots with a creamy, low-fat dip; have a glass of tomato juice; don't leave home without a fruit in your briefcase, purse or knapsack.
3. Have a glass of juice or fresh fruit at breakfast.
4. Add sliced banana or apricots or raisins to your cereal.
5. Enjoy a green salad for lunch, with added veggies, such as carrots, cauliflower or peppers.
6. Comfort yourself with a big bowl of vegetable soup—tomato, minestrone, broccoli or onion.
7. Add vegetables to your sandwiches—lettuce, tomatoes, thinly-sliced onions and peppers.
8. Keep fruit washed and ready to eat in a bowl that's within easy reach—on the counter or table.
9. Add extra veggies such as peas or corn to casseroles and stews.
10. Visualize your dinner plate: half of it should be covered by vegetables; one-quarter by grain products (pasta, rice) and one-quarter by meat or alternatives (lean meat, poultry, fish or legumes).

---

**WHAT'S A SERVING?**
- A medium-sized vegetable or fruit
- 1/2 cup/125mL juice (a juice box is 2 servings' worth)
- 1/2 cup/125mL diced vegetable or fruit
- 1 cup/250mL salad
- 1/4 cup/50 mL dried fruit

---

#### TIPS FOR COOKING VEGETABLES

Some vitamins are destroyed by heat; others dissolve in cooking water. To best preserve vitamins:

- cook vegetables quickly until just tender crisp;
- use cooking methods that require little or no liquid: microwaving, baking, steaming or stir-frying using a small amount of oil;
- use as little water as possible and bring it to a boil before adding vegetables;
- use any leftover cooking liquid in soups or stews.

### *Aim for* 25 to 35 grams of Fiber a Day

*Canada's Guidelines for Healthy Eating* recommends including more dietary fiber in your diet. In addition to the 5 to 10 servings of vegetables and fruit daily, pay attention to these ideas for increasing fiber intake:

- Buy whole-grain foods as much as possible: whole-wheat bread, whole-rye bread, brown rice, whole-grain cereals and crackers. Check the list of ingredients on packages to ensure that the first few ingredients are indeed whole grains.
- Check out the Nutrition Facts box for the fiber content of breakfast cereal. Choose cereals with at least 4 grams of fiber per serving or choose a higher fiber cereal to mix with your usual cereal. See **Label Watch—Fiber,** below, for more information on what fiber content claims mean.
- Try brown rice or kasha from cracked wheat as an alternative to potatoes and pasta.
- Legumes such as canned baked beans or split pea or lentil soup make a great meatless meal. Legumes are the matured, dried seeds of beans, peas and lentils. For easy preparation, buy canned legumes instead of the dried form.
- Try adding chick-peas to salad, lentils to your favorite meat loaf, extra kidney beans to chili and refried beans to tacos and burritos.
- Nuts and seeds are also good sources of fiber. These foods are also high in calories and fat, so they may not be a good choice if you are trying to lose weight.
- See Appendix C for a list of recipes that are high and very high in fiber.

---

**WHAT ARE THE LEGUMES?**
- Beans: black, white, kidney, lima, navy, garbanzo (chick-peas)
- Peas: yellow and green split peas
- Lentils: red and green lentils.

---

### *Label Watch—Fiber*

By law, foods labeled as sources of fiber must meet these standards:

- *Source of fiber*—a serving of a food must contain 2 grams or more of fiber.
- *High source of fiber*—a serving must contain 4 grams or more of fiber.
- *Very high source of fiber*—a serving must contain 6 grams or more of fiber.

Since fiber is a positive feature of food a manufacturer may emphasize the fiber content by making a nutrient claim on the package front. Be careful though, since some foods high in fiber may also be high in fat. The healthiest sources of fiber are lower in fat too.

## GUIDELINE #3: CHOOSE LOWER FAT MILK PRODUCTS, LEANER MEATS AND FOODS PREPARED WITH LITTLE OR NO FAT

This guideline is aimed at reducing fat intake and is in keeping with the Canadian Cancer Society's advice to adopt a lower-fat diet.

Higher-fat diets have been associated with several cancers, including prostate, ovarian and endometrial, but the suggested links between fat intake and breast and colorectal cancer are very controversial at this time. It may be that higher-fat intakes are indirectly linked to higher risks of cancer by contributing to higher energy (calorie) intakes and being overweight. Being overweight and obesity are linked to various cancers, including endometrial cancer, breast cancer in postmenopausal women and bowel cancer in men.

### What's a Healthy Fat Intake?

The emphasis for reducing cancer risk is on eating less fat in total. For the average Canadian, fat should provide 30% or less of the day's calories.

In grams of fat, this means about:

- 90 grams of fat or less for a man age 24-49
- 65 grams of fat or less for a woman age 24-49

Since a healthy fat intake is based on your calorie needs, the amount of fat that is healthy for you can vary with your age and activity.

Younger people and highly active adults who need more calories may be able to eat a little more fat. Older adults and less active people whose daily calorie needs are below this average should aim for a little less fat than is shown here.

### Everyday Ways to Cut back on Fat

Most Canadians can reduce their fat intake to a healthy range by making a few changes in the way they shop, cook and prepare foods. For the average man, age 24-49, a cut-back of 25 grams of fat will bring fat intakes to healthy levels; for a woman of the same age, a cut-back of just 15 grams will do.

Use the Nutrition Facts box on package labels to compare products and make lower-fat choices. It's amazing how easy it is to cut fat from your daily diet. And when eating out at chain restaurants, ask if there is a brochure giving the nutrient breakdown of the menu items offered.

Here are some examples of simple, everyday ways to cut back on total fat:

| CURRENT PRACTICE | ACTION |
| --- | --- |
| You drink 2 glasses of 2% milk a day (10 g fat). | Switch to 1% milk and cut out 4 g of fat. |
| A recipe for 12 muffins calls for 1/2 c/125mL butter or margarine (96 g fat/recipe and 8 g fat/ muffin). | Cut the fat in the recipe by just 2 tbsp/30mL and save 2 g of fat/muffin. |
| You buy lean meat, but you eat 6 ounces. | Reduce the portion size to the recommended 2-3 ounces (50-100 g) and cut out about 9 g of fat for beef, pork and lamb and about 5 g of fat for poultry. |
| You drink only 2 cups of coffee a day, but you like double cream in both. | Switch from cream to 2% milk and cut out about 6 g of fat. Think about what this means if you drink more than 2 cups of coffee a day! |
| Everyone at your house loves pizza and you order in once a week. | Choose a vegetarian pizza with cheese instead of pizza with "the works" and extra cheese, and cut out approximately 13 g of fat for every 2 slices. |
| You like a croissant sandwich for lunch. | Choose almost any other bun and cut out at least 9 g of fat! |

### Shopping and cooking tips for lower-fat eating

- Use the lower fat recipes in this book and apply the ideas for lower-fat cooking to your favourite recipes.
- Buy milk products with 2% or less milk fat (M.F.). The % fat is always on the label.
- Buy lower-fat cheeses (15-20% M.F. or less) for daily use and keep the richer cheeses (30% M.F. or more) for special occasions.
- These days, most cuts of meat are quite lean but avoid the higher-fat processed meats such as sausages, salami, bologna and wieners. Try to include more fish and legumes in your diet.

- Buy fewer prepared foods that are fried or breaded. Check out the Nutrition Facts box on food packages for the fat content and use this information to choose healthier foods.
- Reduce the amount of baked goods and snack items that you buy. Choose lower-fat cookies such as arrowroot biscuits, social teas, gingersnaps or fig Newton-type cookies. Pretzels and popcorn are lower-fat alternatives to chips, cheese-flavored snacks or corn chips.
- To sauté vegetables for making soups and stews, use a nonstick pan and reduce the fat called for by half (1/2 tsp/5-10 mL will do). Add a few tablespoons of water, white wine or stock and cook the vegetables slowly, covered, over low heat. This method brings out the flavors and cooks the onions or other vegetables just as effectively as the traditional method.
- If oil (sesame and extra virgin olive are best) or butter is required for flavor in a stir-fry or pasta sauce, measure a small amount and add it just before serving. Using nonstick or heavy pans is one of the best ways to cut down on the amount of fat used without having food burn or stick.
- Instead of vegetables with a cream sauce, serve a vegetable purée such as Parsnip Purée (page 172) or make a creamy sauce using 2% milk instead of cream and half the usual amount of butter or margarine.
- When cooking meats and poultry, drain fat during cooking. Make meat soups and stews a day in advance and refrigerate overnight. Fat solidifies on top and can be easily lifted off.
- When roasting meat or chicken, use a rack in the roasting pan so that the meat will not be sitting in fat.
- Reduce or omit oil in standard marinades. (See Marinated Leg of Lamb with Coriander, page 110, or Marinated Flank Steak, page 98.)
- If you're making muffins, cakes or other rich desserts, compare recipes for fat or oil content, and choose the one with the lowest amount.
- Use dessert recipes calling for cocoa rather than chocolate, as long as the recipe with cocoa doesn't call for large amounts of fat.

## GUIDELINE # 4: ACHIEVE AND MAINTAIN A HEALTHY BODY WEIGHT BY ENJOYING REGULAR PHYSICAL ACTIVITY AND HEALTHY EATING

This guideline highlights the importance of a healthy weight to overall well-being. Long-term studies show that overweight people are at greater risk for many diseases, including cancers of the endometrium, breast (in postmenopausal women), gallbladder and bile duct.

Being overweight (BMI over 27) and obesity (BMI over 30) is reaching epidemic proportions in Canada, with 57% of adult men and 41% of adult women being overweight or obese.[3]

### What is a Healthy Weight?

A healthy body weight is a weight *range* (not one ideal weight) appropriate for a particular height and body build. It is a weight at which you will:

- be at lower risk for weight-related health problems;
- feel healthy and energetic; and
- feel fit and flexible.

A healthy weight shouldn't be confused with being pencil thin. Being too thin or constantly trying to get thin using one diet after another is not healthy either—physically or emotionally.

---

[3]Macdonald, S.M., Reeder, B.A., Chen, Y., et al. "Obesity in Canada: a descriptive analysis." Can. Med. Assoc. J. 1997: 157 (1suppl): s3-s9.

### *How healthy is your weight?*

The healthiness of your weight is measured using the Body Mass Index, commonly known as the BMI. The BMI is designed for people ages 20-65, not for use with babies, children, adolescents, pregnant or nursing women, older adults or highly muscular people. To find out what your BMI is and to help you establish a realistic healthy weight range for yourself, turn to Appendix A.

### *Losing Weight Successfully*

There is no magic way to lose weight. If there were, this nation wouldn't have the weight problem it does and all the quick-weight-loss schemes would be out of business. What seems to work best in the long run is a combination of daily physical activity and lower-calorie healthy eating.

### *Becoming More Physically Active*

There are many weight experts who believe that people become overweight not from over-eating but from lack of physical activity. The advantages of being more physically active go beyond weight control alone. You'll feel better, stronger, less stressed and more energetic, and enjoy better heart health and a reduced risk of several cancers including colorectal, breast and possibly prostate.

---

**HOW DO YOU BECOME MORE PHYSICALLY ACTIVE?**

*Canada's Physical Activity Guide to Healthy Active Living* from Health Canada says that to stay healthy and improve health you need to accumulate at least 60 minutes a day of light physical activity, such as walking or gardening. You don't have to do 60 minutes at once—10-minute periods of activity can be added up throughout the day.

As you progress to moderate activities such as brisk walking or biking, 30-60 minutes is sufficient and with vigorous activities such as jogging or aerobics, 20-30 minutes will do.

The type of physical activity should vary throughout the week:

- Participate in endurance activities such as walking or cycling 4-7 times a week for the health of heart, lungs and circulatory system.
- Aim for flexibility activities such as yard work, T'ai Chi or yoga 4-7 times a week to keep muscles relaxed and joints mobile.
- Work on strength activities such as heavy yard work or weight training routines 2-4 times a week to keep muscles strong and bones healthy.

Great ways to become more physically active:

- Garden
- Join the kids for basketball
- Play Frisbee
- Run with the dog
- Snowshoe
- Walk...every day!

- Go for a hike
- Kick a soccer ball around
- Ride your bike
- Skate
- Swim

---

### *Tips to Help You Be Successful*

- Make an exercise plan outlining what you want to do and when you're going to do it. Put it on paper. Make up a progress chart to keep yourself on track.
- Choose activities you like to do and can do comfortably. Signing up for an advanced aerobics class when you haven't exercised in years can be very frustrating and discouraging. If you're overweight, try walking to start off. Incorporate physical activity into your daily routine. Walk on your lunch hour; swim if you're near a pool; join a walk program in the local mall; attend an aerobics class that you can catch on the way home from work.

- Join up with a friend if it's helpful and more fun. But don't allow your activity time to become totally dependent on someone else's schedule. Your goal is to be more physically active every day, whether or not you have a friend along.

### Lower-Calorie Healthy Eating for Weight Loss

- Follow the basic principles of healthy eating described in these introductory pages, giving emphasis to lower-calorie and lower-fat choices. *Canada's Food Guide to Healthy Eating* can give you guidance on the number and size of servings to eat.
- Watch portion sizes—big bagels, oversized muffins and super-size fries and beverages make it easy to over-eat without realising it.
- Eat when you're hungry but stop before becoming too full. Fruit, lower-fat yogurt or a light hot chocolate are good choices for snacks between meals.
- Avoid the high-calorie, high-fat snack foods such as chips, cookies and snacking crackers.
- Track what you eat—weighing and measuring servings to make sure your portions are in line with *Canada's Food Guide* recommendations. Research shows that people almost always underestimate what they eat.
- Use the Nutrition Facts box on package labels to compare foods and choose items that are lower in calories and fat.

## GUIDELINE #5: LIMIT SALT, ALCOHOL AND CAFFEINE

This guideline advises a moderate intake of salt, alcohol and caffeine because excessive use of any of these substances is not healthy.

### Salt

Salt is a major source of sodium, a mineral linked to high blood pressure in some people. There is also evidence linking a very high intake of salt with stomach cancer. However, this finding relates mostly to people who eat a lot of salt-preserved foods such as salted cod or pork. The salt intake of the average Canadian is unlikely to be a risk factor for stomach cancer.

For all-round good health consider these tips for keeping your salt intake in check:

- Use pepper, hot pepper sauces, flavored vinegars, herbs and spices to flavor foods instead of reaching for the salt shaker.
- Remove the salt shaker from the table, but leave the pepper handy for a final touch of flavor.
- Use either half or none of the amount of salt called for in recipes.
- Cook from scratch as much as possible. Convenience items such as casseroles and dinner helper mixes, rice mixes, many frozen meals, canned foods and entrées are typically high in salt.
- Avoid eating a lot of salty snack foods and salted crackers.
- Avoid eating frequently at fast-food restaurants. Fast food is notoriously high in salt, even the items that are fat- and calorie-reduced.

### Alcohol

Most people know that alcohol in excess is not good for their health. Alcohol is known to damage the liver, lead to problems of the nervous system, promote high blood pressure and increase the risk of developing certain cancers. Of the dietary factors linked to an increased risk of cancer, the evidence is strongest for alcohol. Alcohol in large amounts increases the risk of breast cancer and cancers of the mouth, larynx, throat and esophagus. The risks linked to alcohol intake are sometimes greater in people who also smoke.

If you choose to drink alcohol, drink in moderation. Low-risk drinking guidelines[4] advise:

- no more than 2 standard drinks on any day; and
- limit weekly intake to 14 or fewer if you are a man, and 9 or fewer if you are a woman.

A standard drink is:

- 12 oz/341 mL or one bottle of beer (5% alcohol);
- 4-5 oz/141 mL wine (12% alcohol); or
- 1 1/2oz/45mL spirits (40% alcohol).

### *Caffeine*

Caffeine may bring on anxiety and irritability and keep you awake at night but there is no evidence that it causes serious harm in the amounts currently consumed.

Methylene chloride, a solvent commonly used to remove the caffeine from coffee and tea, has been the focus of ongoing safety concerns. Only small traces of methylene chloride, if any at all, are detected in decaffeinated beverages. These trace levels are considered harmless. A process that uses water to remove caffeine is growing in popularity, and products decaffeinated in this way are widely available.

## Cancer Issues In the News

### YOUR DIET: KNOW THE RISKS

Consumer polls show that the public is very concerned about the health effects of food additives, agricultural chemicals and environmental pollutants that affect the food chain. However, cancer experts maintain that concern about "chemicals" is not proportional to the actual risk. It is the more common aspects of a person's diet and lifestyle that pose the greatest cancer risks, including:

- not enough vegetables, fruit, whole grains and legumes;
- too much dietary fat;
- too much alcohol;
- too many calories, leading to obesity; and
- lack of physical activity.

Health-related reports appear almost daily in the media; it's difficult sometimes to keep them all in perspective. To help you deal with these "overdoses of information," remember the following points.

### *Don't believe everything you read (or hear)!*

The media like to be the first to report "new findings." Unfortunately, these reports can create false hopes or unfounded fears. Some key questions to ask yourself about these reports are:

- Do these "new findings" come from only one study? It usually takes many studies and years of research before definite conclusions can be drawn.
- If there were other studies done, what did they conclude?
- Are recognized health organizations such as the Canadian Cancer Society issuing statements supporting the findings?

[4]Centre for Addiction and Mental Health, 33 Russell St. Toronto, Canada, M5S 2S1. Endorsed by The College of Family Physicians of Canada and The Canadian Centre on Substance Abuse.

## *Life is a risky business*

This introduction has suggested many positive strategies for reducing the risk of cancer. No food or habit can be described as "no risk" or "zero risk." That's because there is no such thing as "no risk," just as there is no such thing as "absolute safety."

In truth, our food supply contains potential threats to our health. Many exist as natural components in food; others come from additives or environmental pollutants. But our food is also full of anticancer agents and protective factors. More research will help clarify these issues. In the meantime, take action on the dietary factors that we know now will have the most potential to pay off in better health!

## *The dose makes the poison*

There is a saying in science that the dose makes the poison: most things are safe in small amounts but can be harmful in larger amounts. Take vitamins, minerals and dietary fat, for example. All are absolutely essential to life in small amounts but pose a risk to health in larger amounts. The same goes for toxic substances in food, whether they occur naturally, are added in the manufacturing process or are a result of contamination. The tiny amounts normally found in food are harmless, although in large amounts they may be quite harmful.

## COMMON Q & AS

### ARE ORGANIC FOODS ANY HEALTHIER?

Organic food production may be protective of the environment, but there's not much of a nutritional advantage for you. Organic meats are not lower in fat or necessarily lower in chemical residues. Tests of Canadian meat show that both organic and non-organic meats are free of chemical residues. Organically grown produce is the same as non-organic produce in both fiber and vitamin content; both types of produce are exposed to similar environmental pollutants and both contain natural toxic substances such as nitrates. When pesticide residues have been detectable on non-organically grown foods, the amounts have been very small.

### WORRIED ABOUT PESTICIDES ON FRUIT AND VEGETABLES?

Like the natural toxic substances in food, traces of pesticides are not considered a health risk. Canadian authorities spot-check all imported and locally grown produce for pesticide residues. Typically, less than 2% of fresh produce is found to contain residue levels in excess of acceptable limits.

To ensure clean, healthy produce:

- Wash all fresh fruit and vegetables under clean, running tap water. Washing with soap is not needed.
- Throw away outer leaves of cabbages and lettuces.
- Peel fruit and vegetables that have inedible skins.
- Scrub edible skins such as potatoes and carrots to clean well.

### DO NITRITE-CURED FOODS INCREASE CANCER RISK?

The consumption of nitrite-cured foods may increase the risk of stomach cancer for people in some countries, but is not a high-risk factor for Canadians. In Canada, very small amounts of nitrites are used in the preservation of some meats (ham, bacon and luncheon and deli meats) to prevent botulism, a deadly form of food poisoning. In addition, Canadian nitrite-cured meats usually contain vitamin C or erythrobate, a form of vitamin C. Vitamin C is known to block the conversion of nitrite to nitrosamines, the chemical that is actually associated with the increased cancer risk. You can lower any risk associated with these foods by eating plenty of fruit and vegetables rich in vitamin C. Aside from the nitrites, the high fat content of meats such as bacon, salami, sausages and bologna is reason enough to cut down on the consumption of these foods.

### IS IT SAFE TO BARBECUE?
Yes it is, provided you follow these sensible tips:

- Variety, as promoted in these healthy eating guidelines, applies to how you prepare foods too. All forms of high-temperature cooking pose some cancer risk. Barbecuing, pan-frying, broiling and roasting at high temperatures are fine on occasion—but not every day. Cook meat more safely by braising, simmering and roasting at low temperatures.
- Choose the leanest of meats, fish and poultry to barbecue. This will reduce exposure to cancer-causing chemicals that are in the smoke created by burning fat. Raise the grill as far from the coals as possible or cook at medium temperature to discourage flare-ups and smoking. For foods that require a longer cooking time, you can reduce the amount of time that foods are in contact with heat by either precooking in a microwave or wrapping food in foil for most of the grilling time.
- Browning or charring of foods on the barbecue, in a frying pan or in the oven should be avoided. Crispy surfaces will be loaded with substances called polycyclic aromatic hydrocarbons or PAHs. These are the cancer-causing chemicals associated with high-temperature cooking methods.

### WHAT ABOUT SMOKED FOODS?
Foods such as ham and salmon that are preserved by real wood smoking carry a risk similar to that of barbecued foods. Canadians who eat a lot of real smoked foods are at a higher risk for cancer. This advice does not apply to so-called smoked foods that are flavored with liquid smoke. Liquid smoke does not contain PAHs and appears to pose no health risk.

### DO FOOD ADDITIVES CAUSE CANCER?
It is very unlikely. Food additives are subjected to safety testing before they are even considered for approval by Health Canada. Once approved and in use, food additives are continuously monitored and reviewed for adverse reactions and hazards. If at any time the safety of a food additive is shown to be harmful, the additive is removed from the market.

### ISN'T OUR WATER FILLED WITH CANCER-CAUSING CHEMICALS?
The majority of scientists involved in monitoring water quality feel that our water poses no risk to health at this time. However, these same scientists urge Canadians to watch for news regarding continuing safety of drinking water. Public water supplies aren't as pure as they once were. Environmental pollutants are showing up in water tests, although the dangers and long-term effects of these chemicals are not yet clear. Fear about the safety of tap water has driven many people to turn to bottled water or water filtering systems in the belief that these are safer water sources. But these alternatives aren't necessarily safer, say health authorities. Bottled water, which does not fall under any regulatory guidelines, is only as good as the ground that it comes from. In some tests, bottled water has been found to contain undesirable components that are different but just as plentiful as those in municipal tap water. Home water treatment devices are not risk-free either. Some can't even remove the chemicals that pose a potential threat. And dirty filters can release previously removed chemicals back into the water or expose the water to bacterial contamination.

The bottom line? If you have concerns about potential bacterial contamination of the water supply, contact your local Public Health Department. It is responsible for issuing statements about local water. Unless you are advised by public health officials to avoid the municipal water supply, it is probably a safe beverage.

There you have it: answers to common questions about food and the risk of cancer. As issues come and go in the media, remember that a sensible approach to healthy eating is one of your best defenses against cancer. *Canada's Guidelines for Healthy Eating* will help you on your way to a healthier pattern of eating and living.

For more information on nutrition, healthy eating and cooking, contact a dietitian or nutritionist working in:

- the local public health department;
- a community health center;
- a local hospital or cancer clinic;
- a provincial ministry of health or social services;
- the Canadian Cancer Society (1-888-939-3333; *www.cancer.ca*); or
- other health organizations such as the Heart and Stroke Foundation (*www.heartandstroke.ca*) or the Canadian Diabetes Association (*www.diabetes.ca*).

## Planning for Healthy Eating

It is one thing to understand the importance of healthy eating but another challenge altogether to make healthy eating happen in your life. The most noble of intentions are quickly dashed when you arrive home from work pooped at 7:00 PM, and no one feels like cooking and there is no food for a throw-together meal.

If you're serious about healthy eating, a little menu planning in advance goes a long way to keep your good intentions on track. It may sound a little tedious but it takes about 15 minutes maximum to map out your meals for a week. Once you've got your meals planned, shopping and food preparation is much easier and you always have what you need on hand. The only time you'll need to order pizza or Chinese food is when you really want it!

Here are the basics for menu planning:

- Plan your menus using *Canada's Food Guide to Healthy Eating*, which gives you an idea of what foods and how much of each food you need each day. If you don't have a copy of the Food Guide, call your local Cancer Society Office or local health unit for a free copy. You can also view it or download it from Health Canada's web site at *www.hc-sc.gc.ca*.
- In short what you're aiming for each day is:
  - 5-12 servings of grain products
  - 5-10 servings of vegetables and fruit
  - 2-4 servings of milk products
  - 2-3 servings of meat and alternatives

Whether you choose the number of servings in the lower, middle or upper range of the group depends on your age, life stage, gender (in the case of milk products) and how many calories you need. Most women and children have lower calorie needs than teen boys and men, and so need fewer servings of most foods, with the exception of milk products.

- For menu planning, the servings from each group are spread throughout the course of the day as shown in the menu planning chart (pages 16–17). You can either photo enlarge this chart with a copier or replicate it by hand to use in your own planning. All you have to do is fill in what foods your family is going to eat for each day of the week.

- From this weekly menu, prepare a grocery list. Shop once and be done with it!

Menu planning for a day or the week is the big picture. On pages 16–17, Anne shows you how a few meals shape up from a nutrient perspective. With the sample menus provided, you will see where the fat and fiber in a meal comes from.

## Shopping for Healthy Eating–Nutrition Labeling

### SHOPPING FOR HEALTHY FOOD IS GETTING EASIER ALL THE TIME

As this cookbook goes to press, the federal government is about to usher in new nutrition labeling regulations that will help consumers choose foods that meet their needs for healthy eating. The new regulations will make Canadian nutrition labels look more like US food labels.

Some of the key features of nutrition labeling are:

- Nutrition labeling will be mandatory (it was voluntary) on most prepackaged foods. Foods exempt from labeling include: vegetables and fruit, fresh meats, deli counter meats and cheeses, restaurant foods and foods made and sold in small shops such as bakeries.
- Nutrition information will be presented in a box called Nutrition Facts. There are three formats for the box but they are similar enough that it will be easy to compare the nutrition contents of one product with another.
- Calories plus the content of 13 other nutrients must be presented in the Nutrition Facts box in a standard way.

```
Nutrition  Facts
Per 1 cup (264g)
───────────────────────────────
Amount                % Daily Value
───────────────────────────────
Calories 260
───────────────────────────────
Fat 13g                        20%
───────────────────────────────
  Saturated Fat 3g
  + Trans Fat 2g               25%
───────────────────────────────
Cholesterol 30mg
───────────────────────────────
Sodium 660mg                   28%
───────────────────────────────
Carbohydrate 31g               10%
───────────────────────────────
  Fibre 0g                      0%
───────────────────────────────
  Sugars 5g
───────────────────────────────
Protein 5g
───────────────────────────────
Vitamin A 4%  •  Vitamin C 2%
Calcium 15%  •  Iron 4%
```

- Serving sizes for a food category will be set, making serving sizes realistic and allowing for an easier comparison between products.
- A new feature of the Nutrition Label will be the *% Daily Value* of the nutrients. This indicates what percentage of the recommended intake for a given nutrient you're getting when you eat a serving of that food. The *% Daily Value* tells you if you're getting a lot or just a little of a nutrient.
- Nutrient content claims such as "low in energy" (energy means calories), "low in fat" or "high source of fiber" will be strictly defined so you can be assured that the claim always means the same thing. For instance, a "low in fat" claim on a label will always mean that a serving contains 3 grams or less of fat. If a product claims that it is a "very high source of fiber," you will be assured that a serving of that food provides 6 grams or more of fiber.

## Planning for Healthy Eating    Week:_____

| MEALS<br><br>Legend: **GP** – Grain Products   **V&F** – Vegetables & Fruit<br>**MP** – Milk Products   **M&A** – Meat & Alternatives | Sunday | Monday |
|---|---|---|
| **BREAKFAST PATTERN**<br><br>**1-3+ servings GP**<br>**1-3+ servings V&F**<br>**1 serving MP**<br>**1 serving M&A**<br><br>*Sample Menu for a Woman\*:*<br>   1/2 c/125 mL juice (1 V&F)<br>   1 c/250 mL ready-to-eat oat bran cereal (1 GP) with 1/4 c/50mL with<br>      chopped apricots (1 V&F)<br>   1/2 c/125 mL milk (1/2 MP)<br>   *\*The number of servings chosen depends on the age, sex, activity level of the person<br>    but the pattern is the same for everyone.* | | |
| **LUNCH PATTERN**<br><br>**2-3+ servings GP**<br>**2-3+ servings V&F**<br>**1 serving MP**<br>**1 serving M&A**<br><br>*Sample Menu for a Woman:*<br>   Tuna sandwich on whole wheat (1 M&A; 2 GP); Small salad (1 V&F)<br>   Carton of 1% Milk (1 MP)<br>   Pear (1 V&F) | | |
| **DINNER PATTERN**<br><br>**2-3+ servings GP**<br>**2-3+ servings V&F**<br>**1 serving MP**<br>**1 serving M&A**<br><br>*Sample Menu:*<br>   Glass of tomato juice (1 V&F); 1 c/250mL pasta with roasted chicken<br>      breast (2 GP; 1 M&A); 1/2 c/125 mL peas & carrots (1 V&F);<br>      1 c/250 mL 1% milk (1 MP) | | |
| **SNACKS**<br><br>**1 serving V&F**<br>**1 serving MP**<br><br>*Sample Snacks:*<br>   Banana or apple (1 V&F)<br>   Lower-fat yogurt cup (1 MP)<br>   (if not used for a snack, the yogurt should be taken at mealtime so<br>   that at least 3 full servings of MP are obtained) | | |

| uesday | Wednesday | Thursday | Friday | Saturday |
|--------|-----------|----------|--------|----------|
|        |           |          |        |          |
|        |           |          |        |          |
|        |           |          |        |          |
|        |           |          |        |          |

- For the first time ever in Canada, some food labels may make health claims linking the food to the reduction in risk of a disease. The only claim related to cancer risk that will be allowed on the labels of vegetables, fruit and their juices is: "A healthy diet rich in a variety of fruit and vegetables may help reduce the risk of some types of cancer."

Even though nutrition labels provide us with important information on most packaged foods, don't forget to eat healthy but unlabeled foods like fresh produce!

## Eating Out

Most Canadians like to eat out, and *Canada's Guidelines for Healthy Eating* are meant to be flexible to accommodate this option. If menu items are chosen carefully, eating out can be part of a healthy eating pattern and a healthy lifestyle!

Here are examples of simple choices that you can make to avoid some of the pitfalls of eating out:

- Ask for whole-grain bread or buns and go easy on or omit the butter or margarine.
- Order a broth- or milk-based soup rather than a cream-based one. Go for the vegetable, bean or split pea soups for extra nutrition.
- Choose foods that have been broiled, steamed, poached, roasted or grilled. Look for foods served in their own juices or in tomato or wine sauces rather than rich sauces and gravies. Feel free to ask your server how foods have been prepared and if you can have the toppings or gravy "on the side."
- Trim visible fat from meats. If you order chicken, remove the skin before eating.
- Choose a plain hamburger; skip the cheese and bacon.
- Ask for your sandwich to be made without butter or mayonnaise. Mustard and vegetable toppings can provide added moisture.
- Ask if lower-fat dressings are offered—many restaurants provide lower-fat dressings or a lemon wedge as a substitute. Or, ask that the salad be tossed with just a small amount of dressing or that the dressing be served on the side so you can control how much you use.
- At a salad bar, add extra veggies, particularly dark green leafy or orange vegetables, kidney beans or chick-peas.
- Choose rice, baked potato or salad instead of French fries. Go easy on the toppings for baked potatoes. Ask your server for salsa or lower-fat sour cream as a potato topping.
- Consider vegetarian dishes made with legumes, vegetables or whole grains.
- When choosing pasta dishes, avoid sauces made primarily with cream, oil or butter. Instead, choose tomato- or wine-based sauces.
- Having dessert? Have fresh fruit or consider frozen yogurt, sherbet or sorbet. These frozen desserts are usually much lower in fat than ice cream.
- Ask for milk instead of cream in your tea or coffee.
- Some "fast-food" choices to make:
  - lower-fat bran muffins
  - submarine sandwich without the dressing, butter or regular mayonnaise
  - grilled chicken sandwiches
  - rotisserie chicken without the skin
  - chili

# Putting Healthy Meals Together

All the recipes in this book have been chosen on the basis of good taste and good health. They are high in fiber, lower in fat, rich in vitamins and minerals and emphasize fruit and vegetables, whole-grain products, fish and the lean kinds and cuts of meat. Sugar and salt have been kept to a minimum. Some of the recipes are classic favorites, which you will recognize, adapted to reflect the goals of *Canada's Guidelines for Healthy Eating*.

Use the recipes for everyday meals or for entertaining. Suggested menus are included throughout the book and are listed in the index.

To help you plan some meals, each recipe gives you the number of calories and grams of fat per serving, as well as fiber, vitamin and mineral ratings. Remember the daily recommendations:

- 25 to 35 grams of fiber; and
- about 90 grams of fat for a man and 65 grams for a woman.

To see if you need to adjust your eating habits, keep track of your diet for several days. Figure out the amount of fat and fiber you are eating, and whether you are keeping within the guidelines given here.

Once you are familiar with which foods are high in fat and fiber and which are low, you can plan your menus accordingly. For example, if you have a meal with a rich dessert, compensate by choosing other foods low in fat for the rest of the menu: use low-fat salad dressing and broiled chicken instead of a creamy dressing and fried steak. If you aren't getting enough fiber, add a bran muffin, fresh fruit, beans (legumes) or raw vegetables to your diet.

Once you get used to your new way of eating, you will be able to estimate how you are doing without a lot of calculating.

These menus are relatively low in calories and fat. To suit higher calorie needs, serve larger portions and add milk, breads or snacks.

Please note that children need more fat than adults to help them grow and develop properly. This means children can have higher-fat, nutritious snacks such as peanut butter, cheese and ice cream. Infants need about 50% of their calories from fat (in either breast milk or formula). This amount decreases gradually until they reach their full adult height in late adolescence, and from that point, like adults, they should get no more than 30% of their calories from fat.

| PER SERVING<br>*Everyday Family Meals* | *Grams<br>Fiber* | *Grams<br>Fat* | *Calories* | *% Calories<br>from Fat* |
|---|---|---|---|---|
| **Breakfast** | | | | |
| Orange juice (1/2 cup/125 mL) | .4 | .1 | 54 | |
| Raisin-Bran Cereal with<br>    fresh strawberries (1/2 cup/125 mL) | 5.7 | .7 | 141 | |
| Refrigerator Applesauce-Spice Bran Muffin<br>    (1 med.) (page 178) | 5.2 | 6.1 | 206 | |
| Jam or jelly (1 tsp/5 mL) | .1 | 0 | 19 | |
| Milk (skim, 1 cup/250 mL) | 0 | .4 | 85 | |

| PER SERVING Everyday Family Meals | Grams Fiber | Grams Fat | Calories | % Calories from Fat |
|---|---|---|---|---|
| **Lunch** | | | | |
| Bermuda Bean Salad (page 74) | 6.1 | 2.1 | 148 | |
| Cream of Broccoli Soup (page 40) | 1.4 | 1.9 | 87 | |
| Whole-wheat bread (1 slice) | 2.7 | .7 | 68 | |
| 1 tsp. (5 mL) butter or margarine | 0 | 3.7 | 33 | |
| Milk (skim, 1 cup/250 mL) | 0 | .4 | 85 | |
| Banana (1) | 2 | .6 | 106 | |
| **Dinner** | | | | |
| Triple Cheese Lasagna (page 134) | 3.2 | 9.4 | 323 | |
| 1 slice French bread | .4 | .7 | 72 | |
| 1 tsp. (5 mL) butter or margarine | 0 | 3.7 | 33 | |
| Green salad with 1 tbsp (15 mL) low-calorie dressing. | .6 | .4 | 15 | |
| Iced chocolate cake | 1 | 11.3 | 312 | |
| Totals with skim milk | 26.8 | 42.4 | 1786 | 21.4% |
| Totals with 2% milk | 26.8 | 50.9 | 1858 | 24.6% |
| Totals with whole milk | 26.8 | 57.8 | 1916 | 27.1% |
| Totals with 2% milk plus 1 tbsp (15 mL) butter or margarine | 26.8 | 62.3 | 1959 | 28.6% |
| Totals with whole milk plus 1 tbsp (15 mL) butter or margarine | 26.8 | 69.2 | 2017 | 30.9% |
| **Breakfast** | | | | |
| Stewed prunes (3) | 3.7 | .1 | 61 | |
| Corn Flakes (1 1/4 cups/300 mL) | .7 | .1 | 106 | |
| Boiled egg (1) | 0 | 5 | 74 | |
| Slice whole-wheat toast (1) | 2.7 | .7 | 69 | |
| Butter (1 tsp/5 mL) | 0 | 3.7 | 33 | |
| Milk (skim, 1 cup/250 mL) | 0 | .4 | 85 | |
| **Lunch** | | | | |
| Chicken sandwich on whole-wheat (2) with lettuce and light mayonnaise (1 tsp/5 mL) | 5.4 | 3 | 151 | |
| Celery sticks (1/2 cup/125 mL) | .9 | .1 | 10 | |
| Tangerine (1) | .8 | .2 | 37 | |

| PER SERVING | | | | |
| Everyday Family Meals | Grams Fiber | Grams Fat | Calories | % Calories from Fat |
| --- | --- | --- | --- | --- |
| Oatmeal Raisin cookies (2) (page 186) | 2.1 | 6 | 189 | |
| Milk (skim, 1 cup/250 mL) | 0 | .4 | 85 | |
| **Dinner** | | | | |
| Old-Fashioned Meatloaf (page 100) | 3.6 | 11.4 | 238 | |
| Baked potato (1 med.) | 3.2 | .1 | 155 | |
| No-fat sour cream (1 tbsp/15 mL) | 0 | 0 | 9 | |
| Steamed Brussels sprouts (1/2 cup/125 mL) | 2.1 | .2 | 19 | |
| Lemon-Ginger Carrots (page 159) (1/2 cup/125 mL) | 2 | 2.1 | 56 | |
| Pear Crisp with Ginger (page 212) | 4.7 | 4.6 | 255 | |
| Totals with skim milk | 31.9 | 40.2 | 1724 | 21% |
| Totals with 2% milk | 31.9 | 48.7 | 1796 | 24.4% |
| Totals with whole milk | 31.9 | 55.6 | 1854 | 27% |
| Totals with 2% milk plus 1 tbsp (15 mL) butter or margarine | 31.9 | 60.1 | 1897 | 28.5% |
| Totals with whole milk plus 1 tbsp (15 mL) butter or margarine | 31.9 | 67.0 | 1955 | 30.8% |

## About the Nutrient Analysis

Each of the recipes has a helpful nutrient analysis summarizing calories, protein, carbohydrate, fat, dietary fiber and sodium per serving. Saturated fat and cholesterol are also displayed to assist those with specific dietary needs. Nutrient values are rounded to the nearest whole number. Non-zero values less than 0.5 appear as "trace."

On some recipes you will also see nutrition bonus information: vitamin A (which includes beta carotene), vitamin C, calcium, iron and folacin are noted when a recipe is a high or very high source of these nutrients.

According to the criteria for food labeling (*Guide to Food Labeling and Advertising*, Agriculture and Agri-Food Canada, March 1996), a serving supplying 15% of the Recommended Daily Intake (RDI) of a vitamin or mineral (30% for vitamin C) is described as a high source and one supplying 25% of the RDI (50% for vitamin C) is described as a very high source. A serving containing 4 grams of dietary fiber is described as a high source and one containing 6 grams of dietary fiber as a very high source.

Nutrient analysis of the recipes was performed by Info Access (1988) Inc., Don Mills, Ontario, using the Nutritional Accounting component of the CBORD Menu Management System. The nutrient database was the 1991 Canadian Nutrient File, supplemented when necessary with documented data from reliable sources.

The nutrient analysis was based on imperial weights and measures and the first ingredient listed when there was a choice. Unless otherwise stated, the recipes were analyzed using canola oil, 1% milk, 2% yogurt, 2% cottage cheese, light mayonnaise, regular sour cream and canned chicken broth. Salt was included only when a specific quantity was given. Calculations of meat and poultry recipes, including those where fat and skin were not removed before cooking, assumed that only the lean portion was eaten. Optional ingredients and garnishes in unspecified amounts were not included.

*Daily Total Protein, Fat and Carbohydrate Intake (based on 15% of calories from protein, 30% of calories from fat and 55% of calories from carbohydrate) according to Nutrition Recommendations for Canadians, Health and Welfare Canada, 1990.*

| calorie intake day | grams protein per day | grams fat per day | grams carbohydrate per |
|---|---|---|---|
| 1200 | 45 | 40 | 165 |
| 1500 | 56 | 50 | 206 |
| 1800 | 68 | 60 | 248 |
| 2100 | 79 | 70 | 289 |
| 2300 | 86 | 77 | 316 |
| 2600 | 98 | 87 | 357 |
| 2900 | 109 | 97 | 399 |
| 3200 | 120 | 107 | 440 |

# Recipes

# Appetizers

S CRUMPTIOUS SNACKS AND COCKTAIL PARTY TIDBITS are irresistible and first courses are often the most innovative and interesting part of a meal. What's more, they can add valuable nutrients to your diet. But beware, they can also be nutritional hazards. Pâtés, peanuts, potato chips, savory-filled pastries and mayonnaise-based dips are high in fat and should be occasional choices. Instead, choose crudités (raw vegetables, higher in fiber and vitamins) with a yogurt- or low-fat sour-cream-based dip, or savories with a bread casing (lower in fat than pastry cases). Appetizers such as Salmon Mousse with Dill or Teriyaki Beef Rumaki will be favorites with any crowd and are also low in fat. The recipes in this section of the book will help you plan menus for entertaining that are low in fat and calories, yet high in flavor.

Appetizer courses in restaurants can be wonderfully appealing and nutritious. Because some restaurant entrées are very large, appetizers are often just the right size to substitute for a main course.

MAKE AHEAD

Cook shrimp in marinade (don't drain); cover and refrigerate for up to one day. Assembled appetizers can be covered and refrigerated for up to three hours before serving.

Snow peas are a good source of vitamin C and a source of folate and vitamin B6.

## Teriyaki Shrimp Wrapped with Snow Peas

*This colorful, delicious hors d'oeuvre is very easy to prepare. Stick the toothpicks holding these tasty bites into a cauliflower for a novel presentation. Serve any remaining snow peas with a dip or spread, or split them down the center and fill with light sour cream mixed with fresh chopped basil or dill.*

| 1 lb | large raw shrimp (about 18) | 500 g |
| 2 tbsp | soy sauce | 25 mL |
| 2 tbsp | sherry | 25 mL |
| 1 tbsp | sesame oil | 15 mL |
| 1 tbsp | grated fresh gingerroot | 15 mL |
| 2 tsp | granulated sugar | 10 mL |
| 4 oz | snow peas | 125 g |

Remove shell and black intestinal vein from each shrimp; place shrimp in bowl.

Combine soy sauce, sherry, oil, gingerroot and sugar, mixing well. Pour over shrimp; cover and refrigerate for 1 hour.

PER PIECE:
30 calories
4 g protein
1 g total fat
   trace saturated fat
   29 mg cholesterol
1 g carbohydrate
   trace  dietary fiber
90 mg sodium

Transfer shrimp and marinade to nonstick skillet; cook over medium-high heat for 3 to 5 minutes or until shrimp are pink and opaque. Let cool.

Trim snow peas and blanch in boiling water for 2 minutes or just until pliable. Drain and plunge into bowl of ice water to set color and prevent further cooking. Drain.

Wrap 1 snow pea around each shrimp; secure with toothpick. Arrange on serving platter; cover and refrigerate until serving time.

*Makes about 18 pieces.*

## MAKE AHEAD

Filling can be prepared up to six hours in advance. Assembled appetizers can be covered and refrigerated for up to two hours before serving.

### Variations

• Use mini pita rounds to hold many of the salads in the salad section of this book.

• Line pita with leaf lettuce and fill with a spoonful of Hummus (page 34).

• Substitute cooked or canned salmon, shrimp or tuna fish for crab.

• Line pita with lettuce and fill with Roasted Eggplant and Tomato Spread (page 33) or Spinach Dip (page 30) or Tomato Raita (page 65).

PER SERVING:
22 calories
2 g protein
trace total fat
   trace saturated fat
   3 mg cholesterol
3 g carbohydrate
   trace dietary fiber
81 mg sodium

# Crab-Stuffed Mini-Pitas

*Silver-dollar-size pita bread rounds provide quick and easy containers for countless fillings. The packaged varieties are available in the bread sections of some supermarkets and specialty stores. Choose the whole-wheat ones for more flavor and fiber.*

| | | |
|---|---|---|
| 1 | pkg (7 oz/200 g) whole-wheat mini-pitas | 1 |
| 8 oz | crabmeat (canned, fresh or frozen) | 250 g |
| 1/2 cup | Parsley Dressing* (page 81) | 125 mL |
| 2 tbsp | minced green onion | 25 mL |
| 1/2 tsp | fresh lemon juice | 2 mL |
| | Salt, pepper and hot pepper sauce | |
| | Leaf lettuce | |

Cut pita breads in half. Drain crabmeat thoroughly. In bowl, combine crabmeat, Parsley Dressing, onion and lemon juice; season with salt, pepper and hot pepper sauce to taste, mixing lightly. (Add more Parsley Dressing to taste.)

Line pita bread pockets with lettuce. Spoon in crabmeat mixture. Refrigerate until needed.

*Makes 40 pieces.*

*Make the full recipe of Parsley Dressing and use the rest of it as a dip—
   it's delicious!

**MAKE AHEAD**

Rounds can be covered and refrigerated for up to two hours before serving.

# Crab-Cucumber Rounds

*Crisp cucumber slices, instead of pastry or bread, make refreshing low-calorie, low-fat canapé bases. Since such a small amount of sour cream is needed, use no-fat, light or regular.*

| | | |
|---|---|---|
| 1 | seedless English cucumber | 1 |
| 1 | can (6 oz/170 g) crabmeat* | 1 |
| 2 tbsp | sour cream or light cream cheese | 25 mL |
| 2 tbsp | chopped fresh chives or green onion | 25 mL |
| | Salt, pepper and hot pepper sauce | |
| | Paprika | |

Run tines of fork lengthwise along cucumber to make decorative edge; cut into slices 1/4 inch (5 mm) thick.

Drain crabmeat thoroughly. In bowl, mix crab, sour cream, chives; season with salt, pepper and hot pepper sauce to taste. Add more sour cream if necessary to hold mixture together. Place small spoonful of crab mixture onto each cucumber slice. Sprinkle with paprika.

*Makes about 36 pieces.*

*Imitation crabmeat also works well in this recipe. Chop crabmeat and mix with 2 tbsp/25 mL sour cream and an equal amount of light cream cheese.

*Diet Hint*
**REDUCING FAT CONTENT IN HORS D'OEUVRES**
- Instead of pastry cases, use bread cases (see Stuffed Mushroom Croustades, page 27) or whole-wheat mini-pita rounds.
- To hold fillings, use hollowed-out cherry tomatoes, canned lichees and cucumber slices.
- Avoid pâtés and mayonnaise-based dressings.

**PER ROUND:**
5 calories
1 g protein
trace total fat
  trace saturated fat
  2 mg cholesterol
trace carbohydrate
  trace dietary fiber
26 mg sodium

*Hidden Fat in Foods*
*We all know that foods such as mayonnaise, whipped cream and Cheddar cheese are high in fat. Here are some other foods that are also deceptively high in fat.*

| | Grams fat/serving |
|---|---|
| Peanuts, dry roasted (1/2 cup/125 mL) | 37 |
| Ice-cream bar, chocolate-coated (Haagen Dazs) (88 mL) | 22 |
| Cheese scone or biscuit (4 oz/125 g) | 21 |
| Potato chips (1 small bag/55 g) | 19 |
| Eggnog, nonalcoholic (1 cup/250 mL) | 19 |
| Tortilla corn chips (1 small bag/70 g) | 18 |
| Peanut butter (2 tbsp/25 mL) | 16 |
| Half an avocado | 15 |
| Muffin (commercial, avg. 120 g) | 12 |
| Chocolate bar (2 oz/56 g) | 11 |
| Croissant (Sara Lee, frozen) | 11 |
| Olives, green (8 medium) | 8 |
| Popcorn with butter (2 cups/500 mL) | 8 |
| Pâté (2 tbsp/25 mL) | 7 |
| Chocolate chip cookies (3 small) | 7 |
| French-fried potatoes (10 pieces/35 g) | 6 |
| Olives, ripe (6 medium) | 3 |

**MAKE AHEAD**

Bread croustades can be stored in covered container for up to one week. Stuffed mushrooms can be covered and refrigerated up to one day.

# Stuffed Mushroom Croustades

*These mushroom appetizers are so delicious, they'll just disappear from the plate. I first tasted them at Toronto caterer Alison Cummings' home. To keep the fat as low as possible, I reduced the butter and used lower-fat cheese. Other savory fillings are also wonderful nestled in the croustade cases, which are much lower in fat and calories than pastry.*

| | | |
|---|---|---|
| 36 | thin slices whole-wheat bread | 36 |
| 36 | medium-size mushrooms | 36 |
| 1 cup | fresh whole-wheat bread crumbs | 250 mL |
| 1 | large clove garlic, chopped | 1 |
| 1/4 cup | chopped fresh parsley leaves | 50 mL |
| | Salt and pepper | |
| 4 tsp | butter, melted, or olive oil | 20 mL |
| 1/2 cup | shredded part-skim mozzarella cheese | 125 mL |

Using 2 1/2-inch (6 cm) cookie cutter or glass, cut out 36 rounds of bread. Press each into small muffin cups. Bake in 300°F (150°C) oven for 20 to 25 minutes or until light brown. Let cool.

Wash mushrooms and dry with paper towels; remove stems (use in soups).

In food processor or bowl, combine bread crumbs, garlic, parsley, and salt and pepper to taste; process until combined. Add butter and process just until mixed.

Spoon some stuffing into each mushroom cap; top with cheese. Place mushroom into bread case and place on baking sheet; bake in 400°F (200°C) oven for 10 minutes or until hot. If desired, broil for last minute. Serve hot.

*Makes 36 pieces.*

**PER SERVING:**
32 calories
1 g protein
1 g total fat
    trace saturated fat
    2 mg cholesterol
5 g carbohydrate
    1 g dietary fiber
58 mg sodium

**MAKE AHEAD**

Meat can be marinated for up to two days in refrigerator. Wrap meat around water chestnuts; cover and refrigerate for up to six hours.

*Cocktail Party for 25*
- Plan on 6 to 8 pieces per person. Multiply recipes according to number of guests.
- Teriyaki Beef Rumaki (this page)
- Crab-Stuffed Mini-Pitas (page 25)
- Parsley or Watercress Dressing with raw vegetables (page 81)
- Spinach-Stuffed Mushrooms (page 30)
- Teriyaki Shrimp Wrapped with Snow Peas (page 24)
- Salmon Mousse with Dill (page 32)

# Teriyaki Beef Rumaki

*Wrap tender strips of marinated beef around crunchy water chestnuts for a delectable hot appetizer.*

| | | |
|---|---|---|
| 3/4 lb | sirloin, round or flank steak, 1/2 inch (1 cm) thick | 375 g |
| 1/4 cup | soy sauce* | 50 mL |
| 1 | clove garlic, minced | 1 |
| 1 tbsp | minced onion | 15 mL |
| 1 tbsp | granulated sugar | 15 mL |
| 1 tbsp | chopped fresh gingerroot (or 1/2 tsp/2 mL ground ginger) | 15 mL |
| 1/4 tsp | hot pepper sauce | 1 mL |
| 1 | can (10 oz/284 mL) water chestnuts | 1 |

Place meat in freezer for about 30 minutes or until firm for easier slicing. Cut off any fat; slice meat across the grain into very thin strips about 1/8 inch (3 mm) thick and 3 inches (8 cm) long.

In bowl, combine soy sauce, garlic, onion, sugar, gingerroot and hot pepper sauce. Add meat, stirring to coat strips evenly. Marinate for 30 minutes at room temperature, stirring occasionally.

Drain meat. Wrap 1 strip around each water chestnut and secure with toothpick. Arrange on baking sheet; broil for 3 to 4 minutes or until piping hot and meat is medium-rare. (Or microwave on High for 3 to 4 minutes, rotating dish 1/4 turn halfway through cooking time.)

*Makes 25 to 30 pieces.*

*Soy sauce is very high in sodium. If possible, use a sodium-reduced soy sauce. If unavailable, look for naturally brewed soy sauce. The highest amount of sodium is found in chemically brewed soy sauce.

**PER PIECE:**
26 calories
3 g protein
1 g total fat
    trace saturated fat
    7 mg cholesterol
2 g carbohydrate
    trace dietary fiber
87 mg sodium

MAKE AHEAD

Dip can be covered and refrigerated for up to eight hours.

### Beet Greens

Don't throw out the beet tops. Cooked beet greens are an excellent source of vitamin A and folic acid, and a good source of vitamin C, riboflavin and fiber. They're delicious steamed, boiled or used instead of collard leaves in Portuguese Collard Soup (page 54). Beet greens are best when cooked fresh from the garden or within a day or two of picking. They are prepared and cooked like spinach, but require a longer cooking time.

To prepare and cook beet greens: Cut off and discard tough stems or blemished leaves. Either steam in covered steamer over simmering water for 10 to 15 minutes or until wilted and tender, or boil, covered in 1/2 inch (1 cm) of water, in large saucepan for 10 to 15 minutes or until tender. Drain and season with salt, pepper, lemon juice and a dab of butter.

When buying cream cheese, check the b.f. (butterfat) content on the label. Sometimes delicious local regular cream cheese has nearly the same b.f. content as the packaged light cream cheese. Quark (7% b.f.) is a good substitute for higher fat cream cheese in dips and spreads.

**PER TBSP:**
11 calories
1 g protein
1 g total fat
   trace saturated fat
   2 mg cholesterol
1 g carbohydrate
   trace dietary fiber
18 mg sodium

# Fresh Beet and Onion Dip

*Susan Pacaud, who helped with some of the recipe testing for this book, gave me the recipe for this wonderful and intriguingly bright pink dip.*

| | | |
|---|---|---:|
| 2 | green onions, finely chopped | 2 |
| 1/4 cup | grated peeled raw beet | 50 mL |
| 1/2 cup | 2% yogurt or light sour cream | 125 mL |
| 1/2 cup | quark or light cream cheese, softened | 125 mL |
| 2 tsp | fresh lemon juice | 10 mL |
| 1/4 tsp | each salt and pepper | 1 mL |

In small bowl, combine onions, beet, yogurt, quark, lemon juice, and salt and pepper; mix well.

*Makes 1 1/4 cups (300 mL).*

MAKE AHEAD

Dip can be covered and refrigerated for up to one day.

# Spinach Dip

*Perfect as a dip for crunchy fresh vegetables, this is also delicious as a filling for mushrooms and cherry tomatoes. You can even use it as a dressing for salads and chilled cooked vegetables. Spinach is an excellent source of fiber and beta carotene, which the body converts into vitamin A.*

| | | |
|---|---|---|
| 1 | pkg (10 oz/300 g) frozen chopped spinach (or 1 lb/500 g fresh, trimmed) | 1 |
| 1 cup | low-fat plain yogurt | 250 mL |
| 1 cup | light sour cream | 250 mL |
| 1/2 cup | minced fresh parsley leaves | 125 mL |
| 1/4 cup | finely chopped green onions (including tops) | 50 mL |
| 2 tbsp | light mayonnaise | 25 mL |
| 1 | clove garlic, minced | 1 |
| 1 tsp | salt | 5 mL |
| | Pepper | |

### Spinach-Stuffed Mushrooms
Fresh white mushrooms are delicious raw. Remove their stems and they're easy to stuff for a low-fat, low-calorie appetizer. If you're having a party, make the Spinach Dip (this page) or Parsley Dressing (page 81); use as a stuffing for 1/2 lb (250 g) mushrooms or cherry tomatoes, and the rest as a dip.

### Stuffed Cherry Tomatoes
Cherry tomatoes are a colorful, fresh-tasting addition to an hors d'oeuvres platter. To stuff, cut off the top of each tomato, hollow out some of the pulp and fill with Hummus (page 34), Spinach Dip (this page) or Creamy Fresh Dill Dip (page 31).

Serve with broccoli, snow peas, asparagus, carrots, turnip, green beans, cauliflower and/or cherry tomatoes for good to excellent fiber.

Boil or steam spinach just until wilted; drain thoroughly, squeezing out moisture; chop finely.

In bowl, mix together spinach, yogurt, sour cream, parsley, onions, mayonnaise, garlic, salt, and pepper to taste. Cover and refrigerate for at least 4 hours or for up to 1 day to blend flavors.

*Makes 2 1/2 cups (625 mL) dip.*

PER TBSP:
15 calories
1 g protein
1 g total fat
  trace saturated fat
  1 mg cholesterol
2 g carbohydrate
  trace dietary fiber
78 mg sodium

| COMPARE CREAMY FRESH DILL DIP: | | |
|---|---|---|
| *Per 1 1/4 cups (300 mL)* | Calories | Grams fat |
| Dip made with 1 cup (250 mL): | | |
| no-fat sour cream | 184 | 2 |
| 2% cottage cheese | 239 | 6 |
| quark (7% b.f.) | 336 | 19 |
| regular sour cream (14% b.f.) | 388 | 34 |
| light mayonnaise | 762 | 74 |
| regular cream cheese | 846 | 82 |
| mayonnaise | 1641 | 178 |

# Crudités with Creamy Fresh Dill Dip

MAKE AHEAD

Dip can be covered and refrigerated for up to two days.

*Prepare a colorful selection of raw vegetables — cauliflower, carrots, red, yellow and purple peppers, snow peas, baby corn, zucchini, Belgian endive, green and yellow beans, celery, fennel; cut them into strips suitable for dipping and arrange on a large platter with the dip in the center. If I'm using cottage cheese I prefer to make this dip in a blender rather than a food processor for a creamier, smoother consistency. If not using a blender, use quark or low-fat sour cream instead of cottage cheese.*

### Creamy Herb Sauce

Fresh herbs add wonderful flavor to sauces. Creamy Dill Dip is delicious as a sauce and it's low in fat. Instead of fresh dill, you can substitute 1 to 2 tbsp (15 to 25 mL) of chopped fresh tarragon, basil or a combination of whatever fresh herbs you have on hand.

| | | |
|---|---|---|
| 2 | Belgian endive | 2 |
| 4 oz | mushrooms | 125 g |
| 4 | carrots, cut in strips | 4 |
| 2 | sweet red, yellow or green peppers, cut in strips | 2 |
| Half | small cauliflower, cut in florets | Half |

| | *Creamy Dill Dip:* | |
|---|---|---|
| 1/2 cup | chopped fresh dill leaves (or 2 tsp/10 mL dried dillweed*) | 125 mL |
| 2 tbsp | chopped fresh parsley leaves | 25 mL |
| 1 cup | quark or 2% cottage cheese or low-fat sour cream | 250 mL |
| 3 tbsp | 2% plain yogurt | 50 mL |
| | Salt and pepper | |

### Crudités with Creamy Fresh Dill Dip

**PER TBSP:**
53 calories
5 g protein
1 g total fat
  trace saturated fat
  2 mg cholesterol
0 g carbohydrate
  2 g dietary fiber
111 mg sodium

**Vegetable platter:** Separate endive leaves. Halve mushrooms, if large. Arrange endives, mushrooms, carrots, red pepper and cauliflower on platter. Place dip in center.

**Creamy Dill Dip:** In blender, chop dill and parsley. Add cottage cheese, yogurt, and salt and pepper to taste; process until smooth. (Or finely chop dill and parsley, stir in quark or sour cream, yogurt, and salt and pepper to taste.)

*Makes 10 servings (about 1 1/4 cups/300 mL dip).*

*If using dried dillweed, add 1/4 cup (50 mL) more chopped fresh parsley.

### Nutrition Bonus

One serving provides 98% of an adult's daily requirement of vitamin A and 93% of an adult's daily requirement of vitamin C, and is a high source of folacin.

MAKE AHEAD

Can be covered and refrigerated for up to three days.

# Salmon Mousse with Dill

*This is one of my all-time favorite recipes that I continue to make year after year. I always use fresh dill and usually make it in a ring mold or loaf pan, which looks pretty unmolded and surrounded with melba toast or French bread. However, it's just as delicious served straight from a shallow bowl. Be sure to use sockeye salmon for its bright red color.*

| 2 | cans (each 7 3/4 oz/220 g) sockeye salmon | 2 |
|---|---|---|
| 1 | envelope unflavored gelatin | 1 |
| 3/4 cup | 1% yogurt | 175 mL |
| 1/2 cup | sour cream | 125 mL |
| 1/2 cup | finely chopped celery | 125 mL |
| 1/2 cup | chopped fresh dill leaves (or 1 tsp/5 mL dried dillweed*) | 125 mL |
| 2 tbsp | grated onion | 25 mL |
| 1 tbsp | fresh lemon juice | 15 mL |
| 1/2 tsp | salt | 2 mL |
| Dash | hot pepper sauce | Dash |

Drain salmon liquid into measuring cup; add enough water to make 1/2 cup (125 mL). Pour into small saucepan. Sprinkle gelatin over top; let stand until softened, about 5 minutes. Warm over medium heat until dissolved. Let cool to room temperature. Stir in yogurt, sour cream, celery, dill, onion, lemon juice, salt and hot pepper sauce.

Remove skin from salmon (but not bones — they're an excellent source of calcium); mash salmon with fork or process in food processor. Mix into gelatin mixture. Spoon into lightly oiled 4-cup (1 L) mold. Cover and refrigerate until firm, at least 3 hours. Unmold onto serving plate.

*Makes about 3 1/2 cups (875 mL).*

*If using dried dillweed, add 1/4 cup (50 mL) finely chopped fresh parsley.

**PER TBSP:**
18 calories
2 g protein
1 g total fat
   trace saturated fat
   3 mg cholesterol
trace carbohydrate
   0 g dietary fiber
56 mg sodium

**MAKE AHEAD**

Spread can be covered and refrigerated for up to two days.

# Roasted Eggplant and Tomato Spread

*This Mediterranean dip is delicious with raw vegetables or as a spread with melba toast. For a real taste treat, try it as a bruschetta-type topping over toasted bread. Add chopped fresh basil to taste.*

**Roasted Eggplant and Tomato Bruschetta**
Prepare spread and add 1/4 cup (50 mL) chopped fresh basil or more to taste. Toast slices of Italian or French bread; rub 1 side with cut garlic. Spoon eggplant mixture over toast.

| | | |
|---|---|---|
| 1 | large eggplant (about 1 1/4 lb/625 g) | 1 |
| 3 | green onions, finely chopped | 3 |
| 1 | large clove garlic, minced | 1 |
| 1 | large tomato, peeled and chopped | 1 |
| Half | stalk celery, finely chopped | Half |
| 1/4 cup | finely chopped sweet green pepper | 50 mL |
| 1 tbsp | fresh lemon juice or balsamic vinegar | 15 mL |
| 2 tsp | olive oil | 10 mL |
| 1/4 tsp | each salt and pepper | 1 mL |

Prick eggplant in several places with fork. Bake on baking sheet in 400°F (200°C) oven for 45 minutes or until soft, turning once or twice. Let cool, drain, then scoop out flesh and chop finely.

In bowl, combine eggplant, onions, garlic, tomato, celery and green pepper; toss to mix. Add lemon juice, oil, salt and pepper; mix well. Cover and refrigerate for at least 1 hour to blend flavors.

*Makes 3 cups (750 mL).*

**PER 1/4 CUP (50 ML):**
23 calories
1 g protein
1 g total fat
  trace saturated fat
  0 mg cholesterol
4 g carbohydrate
  1 g dietary fiber
52 mg sodium

| **COMPARE:** | | |
|---|---|---|
| *Per 1/4 cup (50 mL) Salmon Mousse* | **Grams fat** | **Calories** |
| Recipe made with: | | |
| • no-fat sour cream | 3.2 | 65 |
| • 1% b.f. sour cream | 3.3 | 69 |
| • 5% b.f. sour cream (light) | 3.6 | 70 |
| • 14 % b.f. sour cream (regular) | 4.4 | 72 |
| • light mayonnaise instead of sour cream | 5.8 | 86 |
| • regular mayonnaise instead of sour cream | 9.5 | 117 |
| • whipping cream instead of yogurt, and mayonnaise instead of sour cream | 13.8 | 151 |
| Chicken liver pâté: 1/4 cup (50 mL) | 15 | 168 |

**MAKE AHEAD**

Can be covered and refrigerated for up to three days.

*Nutrition Bonus*
One serving is a high source of folacin.

*Blender Method*
Purée chick-peas, lemon juice and water in batches; combine with remaining ingredients. If too thick add more water. Or, combine all ingredients in food processor and process until smooth.

*Summer Lunch or Picnic*
White wine spritzers
Whole-wheat pita bread filled with Hummus, topped with alfalfa sprouts or shredded lettuce, and Tomato Raita (page 65) or sliced tomatoes or sweet red peppers and a spoonful of yogurt seasoned with curry or cumin
Strawberries

*Sunday Afternoon Tea*
Crab-Cucumber Rounds (page 26)
Watercress sandwiches
Strawberries with Honey-Lime Fruit Dip (page 35)
Almond Apricot Squares (page 183)
Apricot, Orange and Pecan Loaf (page 188)

**PER 1/4 CUP:**
150 calories
7 g protein
6 g total fat
  1 g saturated fat
  0 mg cholesterol
18 g carbohydrate
  3 g dietary fiber
380 mg sodium

# Hummus

*In 1979, I learned to make Hummus this way from the owner of an Egyptian restaurant in Scarborough, Ontario, and it's still my favorite chick-pea dip. I try to keep a can of chick-peas on hand so I can make this at a moment's notice for an easy appetizer or snack. Serve with pita bread or vegetables as dippers.*

| 1/4 cup | tahini (sesame seed paste) or peanut butter | 50 mL |
|---------|---------------------------------------------|-------|
| 1 tsp | ground cumin | 5 mL |
| 1/2 tsp | salt | 2 mL |
| 2 | large cloves garlic, minced | 2 |
| 2 tbsp | fresh lemon juice | 25 mL |
| 1/4 cup | hot water | 50 mL |
| 1 | can (19 oz/540 mL) chick-peas, drained and rinsed | 1 |
| | Chopped fresh parsley or coriander (cilantro) leaves (optional) | |

In small bowl, combine tahini, cumin, salt and garlic. While stirring, slowly pour in lemon juice, then hot water. Purée chick-peas in food processor, or pass through food mill; add tahini mixture to purée and process or mix well. Season with more cumin and salt to taste. Spread in shallow bowl; sprinkle with parsley.

*Makes 1 1/2 cups (375 mL).*

| COMPARE: | g fat | calories | g protein | g fiber | mg iron |
|----------|-------|----------|-----------|---------|---------|
| Hummus (1/4 cup/50 mL) | 6 | 150 | 7 | 3 | 1 |
| Peanut Butter (2 tbsp/25 mL) | 16 | 190 | 8 | 2 | .5 |

| COMPARE: | grams fat |
|----------|-----------|
| Regular potato chips (55 g) | 19 |
| Baked low-fat potato chips (56 g) | 3 |

# Honey-Lime Fruit Dip

## MAKE AHEAD

Dip can be covered and refrigerated for up to two days.

### Honey Lime Sauce
This dip is equally delicious as a sauce for fruit desserts such as Plum Tart (page 215) or Pear Crisp (page 212).

### To Drain Yogurt
Place 2 cups (500 mL) plain Balkan-style yogurt or a yogurt made without gelatin into sieve lined with cheesecloth or paper towel or yogurt drainer. Set sieve over bowl and refrigerate for 2 to 4 hours or until yogurt is reduced to about 1 cup (250 mL).

**PER 1/4 CUP (50 ML):**
87 calories
3 g protein
1 g total fat
  1 g saturated fat
  4 mg cholesterol
18 g carbohydrate
  trace dietary fiber
44 mg sodium

*Delicious at the beginning or end of a meal, this refreshing dip can be made with lemon or lime. Choose a colorful variety of fruit: melon chunks, strawberries, grapes, or pineapple, apple, mango, papaya, pear and peach wedges, sections of orange or other seasonal fresh fruit. Arrange the fruit on a large platter with the dip in the center and let guests help themselves.*

| | | |
|---|---|---|
| 1 cup | plain yogurt (preferably extra-thick or drained) | 250 mL |
| 3 tbsp | liquid honey | 50 mL |
| | Grated rind of 1 lime | |
| 1 tbsp | fresh lime juice | 15 mL |

In bowl, combine yogurt, honey and lime rind and juice; mix well. Cover and refrigerate for 30 minutes. (Mixture will thicken upon standing.) Before serving, taste and add more honey if necessary.

*Makes 1 cup (250 mL).*

---

### First Courses
When planning menus, first decide on the main course. If it is low in fat and calories, you can then consider a hearty or cream soup or a more filling first course such as pasta or fish. If the main course is high in fat and calories, choose a light green salad or a clear soup for a first course. Many of the recipes in the book make delicious first courses. Here are some suggestions.

**SOUPS**
Any soup recipe in this book can be a first course, but if it is a filling soup, serve in smaller amounts.

**SALADS**
Roasted Red Pepper, Mushroom and Melon Salad (page 56)
Spinach and Red Cabbage Salad with Blue-Cheese Dressing (page 57)
Greek Salad (page 73)
Arugula and Radicchio Salad with Balsamic Vinaigrette (page 62)
Pasta Salad with Sweet Peppers and Dill (page 76)
Julienne Vegetables with Balsamic-Walnut Vinaigrette (page 63)
Artichoke Tomato Salad (page 59)
Melon with Blueberries (page 205)

**FISH**
Lemon-Garlic Salmon and Shrimp Brochettes (page 122), small portions, with Dill Mustard Sauce (page 151)
Mussels Sicilian Style (page 125)
Salmon Mousse with Dill (page 32)
Teriyaki Shrimp Wrapped with Snow Peas (page 24)

**PASTA**
Capellini with Clam Sauce and Sweet Red Peppers (page 124)
Linguine with Shrimp and Tomato (page 123)
Fettuccine with Fresh Tomatoes and Basil (page 132)
Pasta Salad with Sweet Peppers and Dill (page 76)

**VEGETABLES**
Asparagus with Red Pepper Purée (page 158)
Asparagus with Orange Vinaigrette (page 80)
Baked Leeks au Gratin (page 164)
Corn on the Cob (serve, just picked, as a first course)
Broccoli Frittata (page 128)
Spinach and Zucchini Pie (page 139)

# Soups

I F I HAD TO CHOOSE ONLY ONE TYPE of food to exist on, I would quickly choose soups. A warming soup in winter is the best comfort food of all, and nothing beats a chilled soup in summer to cool and refresh. Any time of year I love a large bowl of soup for either lunch or dinner and need nothing more than thick crusty bread, perhaps a wedge of cheese or a salad and fresh fruit for dessert. Some soups, such as Portuguese Collard Soup, Italian Vegetable Soup with Pesto or Split Pea Soup, I can happily eat day after day until a large pot is finished.

When planning your menus, don't forget that soups are ideal for lunch or dinner, as either first courses or main courses, for party fare either after the theater or après ski, or for a midnight meal.

Soups are often a good source of vitamins, particularly A and C, and of fiber. Milk-based soups are usually a good source of calcium, an important addition for adults who don't drink milk and therefore have difficulty meeting their calcium requirements.

## Balkan Beet Cream Soup

**MAKE AHEAD**

Buttermilk mixture can be covered and refrigerated for up to one day.

*On a hot summer evening, this is one of my favorite soups for a first course, or for a light meal along with a pasta or spinach salad and crusty bread. Save any leftover cooked beets for this flavorful chilled soup.*

### To Cook Beets
Cut tops from beets, leaving at least 1 inch (2.5 cm) of greens attached; don't trim off tapering root. (If beets are trimmed too close, color and vitamins are lost in the water.) Cook beets in boiling water or steam for 40 to 60 minutes or until tender when pierced with a fork. Drain under cold running water; slide off skins. Serve hot or let cool and add to salads.

**PER SERVING:**
79 calories
6 g protein
3 g total fat
  2 g saturated fat
  43 mg cholesterol
7 g carbohydrate
  1 g dietary fiber
149 mg sodium

| | | |
|---|---|---|
| 1/4 cup | sour cream | 50 mL |
| 1/4 cup | 2% cottage cheese | 50 mL |
| 2 cups | buttermilk | 500 mL |
| 2 | medium beets, cooked, peeled and cubed | 2 |
| 1 | hard-cooked egg, peeled and chopped | 1 |
| One-third | English cucumber, diced (unpeeled) | One-third |
| 1/2 cup | chopped fresh parsley leaves | 125 mL |
| 3 tbsp | sliced radishes | 50 mL |
| 2 tbsp | chopped fresh chives or green onions | 25 mL |
| | Salt and pepper | |

In blender or food processor, combine sour cream and cottage cheese until smooth. Combine with buttermilk; refrigerate.

Just before serving, divide beets among serving bowls. Stir egg, cucumber, parsley, radishes, chives, and salt and pepper to taste into buttermilk mixture; pour over beets.

*Makes 6 servings, 3/4 cup (175 mL) each.*

MAKE AHEAD

Soup can be covered and refrigerated for up to one day.

# Chilled Melon and Yogurt Soup

*A hint of ginger and fresh mint adds sparkle to this light, refreshing summer soup. Serve it as first course for brunch, lunch or dinner. A ripe cantaloupe is very flavorful; an unripe one is not, so choose one that has a sweet fragrance and yields slightly to pressure at the blossom end.*

***Nutrition Bonus***
One serving provides 105% of an adult's daily requirement of vitamin C and is a very high source of vitamin A.

| | | |
|---|---|---|
| 1 | very ripe cantaloupe | 1 |
| 1 cup | plain low-fat yogurt | 250 mL |
| 3 tbsp | fresh lemon juice | 50 mL |
| 1/2 tsp | grated fresh gingerroot (or 1/4 tsp/1 mL ground ginger) | 2 mL |
| 2 tbsp | chopped fresh mint leaves | 25 mL |

***60-Minute Dinner Party***
Chilled Melon and Yogurt Soup (this page)
Chicken with Snow Peas (page 91)
Rice
Tarragon Carrots (page 159)
Frozen Lemon Cream (page 201)

Cut cantaloupe in half and remove seeds. Scoop out pulp into food processor or blender; purée to make about 1 1/2 cups (375 mL). Add yogurt, lemon juice and ginger; process to mix. Refrigerate until serving.

Divide among small bowls; top with sprinkling of mint.

*Makes 4 servings, about 2/3 cup (150 mL) each.*

**PER SERVING:**
89 calories
4 g protein
1 g total fat
  1 g saturated fat
  4 mg cholesterol
17 g carbohydrate
  1 g dietary fiber
55 mg sodium

**MAKE AHEAD**

Soup can be covered and refrigerated for up to three days. It tastes better the next day. It will thicken upon cooling and standing, so add water to reach desired consistency.

*Nutrition Bonus*
One serving is a very high source of folacin and a high source of dietary fiber.

*Smoked Foods and Nitrites*
Small amounts of nitrites are used in the preservation of some meats such as bacon, ham and cold cuts to prevent botulism, a deadly form of food poisoning. Vitamin C or erythrobate, a form of vitamin C, is usually added to prevent the conversion of nitrites into nitrosamines. Nitrosamines have been associated with increased cancer risk. In any case, many of the nitrite-cured meats such as bacon, salami and bologna often have a higher fat content and should be eaten in moderation.

# Split Pea Soup

*This is one of our family's favorite soups. We use the leftover bone from a cooked ham. Many cooks add carrots and other vegetables, but we don't — my mother said they take away from the flavor of peas. Taste the soup for seasoning just before serving. You might not want to add salt because there is often enough in the ham.*

| 1 | ham bone | 1 |
|---|---|---|
| 8 oz | lean cooked ham*, cubed | 250 g |
| 10 cups | water | 2.5 L |
| 1 1/4 cups | split green peas (12 oz/350 g) | 300 mL |
| 4 | onions, sliced | 4 |
| | Salt and pepper | |

Remove any fat from ham bone. In large saucepan, combine ham bone, ham, water, peas and onions; bring to boil, skimming off any foam.

Reduce heat and simmer, partially covered and stirring occasionally, for 2 to 3 hours or until peas are soft. If too thick; add more water. Season with salt and pepper to taste.

*Makes 10 servings, about 3/4 cup (175 mL) each.*

*Use the meat from the ham bone, or if nothing is left on the bone, buy ham.

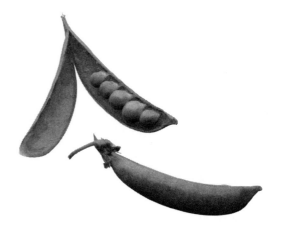

**PER SERVING:**
168 calories
14 g protein
2 g total fat
  trace saturated fat
  12 mg cholesterol
25 g carbohydrate
  5 g dietary fiber
311 mg sodium

**MAKE AHEAD**

Cover and refrigerate for up to one day.

# Gazpacho

*This cold Spanish soup is perfect for a sultry summer evening. It's easy to make in a blender, but tastes best when the vegetables are finely chopped by hand. I like to pass around a bowl of homemade garlic bread croutons and let each person add their own.*

*Nutrition Bonus*
One serving is a high source of vitamin C.

| | | |
|---|---|---|
| 1 | clove garlic | 1 |
| Half | small onion, quartered | Half |
| Half | sweet green or red pepper, seeded and cut in chunks | Half |
| 3 | ripe tomatoes, quartered | 3 |
| 1 | cucumber, cut in chunks* | 1 |
| 2 tbsp | wine vinegar | 25 mL |
| 2 tbsp | olive oil | 25 mL |
| 1/2 cup | vegetable or chicken stock or water (optional) | 125 mL |
| | Salt, pepper and hot pepper sauce | |
| | Chopped fresh basil or coriander | |

For fat-restricted diets, reduce olive oil to 1 tsp (5 mL).

In blender with machine running, drop garlic into feed tube, then onion. Turn machine off. Add green pepper, tomatoes, cucumber, vinegar and oil; blend just until chopped. (Or, finely chop garlic and vegetables; add vinegar and oil.) Add up to 1/2 cup (125 mL) stock if desired. Cover and refrigerate until serving time. Taste and season with salt, pepper, hot pepper sauce and more vinegar, if necessary. Sprinkle each serving with chopped fresh basil or coriander.

*Makes 6 servings, about 3/4 cup (175 mL) each.*

*Peel cucumber only if skin is tough or waxy.

**PER SERVING:**
67 calories
1 g protein
5 g total fat
  1 g saturated fat
  0 mg cholesterol
6 g carbohydrate
  1 g dietary fiber
7 mg sodium

39

MAKE AHEAD

Soup can be covered and refrigerated for up to two days. Serve cold or reheat over medium heat.

# Cream of Broccoli Soup

*One of my favorite soups, this is just as delicious hot as cold. I sometimes top each serving with a spoonful of sour cream and chopped chives, dill or parsley.*

| | | |
|---|---|---|
| 1 | large onion, coarsely chopped | 1 |
| 1 | medium carrot, sliced | 1 |
| 1 | small stalk celery (with leaves), sliced | 1 |
| 1 | clove garlic, minced | 1 |
| 3 cups | chicken stock | 750 mL |
| 1/4 cup | rice | 50 mL |
| 3 cups | coarsely chopped broccoli | 750 mL |
| 2 cups | 2% milk | 500 mL |
| | Salt and cayenne pepper | |

In large saucepan, combine onion, carrot, celery, garlic and chicken stock; bring to boil. Add rice; cover and simmer for 15 to 20 minutes or until rice is tender. Add broccoli; cover and simmer until broccoli is tender, about 5 minutes.

Transfer to blender or food processor, in batches if necessary; purée until smooth. Return to saucepan; add milk, and salt and cayenne to taste. Serve hot or let cool, cover and refrigerate until serving time.

*Makes 8 servings, 3/4 cup (175 mL) each.*

**Nutrition Bonus**
One serving is a very high source of vitamin A and a high source of vitamin C.

Broccoli is a good source of fiber and vitamins C and A.

**Reducing fat content of soups**
When making cream soups, substitute 2% milk or buttermilk for cream or whole milk. When adding milk to a hot soup, especially a tomato-based soup, it is best to warm the milk gradually by slowly adding some of the hot mixture to it, then pouring it into the hot soup. The soup can be reheated, but don't let it boil.

**COMPARE:**

*One serving Cream of Broccoli Soup made with:*

| | Grams fat | Calories |
|---|---|---|
| • 2% milk | 2 | 88 |
| • whole milk | 3 | 95 |
| • light cream (10% b.f.) | 7 | 128 |
| • whipping cream (32% b.f.) | 22 | 252 |

**PER SERVING:**
88 calories
6 g protein
2 g total fat
 1 g saturated fat
 5 mg cholesterol
12 g carbohydrate
 1 g dietary fiber
341 mg sodium

# Fresh Tomato and Basil Soup

**MAKE AHEAD**

Cover and refrigerate stock mixture for up to one day. Reheat and add tomatoes up to one hour before serving. Just before serving, stir in basil and salt and pepper to taste.

*Make the most of our fresh tomato season with this light flavorful soup that's perfect for a first course. If fresh basil is not available, use other fresh herbs such as dill, parsley or a combination of fresh parsley and a teaspoon of dried basil.*

| | | |
|---|---|---|
| 1 tbsp | butter or olive oil | 15 mL |
| 2 | large cloves garlic, minced | 2 |
| 1 | medium carrot, diced | 1 |
| 1 | medium onion, chopped | 1 |
| 4 cups | chicken stock | 1 L |
| 3 cups | diced peeled ripe tomatoes | 750 mL |
| 1/4 cup | chopped fresh basil leaves | 50 mL |
| | Salt and pepper | |

*Nutrition Bonus*
One serving is a very high source of vitamin A.

   In heavy saucepan, melt butter over medium-low heat; cook garlic, carrot and onion, stirring occasionally, until onion is tender. Add stock; cover and simmer for 20 minutes.

   Stir in tomatoes; simmer for 10 minutes. Just before serving, stir in basil. Season with salt, pepper and more basil to taste.

*Makes 6 servings, about 1 cup (250 mL) each.*

**PER SERVING:**
78 calories
5 g protein
3 g total fat
   1 g saturated fat
   5 mg cholesterol
9 g carbohydrate
   2 g dietary fiber
555 mg sodium

# Quick Asian Vegetable-Noodle Soup

*One of the easiest and quickest ways of making soup is simply to cook vegetables in vegetable or chicken stock. The trick is to use a colorful and interesting variety of vegetables, such as in this soup. However, you can substitute any you have on hand, such as squash, turnip, lettuce, potatoes. Add chopped fresh herbs for even more of a flavor boost.*

**Nutrition Bonus**
One serving is a very high source of vitamin A.

| | | |
|---|---|---|
| 5 cups | chicken or vegetable stock | 1.25 L |
| 1 | carrot, diagonally sliced | 1 |
| 1 cup | broccoli florets | 250 mL |
| 1 cup | cauliflower florets | 250 mL |
| 1/2 cup | thinly sliced red cabbage or spinach | 125 mL |
| 1 | pkg (3 oz/90 g) instant (Asian) soup noodles, broken | 1 |
| 1 | green onion, diagonally sliced | 1 |
| 1 tbsp | soy sauce | 15 mL |
| 1/4 tsp | hot pepper sauce | 1 mL |

**Seafood Vegetable Soup**
After vegetables are tender, add 1 cup (250 mL) or 4 oz (125 g) cooked or raw shelled shrimp or scallops, or a combination of both, plus 4 oz (125 g) mussels in shell (optional). Simmer for 2 to 3 minutes longer or until shrimp and scallops are opaque and mussel shells open. (Discard any mussel if shell doesn't open.)

In saucepan, bring stock to boil; add carrot and simmer over medium heat for 5 minutes. Add broccoli, cauliflower and cabbage; simmer for 5 minutes or until vegetables are tender.

Return to boil. Add noodles (discard seasoning packet if in package), onion, soy sauce and hot pepper sauce; simmer for 3 minutes or until noodles are cooked.

*Makes 6 servings, about 1 cup (250 mL) each.*

**Note:** The recipes here were tested and analyzed using canned condensed chicken broth diluted with an equal amount of water. To reduce sodium use a homemade chicken stock or a canned broth diluted with three to four times as much water.

**PER SERVING:**
100 calories
7 g protein
2 g total fat
  trace saturated fat
  0 mg cholesterol
14 g carbohydrate
  2 g dietary fiber
800 mg sodium

**MAKE AHEAD**

Soup can be covered and refrigerated for up to two days.

# Green Pea, Bean and Romaine Soup

*Here is a hearty and rustic, yet low-calorie vegetable soup that's quick to prepare if you slice the vegetables in a food processor. For a creamy, thick soup, purée in a food processor or blender.*

*Nutrition Bonus*
One serving is a very high source of vitamin A and folacin.

| | | |
|---|---|---|
| 6 cups | chicken or vegetable stock | 1.5 L |
| 2 | celery stalks, sliced | 2 |
| 2 | cloves garlic, minced | 2 |
| 1 | large onion, finely chopped | 1 |
| 1 | large carrot, thinly sliced | 1 |
| 1 1/2 cups | green beans, cut in 2-inch (5 cm) lengths (4 oz/125 g) | 375 mL |
| Half | head romaine lettuce, sliced* | Half |
| 1 1/4 cups | frozen peas, thawed | 300 mL |
| 1 cup | sliced mushrooms | 250 mL |
| 1/3 cup | finely chopped fresh parsley leaves | 75 mL |
| 1 tsp | dried dillweed (or 1/4 cup/50 mL chopped fresh dill leaves) | 5 mL |
| 1/4 tsp | pepper | 1 mL |
| Pinch | nutmeg | Pinch |
| | Salt | |

In large saucepan, combine stock, celery, garlic, onion and carrot; bring to boil. Cover, reduce heat and simmer at a low boil for 10 minutes. Add green beans; cook for 5 minutes or until vegetables are tender. Add lettuce, peas and mushrooms; cook for 3 to 5 minutes or until tender. Add parsley, dillweed, pepper, nutmeg, and salt to taste. Serve hot. (Or purée in food processor or blender and serve warm or cold.)

*Makes 8 servings, about 1 cup (250 mL) each.*

*You can substitute half a package (10 oz/284 g) fresh spinach for the romaine lettuce.

**PER SERVING:**
71 calories
6 g protein
1 g total fat
   trace saturated fat
   0 mg cholesterol
9 g carbohydrate
   3 g dietary fiber
621 mg sodium

MAKE AHEAD

Purée can be covered and refrigerated for up to two days or frozen for up to one month. Reheat gently, then add milk; serve hot or cold.

# Leek and Potato Soup

*Entertaining is a breeze when you have the base for this smooth soup on hand in the freezer. Just thaw, add milk and serve hot or cold as a first course at a dinner party. For a lunch main course, top soup with garlic croutons and baby shrimp and chopped chives or green onions.*

| 3 | medium leeks | 3 |
|---|---|---|
| 2 | medium potatoes, peeled and cubed | 2 |
| 1 | clove garlic, minced | 1 |
| 3 cups | chicken stock | 750 mL |
| 1 1/2 cups | 2% milk* | 375 mL |
| | Salt and pepper | |
| 2 tbsp | minced fresh parsley or chives | 25 mL |

*Chunky Leek and Potato Soup*
Add another potato; follow recipe for Leek and Potato Soup except don't purée. Add any other vegetables such as carrots, green beans, sweet potatoes or broccoli. Omit milk if desired. Or for a creamier soup and extra calcium, reduce chicken stock to 2 cups (500 mL) and increase milk to 2 1/2 cups (625 mL).

Trim all dark green parts from leeks. Cut lengthwise and spread apart; wash under cold running water. Slice thinly by hand or in food processor.

In saucepan, combine leeks, potatoes, garlic and chicken stock; simmer, partially covered, for 30 minutes or until vegetables are tender. Pour into blender or food processor; purée until smooth. Return soup to pan. Add milk, and salt and pepper to taste; heat until hot. Sprinkle each serving with parsley.

*Makes 6 servings, about 1 cup (250 mL) each.*

* To serve Leek and Potato Soup cold: For a smoother soup, instead of using 2% milk, substitute 10% light cream. Just before serving, add 1 tbsp (15 mL) fresh lemon juice and salt and pepper to taste.

PER SERVING:
108 calories
6 g protein
2 g total fat
 1 g saturated fat
 5 mg cholesterol
17 g carbohydrate
 1 g dietary fiber
428 mg sodium

**COMPARE:**

*One serving of Leek and Potato Soup made with:*

| | Grams fat | Calories |
|---|---|---|
| • 2% milk | 2 | 108 |
| • whole milk | 3 | 115 |
| • light cream (10% b.f.) | 7 | 149 |
| • whipping cream (32% b.f.) | 22 | 273 |

MAKE AHEAD

Soup can be covered and refrigerated for up to three days or frozen for up to three weeks.

# Vegetable Borscht

*Give a flavor boost to any meal with small portions of this soup for a first course. Or serve larger bowlfuls for a main course. A dollop of sour cream on top adds colorful contrast.*

| | | |
|---|---|---|
| 2 | large fresh beets, peeled and finely chopped | 2 |
| 1 | onion, finely chopped | 1 |
| 1 | medium carrot, diced | 1 |
| 1 | large potato, peeled and diced | 1 |
| 4 cups | beef or vegetable stock | 1 L |
| 1 | tomato, finely chopped | 1 |
| Quarter | small head cabbage, shredded | Quarter |
| 2 tbsp | chopped fresh parsley leaves | 25 mL |
| 1/2 tsp | dried dillweed | 2 mL |
| 2 tsp | fresh lemon juice | 10 mL |
| | Salt and pepper | |
| 3 tbsp | sour cream | 50 mL |

***Nutrition Bonus***
One serving is a very high source of vitamin A.

To reduce the sodium, use sodium- or salt-reduced stock or homemade stock.

Nutrient analysis is based on regular sour cream. If you want to use more than a small spoonful, you might want to use the light sour cream.

If making with a food processor, coarsely chop all vegetables; if not, finely chop.

In large saucepan, combine beets, onion, carrot, potato and beef stock; bring to boil. Reduce heat, cover and simmer for 30 minutes, skimming off foam if necessary. Add tomato, cabbage, parsley and dill; simmer for 15 minutes or until vegetables are tender. Transfer in batches to food processor; finely chop using on-off turns but do not purée. Season with lemon juice, and salt and pepper to taste. Top each serving with spoonful of sour cream.

*Makes 8 servings, 1 cup (250 mL) each.*

**PER SERVING:**
57 calories
3 g protein
1 g total fat
  1 g saturated fat
  2 mg cholesterol
10 g carbohydrate
  2 g dietary fiber
413 mg sodium

**MAKE AHEAD**

Soup can be covered and refrigerated for up to two days. Add pesto just before serving.

# Italian Vegetable Soup with Pesto

*Pesto, a vibrant Italian sauce made with fresh basil and garlic, adds exquisite flavor to this soup. This version of pesto has less oil than most, without any loss in flavor. Add pesto sauce directly to soup before serving, or top each serving with a spoonful.*

*Nutrition Bonus*
One serving is a very high source of vitamin A and a high source of folacin and dietary fiber.

*Pasta with Pesto Sauce*
If making pesto to serve with pasta, use pasta cooking liquid instead of soup liquid and add enough to make sauce thick yet pourable. Plan on at least 2 tbsp (25 mL) pesto sauce per person. Toss with hot cooked pasta and serve.

*Compare:*
This pesto sauce has less than half the amount of fat of most pesto recipes.

| | | |
|---|---|---|
| 1 tbsp | vegetable oil | 15 mL |
| 1 | onion, coarsely chopped | 1 |
| 1 1/2 cups | chicken stock | 375 mL |
| 2 1/2 cups | water | 625 mL |
| 2 | carrots, thinly sliced | 2 |
| 2 | leeks (white part only), coarsely chopped | 2 |
| 1 | potato, diced | 1 |
| 1 | large stalk celery (with leaves), coarsely chopped | 1 |
| 1 | can (19 oz/540 mL) tomatoes (undrained), chopped | 1 |
| 1 cup | sliced green beans | 250 mL |
| 1/2 cup | coarsely chopped zucchini | 125 mL |
| 1/3 cup | broken medium egg noodles or spaghetti | 75 mL |
| 1 | can (19 oz/540 mL) white beans*, drained and rinsed | 1 |
| | Salt and pepper | |

| *Pesto:* | | |
|---|---|---|
| 2 | large cloves garlic | 2 |
| 3/4 cup | lightly packed fresh basil leaves** | 175 mL |
| 1/2 cup | freshly grated Parmesan cheese | 125 mL |
| 2 tbsp | olive oil | 25 mL |
| 1/4 cup | hot soup liquid | 50 mL |

In skillet, heat oil over medium heat; add onion and cook, stirring, for 6 to 8 minutes or until tender.

In large pot, bring chicken stock and water to boil. Add onion mixture, carrots, leeks, potato, celery and tomatoes; cover and simmer for 15 minutes. Add green beans, zucchini, egg noodles and white beans; cover and simmer for 10 to 15 minutes until vegetables are tender, adding more water, if needed. Add salt and pepper to taste.

**PER SERVING:**
169 calories
8 g protein
6 g total fat
  2 g saturated fat
  5 mg cholesterol
22 g carbohydrate
  5 g dietary fiber
490 mg sodium

46

**Pesto:** In food processor, chop garlic and basil. Add Parmesan and oil; process until smooth. Add enough of the warm soup liquid to make consistency of mayonnaise.

Ladle soup into bowls. Top each with spoonful of pesto.

*Makes 10 servings, about 1 cup (250 mL) each.*

*Instead of canned beans, use 2 cups (500 mL) cooked white beans.

**If fresh basil isn't available, substitute 3/4 cup (175 mL) fresh flat-leafed Italian parsley and 2 tsp (10 mL) dried basil. The flavor isn't the same, but it is quite acceptable.

---

To cook beans: Soak 1/2 cup (125 mL) dried white beans (cannellini, white kidney, great northern or pea beans) in water overnight and drain. Or cover beans with cold water and bring to boil; remove from heat and let stand for 1 hour, then drain. Cover well with cold water and bring to boil. Reduce heat and simmer, covered, until beans are tender, about 1 to 2 hours; drain. Time varies with the type and age of bean.

---

MAKE AHEAD

After adding fish, cover and refrigerate for up to one day or freeze for up to two weeks. Thaw; then reheat before adding milk and continuing with recipe.

# Nova Scotia Seafood Chowder

*This flavorful maritime dish is from the Crawford family of Five Islands, Nova Scotia. Serve as a main course along with crusty rolls and a tossed green salad, or for an après-ski dinner buffet or after-theater party. You can make it early in the day to give the flavors a chance to develop. A food processor makes quick work of chopping the onions, celery and carrots.*

***Nutrition Bonus***
One serving of this soup is a very high source of iron (36% of an adult's daily requirement) and vitamin A (100%), and a high source of calcium.

For a creamier soup, use 1 cup (250 mL) chicken stock or clam juice and 3 cups (750 mL) milk.

| | | |
|---|---|---|
| 1 tbsp | butter | 15 mL |
| 1 cup | chopped onions | 250 mL |
| 2 cups | chicken stock or clam juice | 500 mL |
| 1 cup | chopped celery | 250 mL |
| 1 cup | chopped carrots | 250 mL |
| 1 lb | haddock fillets | 500 g |
| 2 cups | whole milk | 500 mL |
| 1/3 cup | all-purpose flour | 75 mL |
| 1 | can (5 oz/142 g) clams (undrained) | 1 |
| 4 oz | cooked small shrimp and/or lobster meat | 125 g |
| | Salt and pepper | |
| 1 to 2 tsp | Pernod (optional) | 5 to 10 mL |

In large saucepan, melt butter over low heat; add onions and cook for a few minutes or until softened. Stir in chicken stock, celery and carrots; bring to boil. Reduce heat, cover and simmer for 20 minutes or until carrots are tender. Add fillets; cover and cook for 5 minutes.

Stir about half of the milk into flour until smooth. Gradually stir flour mixture into soup; stir in remaining milk and simmer until thickened slightly. Stir in clams and shrimp; heat through. Taste and season with salt and pepper. Add Pernod (if using).

*Makes 6 servings, about 1 1/4 cups (300 mL) each.*

**PER SERVING WITH SHRIMP (NO LOBSTER):**
244 calories
28 g protein
6 g total fat
  3 g saturated fat
  106 mg cholesterol
17 g carbohydrate
  2 g dietary fiber
490 mg sodium

MAKE AHEAD

Soup can be covered and refrigerated for up to two days. Reheat, then add parsley or coriander.

# Easy Tomato-Bean Chowder

*I like this soup all year round: it's light enough for a summer supper yet comforting and hearty enough for a cold winter day. Chopped fresh coriander livens up its flavor.*

| | | |
|---|---|---|
| 4 | onions, finely chopped | 4 |
| 2 tsp | chili powder | 10 mL |
| 1 | sweet green pepper, seeded and chopped | 1 |
| 1 | can (28 oz/796 mL) tomatoes (undrained) | 1 |
| 4 cups | water or beef or vegetable stock | 1 L |
| 1 | can (19 oz/540 mL) red kidney beans, drained and rinsed | 1 |
| 1 | can (19 oz/540 mL) chick-peas, drained and rinsed | 1 |
| | Salt and pepper | |
| 1/2 cup | finely chopped fresh parsley or coriander (cilantro) leaves, or both | 125 mL |

*Nutrition Bonus*
One serving is a very high source of folacin and dietary fiber, and a high source of vitamin C.

Legumes such as kidney beans and chick-peas are excellent sources of dietary fiber and contribute iron, calcium and protein to our diet.

The canned beans and peas contribute about 200 mg of sodium per serving. Instead of water, if you use stock from a can or cube, you add another 300 mg of sodium per serving. To further reduce sodium in this recipe, cook your own dried beans and use low-sodium canned tomatoes.

In large heavy saucepan, combine onions, chili powder, green pepper and tomatoes, breaking up tomatoes with back of spoon. Add water; bring to boil. Reduce heat and simmer for 15 minutes.

Add drained beans and peas; simmer for 10 minutes. Season with salt and pepper to taste. Sprinkle each serving with parsley or coriander.

*Makes 10 servings, 1 cup (250 mL) each.*

PER SERVING:
133 calories
7 g protein
1 g total fat
   trace saturated fat
   0 mg cholesterol
25 g carbohydrate
   6 g dietary fiber
347 mg sodium

MAKE AHEAD

Soup can be covered and refrigerated for up to one day. Reheat over medium heat, do not boil. Add parsley and Pernod (if using) just before serving.

*Nutrition Bonus*
One serving is a very high source of vitamin A, and a high source of calcium, vitamin C and folacin.

Pernod, a licorice-flavored liqueur, adds wonderful flavor to fish soups. Other licorice-flavored liqueurs such as Sambuca or Pastis can also be used. Use only a small amount to enhance, not overpower, the other flavors.

*Oyster Chowder*
Prepare Easy Fish Chowder, substituting 1 lb (500 g) shucked oysters for the fish. Just before serving, stir in Pernod.

*Super Supper*
Easy Fish Chowder (this page)
Whole-wheat buns
Tossed salad
Fresh fruit

# Easy Fish Chowder

*Any fresh or frozen fillets can be used in this nutritious recipe, but try monkfish if it's available. It's sometimes called lobster fish because it has a texture like lobster. If using frozen fish, thaw before using. Add a few tablespoons of chopped fresh dill or basil if available.*

| | | |
|---|---|---|
| 1 tbsp | butter | 15 mL |
| 3 | potatoes*, diced | 3 |
| 1 | onion, finely chopped | 1 |
| 1 | carrot, finely chopped | 1 |
| 1 cup | water | 250 mL |
| 3 cups | 2% milk (or 2% evaporated milk) | 750 mL |
| 1 lb | monkfish or other fish fillets (fresh or frozen) | 500 g |
| 1 cup | corn kernels | 250 mL |
| 1/2 cup | chopped fresh parsley leaves | 125 mL |
| 2 to 3 tsp | Pernod (optional) | 10 to 15 mL |
| 1/4 tsp | each salt and pepper | 1 mL |

In heavy saucepan, melt butter over medium heat; add potatoes, onion and carrot and cook, stirring occasionally, for 5 minutes. Add water; cover and simmer for 15 minutes or until vegetables are nearly tender.

Stir in milk, fish (if using monkfish, cut into chunks) and corn; simmer for 5 to 10 minutes or until fish flakes and is opaque. Add parsley, Pernod (if using), salt and pepper.

*Makes 4 main-course servings, about 1 1/2 cups (375 mL) each.*

*Peel potatoes only if skin is tough.

PER MAIN COURSE SERVING:
340 calories
26 g protein
8 g total fat
 4 g saturated fat
 50 mg cholesterol
42 g carbohydrate
 3 g dietary fiber
309 mg sodium

# Corn and Tomato Chowder with Tarragon

## MAKE AHEAD

Soup is best served same day but can be covered and refrigerated for up to two days or frozen for up to one week (stir well after reheating).

*Fresh tarragon adds a burst of flavor to this soup. If it isn't available, use other fresh herbs instead (try basil, rosemary or oregano). If you can't find any fresh herbs, use dried tarragon. Serve soup hot or cold.*

| | | |
|---|---|---|
| 1 tbsp | canola or olive oil | 15 mL |
| 1 | medium onion, chopped | 1 |
| 3 | large cloves garlic, minced | 3 |
| 2 tbsp | all-purpose flour | 25 mL |
| 1 | can (19 oz/540 mL) tomatoes (undrained), chopped | 1 |
| 2 | potatoes, peeled and diced | 2 |
| 1 cup | vegetable or chicken stock | 250 mL |
| 2 cups | 2% evaporated milk or 2% fresh milk | 500 mL |
| 2 cups | corn kernels (canned, frozen or from cooked cob) | 500 mL |
| 2 tbsp | chopped fresh parsley leaves | 25 mL |
| 2 tbsp | chopped fresh chives or green onions | 25 mL |
| 1 tbsp | chopped fresh tarragon leaves (or 1 tsp/5 mL crushed dried) | 15 mL |
| Dash | hot pepper sauce | Dash |
| | Salt and pepper | |

### Nutrition Bonus
One serving is a high source of calcium.

### Nutrition Note
Keep a can of evaporated milk (2%, low-fat or skim) on your shelf. It makes a creamy base for soups and pasta sauces and has the added bonus of twice the amount of calcium and vitamin D as the same amount of fresh milk.

### Curried Corn and Tomato Chowder
For a completely different but appealing flavor, substitute 1 tsp (5 mL) each curry powder and cumin for the tarragon.

In heavy saucepan, heat oil over medium heat; add onion and cook, stirring occasionally, until tender. Stir in garlic and cook for 30 seconds. Sprinkle flour into pan and mix well. Stir in tomatoes, and dried tarragon (if using); bring to boil, stirring. Add potatoes and stock; boil gently for 15 minutes or until potatoes are tender.

In separate saucepan or in microwave oven, heat milk until hot but not boiling; pour into tomato mixture. Stir in corn. Stir in parsley, chives, fresh tarragon (if not using dried) and hot pepper sauce. Season with salt and pepper to taste.

*Makes 8 servings, 3/4 cup (175 mL) each.*

**PER SERVING:**
164 calories
8 g protein
3 g total fat
  1 g saturated fat
  5 mg cholesterol
28 g carbohydrate
  2 g dietary fiber
263 mg sodium

MAKE AHEAD

Soup can be covered and refrigerated for up to three days, or frozen up to one month. This soup tastes best the day after it is made. Soup will thicken upon standing; add water to thin soup if necessary.

# Bean and Vegetable Soup

*This hearty soup is a meal on its own and handy to have ready in the refrigerator or freezer to simplify hectic mealtimes. Individual portions are easy to reheat in the microwave. Serve with homemade bread and a crisp salad.*

| | | |
|---|---|---|
| 6 cups | water | 1.5 L |
| 3 | carrots, thinly sliced | 3 |
| 3 | cloves garlic, minced | 3 |
| 2 | large onions, sliced | 2 |
| 2 | potatoes (unpeeled), cubed | 2 |
| 1 | can (19 oz/540 mL) pinto or romano (cranberry) beans, drained and rinsed* | 1 |
| 1 | can (19 oz/540 mL) kidney beans, baby lima beans, black-eyed peas or flageolets, drained and rinsed | 1 |
| 1 | can (19 oz/540 mL) garbanzo beans (chick-peas), drained and rinsed | 1 |
| 1/2 cup | chopped fresh parsley and/or coriander (cilantro) leaves | 125 mL |
| 1 tbsp | crushed dried basil leaves | 15 mL |
| 2 tsp | crushed dried oregano leaves | 10 mL |
| 1 tsp | each Worcestershire sauce and pepper | 5 mL |
| | Salt | |

**Nutrition Bonus**
One serving is a very high source of vitamin A, dietary fiber and folacin.

**Rush-Hour Family Dinner**
Bean and Vegetable Soup (this page)
Spinach Supper Salad (page 71)
Whole-wheat rolls
Fresh fruit

In large saucepan, combine water, carrots, garlic, onions and potatoes; bring to boil. Reduce heat, cover and simmer for 20 minutes or until vegetables are tender.

Add pinto beans, kidney beans, garbanzo beans, parsley, basil, oregano, Worcestershire sauce and pepper. Simmer for 5 to 10 minutes to blend flavors. Add salt to taste.

*Makes 12 servings, 1 cup (250 mL) each.*

*If unavailable, substitute kidney beans, baby lima beans, black-eyed peas or flageolets.

**PER SERVING:**
157 calories
8 g protein
1 g total fat
 trace saturated fat
 0 mg cholesterol
30 g carbohydrate
 7 g dietary fiber
307 mg sodium

MAKE AHEAD

Soup can be covered and refrigerated for up to three days or frozen for up to one month.

# Red Lentil Soup

*Make this the taste centerpiece of a meal and add grilled cheese sandwiches or a salad depending on your appetite. Use 2 tbsp (25 mL) each of chopped fresh thyme and oregano leaves if available.*

| | | |
|---|---|---|
| 1/2 cup | dried red lentils | 125 mL |
| 2 | small onions, coarsely chopped | 2 |
| 4 cups | vegetable or chicken stock | 1 L |
| 1 | bay leaf | 1 |
| 1 | large clove garlic, minced | 1 |
| 1 cup | sliced carrots | 250 mL |
| 2 tbsp | long-grain rice | 25 mL |
| 1 | can (14 oz/398 mL) tomatoes (undrained), chopped | 1 |
| 1 tsp | each crushed dried thyme and oregano leaves | 5 mL |
| 1 tsp | ground cumin | 5 mL |
| 1/4 cup | chopped fresh parsley and/or coriander (cilantro) leaves | 50 mL |
| | Salt and pepper | |

Wash and drain lentils. In large saucepan, combine lentils, onions, stock, bay leaf and garlic; cover and simmer for 30 minutes.

Add carrots, rice, tomatoes, thyme, oregano and cumin; simmer, covered, for 20 minutes or until carrots are tender and lentils are soft. Remove bay leaf. Add parsley and/or coriander; season with salt and pepper to taste.

*Makes 8 servings, 3/4 cup (175 mL) each.*

*Nutrition Bonus*
One serving is a very high source of vitamin A and folacin, and a high source of iron.

*Brown, Green or Red Lentils – Is there a difference?*
Yes. When cooked, red (often called Egyptian) lentils are soft, while brown or green lentils retain their shape. Use red lentils for soups and dishes (such as patties) where you want the lentils to be soft. Use brown lentils in salads, soups or in dishes where you want the lentils to retain their shape.

Because lentils are a good source of protein, they are often included in meatless meals. One cup (250 mL) of cooked lentils is a very high source of fiber.

**PER SERVING:**
91 calories
5 g protein
1 g total fat
  trace saturated fat
  0 mg cholesterol
17 g carbohydrate
  3 g dietary fiber
417 mg sodium

**MAKE AHEAD**

Soup can be covered and refrigerated for up to two days.

# Portuguese Collard Soup

*My Canadian-Portuguese friend, Albino Santos, taught me how to make this savory soup. Collard greens are similar in shape to large beet green but look like dark green, flat cabbage leaves with coarse stems. This soup is so popular in Portugal that the grocery stores sell plastic bags full of thinly sliced collard leaves. Use spinach if collard leaves are not available.*

| | | |
|---|---|---|
| 6 cups | water | 1.5 L |
| 5 | large potatoes, peeled and coarsely chopped | 5 |
| 1 | large carrot, thinly sliced | 1 |
| 14 | large collard leaves | 14 |
| 2 oz | chorizo* (sweet smoked pork sausage), about 3 1/2 inches (9 cm) long | 60 g |
| 2 tbsp | olive oil | 25 mL |
| 1 tsp | salt | 5 mL |
| Dash | hot pepper sauce | Dash |

*Nutrition Bonus*
One serving is a very high source of vitamin A.

*Spinach Soup*
Substitute 1 package (10 oz/284 g) fresh spinach, thinly sliced, for the collard.

For a very low-fat choice, you can omit oil without sacrificing taste.

In large saucepan, combine water, potatoes and carrot; simmer over medium heat until vegetables are tender. With a hand-held blender, purée in pot until smooth. (Or use slotted spoon to transfer potatoes and carrot to food processor; blend until smooth. and return to cooking liquid and stir until combined.)

Remove tough stems from collard leaves. Thinly slice leaves into 1/8-inch (3 mm) or less strips to make about 8 cups (2 L) lightly packed. (Or roll up 4 or 5 leaves at a time and slice crosswise in food processor.)

Peel casing from sausage; slice sausage as thinly as possible (1/16-inch/1 mm thick). Stir sliced collard leaves and sausage into soup; simmer, uncovered, for 10 minutes. Add oil, salt and hot pepper sauce. If soup is too thick, add more water.

*Makes 10 servings, about 1 cup (250 mL) each.*

**PER SERVING:**
144 calories
4 g protein
5 g total fat
  1 g saturated fat
  5 mg cholesterol
22 g carbohydrate
  3 g dietary fiber
323 mg sodium

*Chorizo sausages are available in many European meat stores or delicatessens. Sweet means they are not hot and spicy. If chorizo sausages are not available, use a small pepperoni instead.

**MAKE AHEAD**

Soup can be covered and refrigerated for up to one day or frozen for up to one month. (If freezing, add curry powder just before reheating soup.) Before reheating gently, stir soup with a whisk to regain consistency.

***About Curry Powder and Pastes***

Curry powder is a blend of a number of spices and can vary in taste and degree of hotness or heat. Some are labelled mild or medium. Most lose intensity of flavor over time. Curry pastes are now available in many Canadian grocery stores. The paste has a wonderful, fresh flavor and can be used instead of curry powder. They also vary in taste and degree of hotness. Add a small amount of powder or paste to your recipe, then add more to suit your tastes.

# Curried Apple and Zucchini Soup

*The lovely delicate flavor of this light cream soup makes it a good choice for a first course at a dinner party that has a variety of tastes and texture to follow.*

| | | |
|---|---|---|
| 2 tbsp | butter or olive oil | 25 mL |
| 2 | apples, peeled, cored and chopped | 2 |
| 1 | large onion, chopped | 1 |
| 1 to 3 tsp | curry powder (or 2 tbsp/25 mL medium-hot curry paste)* | 5 to 15 mL |
| 4 cups | chicken stock | 1 L |
| 3 cups | diced (unpeeled) zucchini (12 oz/375 g) | 750 mL |
| 1/4 cup | rice | 50 mL |
| 1/2 tsp | salt | 2 mL |
| 1 cup | 2% milk | 250 mL |

In saucepan, melt butter; over medium-high heat, sauté apples and onions for 5 minutes or until softened. Sprinkle with curry powder; cook, stirring, for a few seconds. Pour in chicken stock; bring to boil.

Add zucchini, rice and salt; cover and simmer over low heat until zucchini and rice are very soft and soup is slightly thickened. In batches, pour into food processor or blender; blend until smooth. Return to pan and add milk; heat through.

*Makes 10 servings, about 3/4 cup (175 mL) each.*

**PER SERVING:**
90 calories
4 g protein
3 g total fat
  1 g saturated fat
  2 mg cholesterol
12 g carbohydrate
  1 g dietary fiber
470 mg sodium

# Salads

SALADS HAVE A NEW STATUS IN OUR MEALS and deservedly so. They are no longer reserved only for side dishes. And rock-hard tomatoes and flavorless iceberg lettuce have been pushed aside by crisp romaine and tender buttery Boston lettuce. We now have so many wonderful fresh ingredients to work with that there has been a breakthrough in imaginative combinations of foods — the Melon and Bean Salad (page 68) is just one example. In fact, we could feast on salads for months and never taste the same one. Red radicchio lettuce and nutty arugula are special treats to excite your palate. Pasta salads (now much more than macaroni with mayonnaise), Greek Salad (page 73), Chick-Pea Salad with Red Onion and Tomato (page 77), plus many others are delicious as a main course as well as a side salad.

Moreover, health-conscious gourmets realize that salads are a good way to get fiber, vitamins and minerals into our diet. When combined with high-fiber vegetables, such as spinach, beans and chick-peas, and tossed with a low-fat dressing, such as Creamy Caesar (page 81) or Blue Cheese Dressing (page 80), they are low in calories and fat, and high in fiber. These salads are made to order for the Canadian Cancer Society's recommendations for a low-fat, high-fiber diet.

**MAKE AHEAD**

Roast red peppers; cover and refrigerate up to three days. Wash lettuce; dry well. Wrap in paper towels and place in plastic bag; refrigerate up to one day.

**Nutrition Bonus**
One serving provides 153% of an adult's daily requirement of vitamin C (a very high source) and is also a very high source of folacin.

In the winter or if time is short, use the peppers raw or use canned or bottled roasted red peppers.

Photo:
*Crudités with Creamy Fresh Dill Dip (page 31)*

## Roasted Red Pepper, Mushroom and Melon Salad

*Roasted peppers have a rich, delicious flavor and a soft yet still firm texture that makes this salad spectacular as an appetizer or for lunch. Increase the shrimp and serve as a main-course salad for a light supper.*

| | | |
|---|---|---|
| 1 | large sweet red pepper | 1 |
| 1 | head Boston lettuce, separated | 1 |
| 1 | honeydew melon or cantaloupe, seeded and cut in wedges | 1 |
| 12 | white mushrooms, sliced | 12 |
| 2 | tomatoes, sliced | 2 |
| 8 oz | cooked salad shrimp (optional) | 250 g |
| 1 cup | Orange Vinaigrette (page 80) | 250 mL |

On a baking sheet, roast red pepper in 375°F (190°C) oven for 20 minutes; turn and roast on other side for 20 minutes longer or until soft and blistered. Let cool. Peel off skin (it should come off easily); remove seeds and ribs and cut into strips.

**PER SERVING:**
149 calories
2 g protein
7 g total fat
 1 g saturated fat
 0 mg cholesterol
22 g carbohydrate
 3 g dietary fiber
176 mg sodium

Line 8 salad plates with lettuce. Arrange melon wedges in center; top with red pepper strips. Arrange mushrooms on one side, tomatoes on other. Arrange shrimp (if using) over remaining lettuce. Drizzle with Orange Vinaigrette.

*Makes 8 appetizers.*

---

***Menu-Planning Tip for Busy Cooks***

Once a week, make a large amount of a hearty soup, such as Bean and Vegetable Soup (page 52), Italian Vegetable Soup with Pesto (page 46) or Nova Scotia Seafood Chowder (page 48), and a salad that keeps well, such as Bermuda Bean Salad (page 74), Tabbouleh (page 60) or Chick-Pea Salad with Red Onion and Tomato (page 77). Along with thick fresh bread or toast, you'll be ready for rush-hour meals. Or for a fast, nutritious meal, serve either the salad or the soup with open-face grilled sandwiches, such as mozzarella on whole-wheat buns sprinkled with oregano.

---

MAKE AHEAD

Prepare spinach and wrap in paper towels. Place in plastic bag; refrigerate up to one day.

*Nutrition Bonus*
One serving is a very high source of folacin, and a high source of vitamin A.

**PER SERVING:**
28 calories
2 g protein
1 g total fat
 1 g saturated fat
 3 mg cholesterol
2 g carbohydrate
 1 g dietary fiber
79 mg sodium

Photo:
***Italian Vegetable Soup with Pesto (page 46)***
***Olive and Rosemary Soda Bread (page 181)***

# Spinach and Red Cabbage Salad with Blue Cheese Dressing

*Red cabbage on dark green spinach is a striking color combination. Team it with Blue Cheese Dressing (page 80) for a punch of flavor and a creamy texture.*

| | | |
|---|---|---|
| 2 cups | packed fresh spinach leaves (5 oz/140 g) | 500 mL |
| 1/2 cup | thinly sliced red cabbage | 125 mL |
| 1/4 cup | Blue Cheese Dressing (page 80) | 50 mL |

Wash spinach and dry well; discard tough stems and tear large leaves into 2 or 3 pieces. In salad bowl, toss spinach with cabbage and dressing.

*Makes 4 servings.*

**MAKE AHEAD**

Salad ingredients and vinaigrette can be covered and refrigerated separately for up to eight hours; toss together just before serving. (If vinaigrette and vegetables are combined in advance, broccoli will lose its color.)

*Nutrition Bonus*
One serving provides 87% of an adult's daily requirement of vitamin C (a very high source), and is a high source of folacin.

*Winter Family Supper*
Broccoli Buffet Salad (this page)
Omelet à la Jardinière (page 131)
Apricot, Orange and Pecan Loaf
(page 188)
Cinnamon Applesauce (page 206)

*To toast almonds*
Place almonds in baking pan and bake in 350°F (180°C) oven for 8 to 10 minutes or until golden and fragrant. Toasting almonds enhances their flavor.

# Broccoli Buffet Salad

*Serve this colorful any-time-of-year salad as a first course, or as a main course with an omelet, soup or grilled meat or chicken. Use a mild red onion or a sweet white onion.*

| | | |
|---|---|---|
| 1 | large bunch broccoli (1 1/2 lb/750 g) | 1 |
| 1 1/2 cups | thickly sliced small mushrooms | 375 mL |
| 1 cup | crumbled feta cheese (4 oz/125 g) | 250 mL |
| 1/2 cup | thinly sliced mild red or Spanish onion, separated in rings | 125 mL |
| 2 tbsp | toasted sliced almonds | 25 mL |

| *Vinaigrette Dressing:* | | |
|---|---|---|
| 3 tbsp | water | 50 mL |
| 2 tbsp | olive oil | 25 mL |
| 2 tbsp | fresh lemon juice | 25 mL |
| 1 | clove garlic, minced | 1 |
| 1/2 tsp | crumbled dried oregano leaves | 2 mL |
| 1/4 tsp | each salt and pepper | 1 mL |

Trim ends of broccoli. Cut into florets. Peel stalks and cut in 1-inch (2.5 cm) long strips about 1/4 inch (5 mm) wide to make about 6 cups (1.5 L).

In large pot of rapidly boiling water, cook broccoli for 2 minutes; drain and refresh under cold running water to set color and prevent further cooking. Drain and dry with paper towels. Place in salad bowl and toss with mushrooms, cheese and onion.

**Vinaigrette Dressing:** Combine water, oil, lemon juice, garlic and oregano, mixing well; pour over vegetables and toss to mix. Season with salt and pepper; toss again. Sprinkle almonds over top.

*Makes 8 servings, about 1 cup (250 mL) each.*

**PER SERVING:**
108 calories
5 g protein
8 g total fat
  3 g saturated fat
  14 mg cholesterol
6 g carbohydrate
  2 g dietary fiber
263 mg sodium

MAKE AHEAD

Salad can be covered and refrigerated for up to three hours. Let stand at room temperature before serving.

# Artichoke Tomato Salad

*Tasty chunks of artichoke heart combine with cucumbers, tomatoes and green onions for a sensational summer salad. Serve with soup or cheese and fresh bread for lunch or supper.*

| | | |
|---|---|---|
| 2 tbsp | red wine vinegar | 25 mL |
| 1/2 tsp | Dijon mustard | 2 mL |
| 1 | clove garlic, minced | 1 |
| 1/4 cup | olive or vegetable oil | 50 mL |
| 4 | green onions, chopped | 4 |
| 1 | English cucumber, cut in chunks | 1 |
| 5 | tomatoes, coarsely chopped | 5 |
| 1 | can (14 oz/398 mL) artichoke hearts, drained and quartered | 1 |
| 2 | hard-cooked eggs, grated or chopped | 2 |
| | Salt and pepper | |
| | Lemon juice | |

In large salad bowl, mix together vinegar, mustard and garlic; gradually whisk in oil. Layer with onions, then cucumber, then tomatoes and artichokes. Sprinkle eggs over top. Cover and refrigerate.

About 15 minutes before serving, toss salad. Season with salt, pepper and lemon juice to taste.

*Makes 6 servings, about 1 cup (250 mL) each.*

*Nutrition Bonus*
One serving is a very high source of folacin and a high source of vitamin C and dietary fiber.

*Perfect Hard-Cooked Eggs*
For tender hard-cooked eggs without a dark ring, cover eggs with cold water and bring to boil. Remove pan from heat; cover and let stand for 20 minutes. Rinse eggs in cold water and peel off shell. Unpeeled hard-cooked eggs can be stored for up to one week in the refrigerator.

| COMPARE: | |
|---|---|
| *Per 3 1/2 oz/100g:* | **Grams fiber** |
| • Lettuce (iceberg, romaine or Boston) | 1.5 |
| • Cabbage (red, green or Savoy), raw | 2.0 |
| • Spinach, raw | 4.0 |

PER SERVING:
119 calories
5 g protein
7 g total fat
  1 g saturated fat
  72 mg cholesterol
12 g carbohydrate
  4 g dietary fiber
170 mg sodium

**MAKE AHEAD**

Salad can be covered and refrigerated for up to one day.

# Tabbouleh

*One of my favorite summer salads, this Mediterranean dish is delicious as part of a salad plate for picnics or lunches, and keeps well in the refrigerator. Bulgur adds a nutty flavor and texture, and mint lends a special fresh touch. If fresh mint isn't available, simply omit it.*

| | | |
|---|---|---|
| 1 cup | bulgur | 250 mL |
| 2 cups | lightly packed chopped fresh parsley | 500 mL |
| 1 cup | finely chopped green onions | 250 mL |
| 1/3 cup | olive oil | 75 mL |
| 1/3 cup | fresh lemon juice | 75 mL |
| 1/4 to 1/2 cup | chopped fresh mint leaves | 50 to 125 mL |
| 3 | tomatoes, diced | 3 |
| 1 | cucumber, peeled, seeded and chopped | 1 |
| 1 tsp | salt | 5 mL |
| | Pepper | |

Soak bulgur for 30 minutes in enough hot water to cover by 2 inches (5 cm); drain well, pressing out excess water. Toss with parsley, onions, oil, lemon juice, mint, tomatoes and cucumber. Cover and refrigerate for at least 1 hour. Add salt; season with pepper to taste.

*Makes 10 servings, about 2/3 cup (150 mL) each.*

***Nutrition Bonus***
One serving is a high source of vitamin C, folacin and dietary fiber.

***Picnic Salad Supper***
White Kidney Bean Salad (page 70)
Pasta Salad with Sweet Peppers and Dill (page 76)
Tabbouleh (this page)
Whole-wheat pita bread
Fresh peaches

**PER SERVING:**
132 calories
3 g protein
8 g total fat
  1 g saturated fat
  0 mg cholesterol
15 g carbohydrate
  4 g dietary fiber
244 mg sodium

> ### Bulgur and Cracked Wheat
> Bulgur and cracked wheat add a new dimension in texture, a nutty flavor, good nutrients and fiber to dishes. They are both made from wheat berries. Cracked wheat is basically made from wheat berries that have been cracked, then coarsely milled. Bulgur is made from wheat berries that have been crushed, then either parboiled (European) or steamed (American), then dried. Bulgur is a very high source of fiber. One cup (250 mL) of cooked bulgur has 8 grams of dietary fiber.
>
> Bulgur is available in some supermarkets and bulk food stores, but you can always find it in health food stores. I usually buy medium grind bulgur and use it in salads (Tabbouleh, this page) or stuffings, or mix with other grains or vegetables. Fine grind bulgur is used in breads; coarse grind is often used in pilafs. To use, combine with twice as much hot water as bulgur and soak bulgur for about 20 minutes or until tender but not mushy (soaking time may vary depending on grind and processing); drain. I prefer bulgur to cracked wheat in salads and pilafs.

MAKE AHEAD

Salad can be covered and refrigerated for up to one day. Drain and season before serving.

# Danish Cucumber Salad

*Danes serve this salad often, especially with chicken or as a topping for open-face sandwiches. Sprinkling the cucumbers with salt draws out the water and makes the cucumbers crisp. The dressing has virtually no fat. When I had this dish in Denmark, it was beautifully garnished with blue cornflowers.*

| 1 | English cucumber (unpeeled) | 1 |
|---|---|---|
| 1 tsp | salt | 5 mL |
| 1/2 cup | granulated sugar | 125 mL |
| 1/2 cup | vinegar | 125 mL |
| | Salt and pepper | |
| | Chopped fresh dill leaves | |

Thinly slice cucumbers and place in bowl or sieve. Sprinkle with salt and let stand for 1 hour. Pour off liquid and pat dry; transfer to bowl.

In small saucepan or microwaveable dish, combine sugar and vinegar; stir over low heat or microwave until sugar is dissolved; let cool. Pour over cucumbers; let stand for 30 to 60 minutes. Drain cucumbers; season with salt and pepper to taste. Garnish generously with dill.

*Makes 4 servings.*

PER SERVING:
111 calories
1 g protein
trace total fat
 0 g saturated fat
 0 mg cholesterol
29 g carbohydrate
 1 g dietary fiber
2 mg sodium

MAKE AHEAD

Greens can be washed and dried, then loosely rolled in paper towels and refrigerated in plastic bag for up to 24 hours. Oranges can be sliced, covered with plastic and refrigerated up to 24 hours as well. Toss with dressing just before serving.

**Nutrition Bonus**
One serving is a very high source of folacin.

Balsamic vinegar from Italy is dark colored and has a mellow, slightly sweet wonderful flavor that is delicious in salad dressings. It is available at most grocery stores and varies considerably in quality and price. The higher the quality, the more the balance between sweetness and acid.

**Easter Luncheon**
Melon with fresh lime
Eggs with Curry Sauce over rice
(page 94)
Arugula and Radicchio Salad with
Balsamic Vinaigrette (this page)
Rhubarb Crumb Pie (page 216)

**PER SERVING:**
56 calories
1 g protein
5 g total fat
  1 g saturated fat
  0 mg cholesterol
3 g carbohydrate
  1 g dietary fiber
16 mg sodium

# Arugula and Radicchio Salad with Balsamic Vinaigrette

*Arugula is a tender salad green with a delightful peppery nutty flavor. It's very special and often expensive. Radicchio, a red leaf lettuce, is much like a small cabbage in appearance. When these two are combined, they make a colorful, elegant salad. The flavors are wonderful, so it isn't necessary to add a lot of other ingredients.*

| | | |
|---|---|---|
| 1 | small head radicchio | 1 |
| 1 | bunch arugula or lamb's lettuce or watercress | 1 |
| 1 | head Boston or Bibb lettuce | 1 |
| 1 | orange (optional) | 1 |
| 2 tbsp | balsamic vinegar | 25 mL |
| 2 tbsp | extra virgin olive oil | 25 mL |
| 1/4 tsp | Dijon mustard | 1 mL |
| | Salt and pepper | |
| 1/4 cup | coarsely chopped fresh parsley leaves | 50 mL |

Separate radicchio, arugula and Boston lettuce leaves and wash thoroughly. Spin or pat dry on paper towels. Cut off rind and white pith from orange (if using); cut into thin slices.

In large salad bowl, whisk together vinegar, oil, mustard, and salt and pepper to taste. Tear lettuce into large pieces. Add to bowl along with orange slices; toss well. (Or arrange tossed lettuce on salad plates; garnish with orange slices.) Sprinkle with parsley.

*Makes 6 servings.*

**MAKE AHEAD**

Vegetables and vinaigrette can be prepared and set aside separately for up to two hours.

# Julienne Vegetables with Balsamic-Walnut Vinaigrette

*White or yellow turnip or tender parsnips cut into julienne, or matchstick-size, strips make an interestingly different salad. Serve with grilled meats or fish or as part of a buffet.*

|  | *Balsamic-Walnut Vinaigrette:* |  |
|---|---|---|
| 1 | clove garlic, minced | 1 |
| 1/2 tsp | salt | 2 mL |
| 4 tsp | balsamic vinegar | 20 mL |
| 4 tsp | walnut oil | 20 mL |
| 1 cup | julienned carrot | 250 mL |
| 1 cup | green beans, cut in 1 1/2-inch (4 cm) lengths | 250 mL |
| 1 cup | julienned zucchini | 250 mL |
| 1 cup | julienned celery | 250 mL |
| 2 tbsp | chopped green onions or fresh chives | 25 mL |
| 1/2 tsp | pepper | 2 mL |

*Nutrition Bonus*
One serving is a very high source of vitamin A.

*Making the Most of Salad Oils*
One tablespoon (15 mL) of oil contains 14 grams of fat, so use it sparingly. You can often use less if you use a stronger, more flavorful oil such as extra virgin olive or walnut.

*Lemon Vinaigrette*
Substitute fresh lemon juice and extra-virgin olive oil for the balsamic vinegar and walnut oil.

**Balsamic-Walnut Vinaigrette:** In shallow salad bowl, mash garlic with salt; whisk in vinegar, then oil. Set aside.
**Salad:** In saucepan of boiling water, cook carrot and beans for 3 minutes or until crisp-tender; drain and rinse under cold running water. Drain again. Add to vinaigrette along with zucchini and celery; toss until well mixed. Sprinkle with green onions and pepper.

*Makes 6 servings, about 2/3 cup (150 mL) each.*

**PER SERVING:**
50 calories
1 g protein
3 g total fat
  trace saturated fat
  0 mg cholesterol
5 g carbohydrate
  2 g dietary fiber
223 mg sodium

63

MAKE AHEAD

Salad can be covered and refrigerated for up to one day.

# Coleslaw with Apple and Onion

*This is a tasty everyday summer salad using new-crop, mild-flavored, crisp cabbage. It also makes a fine winter salad when lettuce and tomatoes aren't plentiful or flavorful.*

| | | |
|---|---|---|
| 2 cups | finely shredded cabbage | 500 mL |
| 1 | medium carrot, grated | 1 |
| Half | sweet green pepper, chopped | Half |
| 1 | apple, chopped | 1 |
| 2 | green onions, chopped | 2 |
| | Salt and pepper | |

| *Yogurt Dressing:* | | |
|---|---|---|
| 1/4 cup | plain yogurt | 50 mL |
| 2 tbsp | light mayonnaise | 25 mL |
| 1 tsp | fresh lemon juice | 5 mL |
| 1/4 tsp | dried dillweed or 2 tbsp (25 mL) chopped fresh | 1 mL |

*Nutrition Bonus*
One serving is a very high source of vitamins A and C, and a high source of folacin.

In serving bowl, combine cabbage, carrot, green pepper, apple and onions.

**Yogurt Dressing:** Combine yogurt, mayonnaise, lemon juice and dillweed, mixing well. Pour over salad and toss to mix. Season with salt and pepper to taste.

*Makes 4 servings, about 1/2 cup (125 mL) each.*

To reduce the fat content and give a lighter flavor and texture, substitute low-fat yogurt for mayonnaise in salad dressing recipes, or use half yogurt and half sour cream or light mayonnaise.

**PER SERVING:**
77 calories
2 g protein
3 g total fat
  trace saturated fat
  1 mg cholesterol
13 g carbohydrate
  2 g dietary fiber
76 mg sodium

**MAKE AHEAD**

Omitting tomatoes, salad can be covered and refrigerated for up to four hours; add tomatoes just before serving.

# Tomato Raita

*Raita is an East Indian type of salad. Delicious with curries or spicy foods, it adds a colorful note to the meal. I also like to have it for lunch spooned into pita bread pockets along with hummus and shredded lettuce.*

| | | |
|---|---|---:|
| 1 1/2 cups | chopped seeded peeled cucumber | 375 mL |
| 1 tsp | salt | 5 mL |
| 2 | medium tomatoes | 2 |
| 1 tbsp | finely chopped onion | 15 mL |
| 1 cup | plain low-fat or extra-thick yogurt | 250 mL |
| 1/4 cup | chopped fresh parsley leaves | 50 mL |
| 2 tbsp | chopped fresh coriander (cilantro) leaves | 25 mL |
| 1 tsp | ground cumin | 5 mL |

***Cucumber Raita***
Use 3 cups (750 mL) chopped cucumbers; omit tomatoes.

Sprinkle cucumber with salt; let stand for about 40 minutes. Rinse under cold running water; pat dry. Core tomatoes; cut into 1/2-inch (1 cm) cubes. In bowl, toss together cucumber, tomatoes and onion; drain off any liquid.

Combine yogurt, parsley, coriander and cumin; pour over vegetables and mix lightly.

*Makes 6 servings, about 3/4 cup (175 mL) each.*

**PER SERVING:**
43 calories
3 g protein
1 g total fat
  trace saturated fat
  2 mg cholesterol
7 g carbohydrate
  1 g dietary fiber
35 mg sodium

**MAKE AHEAD**

Salad can be covered and refrigerated for up to eight hours.

# Red Potato Salad with Sour Cream and Chives

*Red-skinned potatoes add color, but any kind of new potato can be used. Be sure to leave the skin on for additional flavor and fiber. Sour cream and yogurt combine to make a light yet creamy dressing that is much lower in fat than traditional mayonnaise, or use light mayonnaise mixed with no-fat sour cream or yogurt (see chart below).*

| | | |
|---|---|---|
| 6 | medium red-skinned potatoes | 6 |
| 1/2 cup | sour cream | 125 mL |
| 1/2 cup | plain yogurt | 125 mL |
| 1/3 to 1/2 cup | finely chopped fresh chives or green onions | 75 to 125 mL |
| 1/2 tsp | salt | 2 mL |
| | Pepper | |

Scrub potatoes but do not peel. If large, cut in half or quarters. In saucepan of boiling water cook potatoes until fork-tender; drain and return to pot. Shake in pan over medium heat for a few seconds to dry potatoes. Cut into 1/2-inch (1 cm) cubes; let cool and place in bowl.

Combine sour cream, yogurt and chives; toss with potatoes. Add salt, and pepper to taste. Refrigerate until serving.

*Makes 10 servings, 1/2 cup (125 mL) each.*

**PER SERVING:**
103 calories
3 g protein
2 g total fat
  1 g saturated fat
  5 mg cholesterol
19 g carbohydrate
  2 g dietary fiber
133 mg sodium

| COMPARE: | | |
|---|---|---|
| *Per 1/2 cup (125 mL)* | **g fat** | **calories** |
| Potato salad made with: | | |
| • 1 cup (250 mL) mayonnaise | 18 | 238 |
| *Or with* | | |
| • 1/2 cup (125 mL) 1% yogurt and 1/2 cup (125 mL): | | |
| • mayonnaise | 9 | 165 |
| • light mayonnaise | 4 | 121 |
| • regular sour cream (14% m.f.) | 2 | 103 |
| • light sour cream (5% m.f.) | 1 | 99 |
| • no-fat sour cream | 0.3 | 92 |

MAKE AHEAD

Cover and refrigerate cooked chicken and dressing separately for up to one day. Assemble salad up to one hour before serving.

# Chicken and Melon Salad

*This delicious main-course salad makes an elegant but easy lunch. The chicken can be cooked and all ingredients chopped a day in advance; then simply assemble the salad an hour or so before serving. Instead of grapes or honeydew melon, you can substitute other melons, or papaya, pineapple, mushrooms or water chestnuts.*

| | | |
|---|---|---|
| 6 cups | cubed cooked skinless chicken* | 1.5 L |
| 2 cups | honeydew melon or cantaloupe balls | 500 mL |
| 2 cups | chopped celery | 500 mL |
| 1 cup | seedless green or red grapes, cut in half | 250 mL |
| 1 cup | sliced water chestnuts (optional) | 250 mL |
| 1/2 cup | 5% or regular sour cream | 125 mL |
| 1/2 cup | 2% plain yogurt | 125 mL |
| 1 tsp | grated fresh gingerroot (optional) | 5 mL |
| 1/2 tsp | curry powder | 2 mL |
| | Salt and pepper | |

In large bowl, combine chicken, melon balls, celery, grapes, and water chestnuts (if using).

Combine sour cream, yogurt, ginger (if using) and curry powder until smooth; stir gently into salad. Season with salt and pepper to taste.

*Makes 8 servings, about 1 cup (250 mL) each.*

*For 6 cups (1.5 L) cubed cooked chicken, use two 2 1/2 lb (1.25 kg) roasting chickens or 8 chicken breasts. To cook 1 whole chicken in microwave oven, put chicken on rack in microwave dish; cover dish with waxed paper. Microwave on High for about 17 minutes, rotating a few times, or until juices run clear when thigh is pierced or until meat thermometer registers 185°F (85°C) when inserted in thickest part. To cook conventionally, cover whole chicken with water and simmer for 1 hour or until tender, skimming off foam occasionally. Let cool; discard skin and bones.

**PER SERVING:**
262 calories
33 g protein
9 g total fat
  3 g saturated fat
  97 mg cholesterol
11 g carbohydrate
  1 g dietary fiber
144 mg sodium

**MAKE AHEAD**

Salad can be covered and refrigerated for up to two days.

# Melon and Bean Salad

*Red kidney beans, juicy melon balls and strips of sweet red pepper make a colorful combination that will perk up anything from cold turkey to meat loaf to sandwiches.*

| | | |
|---|---|---|
| 1 | small cantaloupe or honeydew melon | 1 |
| 2 | green onions (including tops) | 2 |
| 1 | small sweet red pepper | 1 |
| 1 | can (19 oz/540 mL) red or white kidney beans, drained and rinsed | 1 |
| 1 | clove garlic, minced | 1 |
| 2 tbsp | chopped fresh parsley leaves | 25 mL |
| 2 tbsp | fresh lemon juice | 25 mL |
| 2 tbsp | olive oil | 25 mL |
| | Salt and pepper | |

*Nutrition Bonus*
One serving is a very high source of vitamin C and a high source of vitamin A, dietary fiber and folacin.

Cut melon in half; scoop out seeds. With melon baller, scoop out pulp (or cut into cubes) to make about 2 cups (500 mL). Cut onions and red pepper into thin 1-inch (2.5 cm) long strips. In salad bowl, combine melon, onions, red pepper, beans, garlic and parsley; toss to mix.

Whisk together lemon juice and oil; pour over salad and toss to mix. Season with salt and pepper to taste; toss again. Cover and refrigerate until serving time.

*Makes 8 servings, about 1/2 cup (125 mL) each.*

*Summer Salad Buffet*
Melon and Bean Salad (this page)
Julienne Vegetables with Balsamic-Walnut Vinaigrette (page 63)
Red Potato Salad with Sour Cream and Chives (page 66)
Sliced tomatoes and cucumbers
Toasted French bread with Tomato Salsa Topping (page 154)
Fresh fruit in watermelon boat

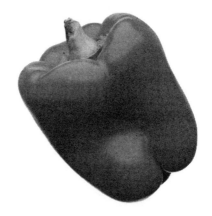

**PER SERVING:**
109 calories
5 g protein
4 g total fat
  trace saturated fat
  0 mg cholesterol
15 g carbohydrate
  5 g dietary fiber
161 mg sodium

**MAKE AHEAD**

Omitting peas, salad can be covered and refrigerated for up to one day. Add peas up to one hour before serving (after a few hours, peas will turn yellow).

# Bulgur Salad with Peas and Onions

*Served instead of a starchy vegetable such as potatoes, this salad pairs beautifully with beef, chicken and fish. Bulgur is available at some supermarkets and most health food stores.*

| | | |
|---|---|---|
| 3/4 cup | bulgur | 175 mL |
| 2 cups | green peas (fresh or frozen) | 500 mL |
| 1/2 cup | chopped green onions | 125 mL |
| 1/2 cup | chopped fresh parsley leaves | 125 mL |
| 1/4 cup | each chopped fresh mint and coriander (cilantro) leaves* | 50 mL |
| 3 tbsp | fresh lemon juice | 50 mL |
| 1/2 tsp | salt | 2 mL |
| 1/4 tsp | pepper | 1 mL |

*Nutrition Bonus*
One serving is a high source of folacin and dietary fiber.

Pour enough boiling water over bulgur to cover by at least 2 inches (5 cm); let stand for 20 to 30 minutes or until tender and doubled in volume. Drain thoroughly, pressing out excess water.

In saucepan of boiling water, cook peas for 1 minute; drain and cool under cold running water. Drain again.

In bowl, combine bulgur, peas, onions, parsley, mint, coriander, lemon juice, salt and pepper; toss to mix. Serve cold or at room temperature.

*Makes 8 servings, 1/2 cup (125 mL) each.*

*Instead of fresh mint and coriander, add 1/2 to 1 tsp (2 mL to 5 mL) ground cumin and 1 tbsp (15 mL) sesame oil.

**PER SERVING:**
78 calories
4 g protein
trace total fat
  trace saturated fat
  0 mg cholesterol
16 g carbohydrate
  4 g dietary fiber
189 mg sodium

MAKE AHEAD

Salad can be covered and refrigerated for up to three days.

# White Kidney Bean Salad

*Cannellini, or white kidney beans, make a delicious salad when teamed with summer garden vegetables. Add cucumber and tomato and you have a gazpacho-like flavor. If white kidney beans are not available, use red. Serve as part of a salad plate, with hamburgers or cold chicken, or toss with spinach for a substantial salad.*

**Nutrition Bonus**
One serving is a very high source of dietary fiber and a high source of vitamin C and folacin.

***Jiffy White Kidney Bean Salad***
Keep a can of white kidney beans on hand for a salad you can make at a moment's notice without the bother of chopping vegetables. Toss 1 can (19 oz/540 mL) drained and rinsed white kidney beans with 2 tbsp (25 mL) olive oil; 2 cloves garlic, minced; 1 cup (250 mL) chopped fresh parsley leaves, and salt, pepper and fresh lemon juice to taste. Makes 4 servings.

***Summer Salad Plate***
White Kidney Bean Salad (this page)
Devilled eggs
Spinach greens with Buttermilk Herb Dressing (page 78)

| | | |
|---|---|---|
| 1 | can (19 oz/540 mL) white kidney beans, drained and rinsed (about 2 cups/500 mL) | 1 |
| 2/3 cup | chopped English cucumber | 150 mL |
| 2/3 cup | chopped Spanish or sweet onion | 150 mL |
| 1 | sweet green pepper, chopped | 1 |
| 1 | large tomato, chopped | 1 |
| 1/4 cup | chopped fresh coriander (cilantro) or parsley leaves | 50 mL |
| 2 tbsp | (approx) fresh lemon juice | 25 mL |
| 1 tbsp | olive oil | 15 mL |
| 3/4 tsp | (approx) ground cumin | 4 mL |
| | Salt and pepper | |
| | Lettuce (optional) | |

In bowl, combine beans, cucumber, onion, green pepper, tomato, coriander, lemon juice, oil and cumin. Taste and season with more lemon juice, cumin, and salt and pepper. Serve alone or on lettuce.

*Makes 6 servings, 3/4 cup (175 mL) each.*

**PER SERVING:**
117 calories
6 g protein
3 g total fat
   trace saturated fat
   0 mg cholesterol
18 g carbohydrate
   7 g dietary fiber
211 mg sodium

# Spinach Supper Salad

*On a hot summer night, this is a perfect light meal with French bread, cold soup and, for dessert, fresh fruit. Present it attractively mounded in a large shallow bowl or arrange it on individual salad plates. This salad is also delicious with Oil and Vinegar Dressing (page 79).*

*This salad is also delicious with Oil and Vinegar Dressing (page 79).*

### Nutrition Bonus

One main-course serving contributes 104% of an adult's daily requirement for vitamin A , 117% vitamin C, and is also a very high source of calcium, iron, folacin and dietary fiber.

| | | |
|---|---|---|
| 4 cups | torn fresh spinach leaves (4 oz/125 g) | 1 L |
| Half | head leaf lettuce, torn in bite-size pieces | Half |
| 2 cups | alfalfa sprouts | 500 mL |
| 1/4 cup | Buttermilk Herb Dressing (page 78) | 50 mL |
| 4 oz | mushrooms, sliced | 125 g |
| 1 | large tomato, cut in chunks | 1 |
| 2 | green onions, chopped | 2 |
| 1/2 cup | crumbled feta cheese (2 oz/60 g) | 125 mL |
| 1 | hard-cooked egg, coarsely chopped | 1 |

In large shallow salad bowl, toss spinach, lettuce and alfalfa sprouts with dressing. Sprinkle with mushrooms, then tomato, onions, feta cheese and egg.

*Makes 2 main-course or 6 side-salad servings.*

### 10-Minute August Supper

Corn on the cob
Sliced tomatoes
Jiffy White Kidney Bean Salad
(page 70)
Whole-wheat bread
Fresh blueberries or peaches
Milk

Herbs and spices vary in intensity of flavor from one brand to another and lose flavor over time. Always taste and correct seasonings before serving.

| **COMPARE:** | | |
|---|---|---|
| *Main course serving:* | **g fat** | **calories** |
| Spinach Supper Salad: | | |
| • without dressing | 11 | 203 |
| • with oil and vinegar dressing | 22 | 306 |
| • with Buttermilk Herb Dressing | 11 | 216 |

| **COMPARE:** | | |
|---|---|---|
| *Side-salad serving:* | **g fat** | **calories** |
| Spinach Supper Salad: | | |
| • with oil and vinegar dressing | 7 | 102 |
| • with Buttermilk Herb Dressing | 4 | 72 |

**PER MAIN-COURSE SERVING:**
216 calories
16 g protein
11 g total fat
  6 g saturated fat
  135 mg cholesterol
18 g carbohydrate
  7 g dietary fiber
592 mg sodium

MAKE AHEAD

Salad can be covered and
refrigerated for up to two days.

# Mediterranean Lentil Salad

*Brown or green lentils instead of red are better for salads
because they retain their shape after cooking and are tender
but not mushy. This salad is delicious as part of a buffet or
served on salad plates along with sliced tomatoes, artichoke
hearts, cooked green beans or asparagus drizzled with a
vinaigrette.*

| | | |
|---|---|---|
| 1 cup | green or brown lentils | 250 mL |
| 1 cup | diced carrots | 250 mL |
| 1 cup | diced onion | 250 mL |
| 3 | large cloves garlic, minced | 3 |
| 1 | bay leaf | 1 |
| 1/2 tsp | crushed dried thyme leaves | 2 mL |
| 1 cup | diced celery | 250 mL |
| 1 cup | chopped fresh parsley leaves | 250 mL |
| 1/4 cup | fresh lemon juice | 50 mL |
| 2 tbsp | extra virgin olive oil | 25 mL |
| 1 tsp | salt | 5 mL |
| 1/4 tsp | pepper | 1 mL |

*Nutrition Bonus*
One serving of this salad contributes
22% of an adult's recommended daily
intake of iron and is high in dietary
fiber.

Lentils, like other legumes, are an
excellent source of dietary fiber, are
high in iron and a good source of
vegetable protein.

Brown lentils are usually smaller
than green lentils. Use either in this
salad. Cooking time will vary depending
on age and type. Cook until tender. If
overcooked, they fall apart.

In saucepan, combine lentils, carrots, onion, 2 of the garlic
cloves, bay leaf and thyme. Add enough water to cover by at
least 1 inch (2.5 cm); bring to boil. Reduce heat and simmer,
uncovered, until lentils are tender but not mushy, 15 to 20
minutes. Drain and remove bay leaf. Add celery, parsley,
lemon juice, oil, remaining garlic, salt and pepper; toss to
mix. Serve at room temperature.

*Makes 8 servings, 1/2 cup (125 mL) each.*

**PER SERVING:**
134 calories
7 g protein
4 g total fat
  1 g saturated fat
  0 mg cholesterol
19 g carbohydrate
  4 g dietary fiber
314 mg sodium

**MAKE AHEAD**

Chop vegetables up to two hours in advance; sprinkle with remaining ingredients 20 minutes before serving.

# Greek Salad

*This salad is wonderful made with home-grown sun-ripened tomatoes that haven't seen the inside of a refrigerator. In fact, for the best full flavor, be sure all the vegetables are at room temperature when serving. Serve with soup, an omelet or as part of a salad plate.*

| | | |
|---|---|---|
| 3 | large tomatoes, chopped | 3 |
| 2 | cucumbers, peeled and chopped | 2 |
| Half | small red onion or 2 green onions, finely chopped (optional) | Half |
| 2 tbsp | extra-virgin olive oil | 25 mL |
| 1 tbsp | fresh lemon juice | 15 mL |
| 1 1/2 tsp | crumbled dried oregano leaves | 7 mL |
| | Salt and pepper | |
| 1 cup | crumbled feta cheese (4 oz/125 g) | 250 mL |
| 6 | black olives (preferably Greek), sliced | 6 |

***Nutrition Bonus***
One serving is a high source of vitamin C and folacin.

In shallow salad bowl or on serving platter, combine tomatoes, cucumber and onion (if using). Sprinkle with oil, then with lemon juice, oregano, and salt and pepper to taste. Sprinkle feta cheese and olives over salad.

*Makes 6 servings, about 3/4 cup (175 mL) each.*

**PER SERVING:**
138 calories
4 g protein
10 g total fat
  4 g saturated fat
  18 mg cholesterol
9 g carbohydrate
  2 g dietary fiber
321 mg sodium

## MAKE AHEAD

Salad can be covered and refrigerated for up to three days.

**Nutrition Bonus**

One serving is a very high source of folacin and dietary fiber and a high source of vitamin C.

**Dried Beans**

Instead of using canned beans in any of the bean recipes in this book, you can cook dried beans. They have a much nicer, firmer texture and are less expensive. One pound (500 g) dried beans (about 2 cups/500 mL) equals 5 to 6 cups (1.25 to 1.5 L) cooked beans. Cooked beans freeze for up to 6 months. One can (19 oz/540 mL) beans equals 2 cups (500 mL) drained beans.

To soak dried peas or beans: Soak well covered in water overnight OR quick-soak by covering with water and bringing to boil; boil for 2 minutes. Remove from heat; cover and let stand for 1 hour. Drain.

To cook soaked beans or peas: cover with water and bring to boil; reduce heat, partially cover and simmer for 1 to 2 hours or until tender. Add more water if necessary. Don't add salt until beans are tender or they will take longer to cook.

**PER SERVING:**

148 calories
7 g protein
2 g total fat
  trace saturated fat
  0 mg cholesterol
27 g carbohydrate
  6 g dietary fiber
250 mg sodium

# Bermuda Bean Salad

*This salad is good with just about any meal, and is handy at a picnic or the cottage for crowd-size entertaining. The recipe can easily be halved by using 10 oz (284 mL) cans of beans and half a pound (250 g) each of fresh beans, but make the same amount of marinade. Bermuda onions — white and slightly flattened at the ends — have a wonderful sweet, mild flavor, but you can use any sweet, mild onion.*

| | | |
|---|---|---|
| 6 cups | cut fresh wax beans (1 lb/500 g) | 1.5 L |
| 6 cups | cut fresh green beans (1 lb/500 g) | 1.5 L |
| 1 | can (19 oz/540 mL) red kidney beans, drained and rinsed | 1 |
| 1 | can (19 oz/540 mL) lima or broad beans, drained and rinsed | 1 |
| 1 | can (19 oz/540 mL) chick-peas, drained and rinsed | 1 |
| 1 | can (19 oz/540 mL) pinto, romano or white kidney beans, drained and rinsed | 1 |
| 2 | sweet green peppers, chopped | 2 |
| 2 | Bermuda onions, thinly sliced in rings | 2 |

| *Marinade:* | | |
|---|---|---|
| 1/2 cup | red wine vinegar | 125 mL |
| 1/3 cup | granulated sugar | 75 mL |
| 1/3 cup | packed brown sugar | 75 mL |
| 1/4 cup | vegetable oil | 50 mL |
| 1 tsp | pepper | 5 mL |
| 1/2 tsp | salt | 2 mL |

Snap ends off fresh beans; cut into 1 1/2-inch (4 cm) pieces. In large pot of rapidly boiling water, cook wax and green beans for 3 minutes; plunge into cold water until cool. Drain and pat dry. In large bowl, combine cooked beans, kidney beans, lima beans, chick-peas, pinto beans, green peppers and onions.

**Marinade:** In small bowl, combine vinegar, white sugar, brown sugar, oil, pepper and salt, stirring until sugar is dissolved. Stir into bean mixture. Marinate in refrigerator for at least 12 hours.

*Makes 20 servings, 1/2 cup (125 mL) each.*

MAKE AHEAD

Salad can be covered and refrigerated for up to two days. Add sesame seeds just before serving.

# Crunchy Green Bean Salad with Asian Dressing

*Let your imagination be your guide and add other raw vegetables such as carrots, kohlrabi, fennel and turnip to this easy make-ahead salad that's perfect for a buffet.*

| | | |
|---|---|---|
| 1 1/2 lb | green beans* | 750 g |
| Half | small head cauliflower | Half |
| 1 | onion, chopped | 1 |
| 1 | large clove garlic | 1 |
| 1/4 cup | soy sauce** | 50 mL |
| 1/4 cup | water | 50 mL |
| 1 tbsp | olive or sesame oil | 15 mL |
| 1 tbsp | sesame seeds | 15 mL |
| 8 | large leaves Boston lettuce (optional) | 8 |

*Nutrition Bonus*

One serving is a high source of vitamin C and folacin.

Remove stem end of green beans. Leave whole or cut into 1 1/2-inch (4 cm) pieces. Cut cauliflower into small florets. In large saucepan, bring 1 cup (250 mL) water to boil; add onion, garlic, beans and cauliflower. Reduce heat, cover and simmer until vegetables are tender-crisp, about 8 minutes; drain and refresh under cold running water. Drain well. Discard garlic.

Combine soy sauce, water and oil; pour over vegetables. Cover and refrigerate for at least 1 hour.

Meanwhile, in skillet, toast sesame seeds over medium-high heat, stirring, for about 3 minutes or until golden.

Place lettuce leaf (if using) on each plate. Toss vegetable mixture; remove from marinade and spoon onto lettuce. Sprinkle with sesame seeds.

*Makes 8 servings.*

*1 1/2 lb (750 g) green beans cut into 1 1/2-inch (4 cm) lengths yields 9 cups (2.2 L).

**Soy sauce is very high in sodium. If possible, use a sodium-reduced soy sauce. If unavailable, look for naturally brewed soy sauce. The highest amount of sodium is found in chemically brewed soy sauce.

*Lunch Menus for Entertaining*

**SPRING**

Chicken and Melon Salad (page 67)
Tossed green salad
Asparagus with Orange Vinaigrette (page 80)
Apricot, Orange and Pecan Loaf (page 188)
Strawberry Meringue Torte (page 210)

**SUMMER**

Pasta Salad with Sweet Peppers and Dill (page 76)
Sliced tomatoes with basil
Peaches with Raspberry Coulis (page 199)

**PER SERVING:**
47 calories
2 g protein
1 g total fat
  trace saturated fat
  0 mg cholesterol
9 g carbohydrate
  3 g dietary fiber
51 mg sodium

## MAKE AHEAD

Prepare salad but only add half of the dressing; cover and refrigerate for up to one day. Add remaining dressing just before serving.

### Nutrition Bonus

One serving provides 113% of an adult's daily requirement of vitamin C (a very high source), and is also a very high source of vitamin A and a high source of folacin.

You can make this salad with 8 oz (250 g) of rotini, fusilli, truciolotti or broken lasagne noodles.

### Lunch Menus for Entertaining

**FALL**

Nova Scotia Seafood Chowder (page 48)
Artichoke Tomato Salad (page 59)
Olive and Rosemary Soda Bread (page 181)
Apple Cinnamon Sorbet (page 200)
Almond Meringues (page 185)

**WINTER**

Tex-Mex Chili (page 100) or Fettuccine with Clam Sauce (page 124)
Whole-wheat toast
Broccoli Buffet Salad (page 58) or Spinach and Red Cabbage Salad (page 57)
Applesauce Raisin Spice Cake (page 191)
Grapefruit Ice (page 202)

**PER SERVING:**
161 calories
4 g protein
6 g total fat
  1 g saturated fat
  0 mg cholesterol
24 g carbohydrate
  3 g dietary fiber
126 mg sodium

# Pasta Salad with Sweet Peppers and Dill

*You can add any of the usual salad ingredients to this dish except lettuce. It's a terrific salad to have on hand in the refrigerator for a ready-made summer meal or a picnic. Vegetables can be crisply cooked, but I like the crunch of them raw. To serve as a main course, add shrimp, julienne strips of ham, chicken and/or cheese.*

| | | |
|---|---|---|
| 3 cups | penne (or 8 oz/250 g pasta) | 750 mL |
| 1 1/4 cups | snow peas or green beans (4 oz/125 g) | 300 mL |
| 3 cups | small cauliflower pieces | 750 mL |
| 1 cup | thinly sliced carrots | 250 mL |
| 2 | sweet peppers (red, yellow, green or purple or combination), chopped | 2 |
| 2 | green onions, chopped | 2 |
| 1 1/2 lb | large, cooked shrimp (optional) | 750 g |
| 1/2 cup | chopped fresh dill leaves* | 125 mL |

*Dressing:*

| | | |
|---|---|---|
| 2 | cloves garlic, minced | 2 |
| 1/4 cup | balsamic or red wine vinegar | 50 mL |
| 1/4 cup | fresh lemon juice | 50 mL |
| 1 tsp | granulated sugar | 5 mL |
| 1 tsp | crushed dried oregano leaves | 5 mL |
| 1/2 tsp | each salt and pepper | 2 mL |
| 1/3 cup | water | 75 mL |
| 1/4 cup | olive oil | 50 mL |

In large saucepan of boiling water, cook pasta until tender but firm (taste for doneness after 2 minutes for fresh pasta, 5 minutes for dry). Drain and rinse under cold running water; drain again.

Blanch snow peas or green beans in boiling water for 2 minutes. Drain and rinse under cold running water; drain again. Cut diagonally into 2-inch (5 cm) lengths.

In large bowl, combine cauliflower, carrots, sweet peppers, green onions, dill, snow peas and pasta; toss to mix.

**Dressing:** In food processor or bowl, combine garlic, vinegar, lemon juice, sugar, oregano, salt and pepper, mixing well. While processing or whisking, add water and oil, mixing well. Pour over salad and toss to mix.

*Makes about 10 servings, 1 cup (250 mL) each.*

*If fresh dill isn't available, substitute fresh parsley and/or basil.

**MAKE AHEAD**

Salad can be covered and refrigerated for up to one day.

# Chick-Pea Salad with Red Onion and Tomato

*Chick-peas, or garbanzo beans, are becoming as popular here as they are in Mediterranean countries. Serve this substantial salad as part of a salad plate with a green salad and dark bread for a light yet high-fiber lunch or supper. It's ideal as part of a meatless meal — chick-peas are high in protein as well as in fiber and iron.*

**Nutrition Bonus**
One serving is a high source of folacin.

**Summer Picnic in the Park**
Broccoli Buffet Salad (page 58)
Red Potato Salad with Sour Cream and Chives (page 66)
Sliced cucumbers
Chick-Pea Salad with Red Onion and Tomato (this page)
Olive and Rosemary Soda Bread (page 181)
Fresh peaches

| 1 | can (19 oz/540 mL) chick-peas, drained and rinsed | 1 |
| 2 tbsp | finely chopped red onion or green onions | 25 mL |
| 2 | cloves garlic, minced | 2 |
| 1 | tomato, diced | 1 |
| 1/2 cup | chopped fresh parsley leaves | 125 mL |
| 2 tbsp | fresh lemon juice | 25 mL |
| 1 tbsp | extra-virgin olive oil | 15 mL |
| 1/4 tsp | each salt and pepper | 1 mL |

In salad bowl, combine chick-peas, onion, garlic, tomato, parsley, lemon juice, oil, salt and pepper; toss to mix. Chill for 2 hours to develop flavors before serving.

*Makes 6 servings, about 1/2 cup (125 mL) each.*

**PER SERVING:**
113 calories
5 g protein
3 g total fat
  trace saturated fat
  0 mg cholesterol
17 g carbohydrate
  3 g dietary fiber
236 mg sodium

# Salad Dressings

BEWARE OF SALAD DRESSINGS: WHEN MADE with mayonnaise, cream or oil, they can add a wicked amount of fat to your diet. You can make delicious dressings with low-fat yogurt or buttermilk, and either light mayonnaise or just a touch of oil, with fresh herbs, mustard or garlic for added flavor.

To reduce the fat in your usual recipes, substitute plain low-fat yogurt, buttermilk or low-fat sour cream for half of the mayonnaise or sour cream you usually use. You'll be surprised at the results — the dressing will be lighter and have added flavor.

Try some of these dressings. Most of them are very low in fat compared to traditional recipes for dressings. If buying commercial varieties, choose the lower fat and calorie-reduced kind.

**MAKE AHEAD**

Dressing can be covered and refrigerated for up to four days.

## Buttermilk Herb Dressing

*Buttermilk, made from low-fat milk, has only a trace of fat, yet it gives body and a wonderful flavor to this creamy salad dressing.*

| | | |
|---|---|---|
| 3/4 cup | buttermilk | 175 mL |
| 1/4 cup | light mayonnaise | 50 mL |
| 3 tbsp | chopped fresh parsley leaves | 50 mL |
| 1 | small clove garlic, minced | 1 |
| 1/2 tsp | Dijon mustard | 2 mL |
| 1/2 tsp | dried dillweed (or 3 tbsp /50 mL chopped fresh dill leaves) | 2 mL |
| 1/4 tsp | each salt and pepper | 1 mL |

In small bowl, whisk together buttermilk, mayonnaise, parsley, garlic, mustard, dill, salt and pepper. Cover and refrigerate.

*Makes 1 cup (250 mL).*

**PER TBSP:**
6 calories
trace protein
trace total fat
  trace saturated fat
  0 mg cholesterol
1 g carbohydrate
  0 g dietary fiber
52 mg sodium

# Oil and Vinegar Dressing

MAKE AHEAD

Dressing can be covered and refrigerated for up to four days.

*Use this all-purpose dressing on green salads, pasta salads and as a marinade for vegetables. It has about half the fat content of a traditional oil-and-vinegar dressing, but use it sparingly because it is still high in fat.*

| | | |
|---|---|---|
| 1 tbsp | cider vinegar | 15 mL |
| 1/2 tsp | Dijon mustard | 2 mL |
| 1 | small clove garlic, minced | 1 |
| | Salt and pepper | |
| 3 tbsp | canola or olive oil | 50 mL |
| 3 tbsp | water | 50 mL |
| 1/8 tsp | granulated sugar (optional) | 0.5 mL |

*Herb Vinaigrette*
Add 1 tbsp (15 mL) chopped fresh herbs or parsley leaves and 1/4 tsp (1 mL) each crumbled dried thyme leaves and celery seed.

*Tarragon Vinaigrette*
Substitute 1 tbsp (15 mL) tarragon vinegar for cider vinegar or add 1/4 tsp (1 mL) dried tarragon leaves.

A classic oil-and-vinegar dressing uses 3 parts oil to 1 part vinegar (e.g., 3/4 cup/175 mL oil and 1/4 cup/50 mL vinegar), and has about 10 grams fat per 1 tbsp (15 mL). To reduce the fat content, replace half of the oil with water, orange juice, or beef or chicken stock, and add a pinch of sugar.

In small bowl, whisk together vinegar, mustard, garlic, and salt and pepper to taste; gradually whisk in oil. Whisk in water; add sugar (if desired). *Makes about 1/2 cup (125 mL).*

**COMPARE:**

| | g fat per 1 tbsp (15 mL) |
|---|---|
| *Salad Dressings from this book:* | |
| Buttermilk Herb | trace |
| Parsley Dressing | 1 |
| Blue Cheese | 1 |
| Tomato-French | 1 |
| Creamy Caesar | 1 |
| Orange Vinaigrette | 3 |
| Oil and Vinegar | 5 |
| *Commercial Salad Dressings:* | |
| Ultra Low Fat Honey Dijon | trace |
| Thousand Island - light | 2 |
| Creamy Caesar Light | 3 |
| Miracle Whip Light | 3 |
| Mayonnaise - light | 5 |
| Blue Cheese with Sour Cream | 6 |
| Miracle Whip Regular | 7 |
| Thousand Island - regular | 7 |
| Creamy Caesar | 8 |
| Mayonnaise - regular | 11 |

PER TBSP:
46 calories
0 g protein
6 g total fat
1 g saturated fat
0 mg cholesterol
trace carbohydrate
0 g dietary fiber
5 mg sodium

**MAKE AHEAD**

Dressing can be covered and refrigerated for up to five days.

*Spring Appetizer*
**Asparagus with Orange Vinaigrette**
Enjoy tender-crisp asparagus with a touch of tangy flavor. Sprinkle 1/2 cup (125 mL) Orange Vinaigrette over 1 1/4 lb (625 g) cooked asparagus. Makes 4 servings.

**PER TBSP:**
36 calories
trace protein
3 g total fat
  trace saturated fat
  0 mg cholesterol
1 g carbohydrate
  trace dietary fiber
77 mg sodium

# Orange Vinaigrette

*Use this citrusy dressing with a tossed green salad or drizzle over cooked, cooled vegetables such as asparagus or green beans.*

| | | |
|---|---|---|
| 1 | small clove garlic, minced | 1 |
| 1 tbsp | fresh lemon juice | 15 mL |
| 1/2 tsp | Dijon mustard | 2 mL |
| 1/4 tsp | granulated sugar | 1 mL |
| 1/4 tsp | salt | 1 mL |
| | Pepper | |
| 2 tbsp | olive oil | 25 mL |
| 1/4 cup | fresh orange juice | 50 mL |
| 2 tbsp | finely chopped fresh parsley leaves | 25 mL |

In small bowl, whisk together garlic, lemon juice, mustard, sugar, salt, and pepper to taste; gradually whisk in oil. Whisk in orange juice, then parsley.
*Makes about 1/2 cup (125 mL).*

**MAKE AHEAD**

Dressing can be covered and refrigerated for up to three days.

**PER TBSP:**
21 calories
1 g protein
1 g total fat
  1 g saturated fat
  3 mg cholesterol
1 g carbohydrate
  0 g dietary fiber
60 mg sodium

# Blue Cheese Dressing

*Using low-fat yogurt instead of the traditional mayonnaise makes a lighter but equally good tasting dressing that is much lower in fat and calories. It's perfect tossed with greens or spinach salad.*

| | | |
|---|---|---|
| 1/4 cup | blue cheese, crumbled (about 1 1/4 oz/35 g) | 50 mL |
| 1/2 cup | 1% plain yogurt | 125 mL |
| Half | clove garlic, minced | Half |
| 1/4 tsp | Dijon mustard (or pinch dry mustard) | 1 mL |
| | Pepper | |

In small bowl and using fork, mash half of the cheese until smooth. Stir in yogurt, garlic, mustard, and pepper to taste, mixing well. Stir in remaining cheese.
*Makes about 2/3 cup (150 mL).*

MAKE AHEAD

Dressing can be covered and refrigerated for up to three days.

## Watercress Dressing

Substitute watercress leaves (stems removed because they have too strong a flavor, and also won't chop finely in food processor) for the parsley.

PER TBSP:
16 calories
2 g protein
1 g total fat
 trace saturated fat
 1 mg cholesterol
1 g carbohydrate
 trace dietary fiber
62 mg sodium

# Parsley Dressing

*This thick, creamy dressing is one of my favorites. Perfect to lightly coat spinach and green salads, it can also be served as a dip for vegetables. It is much smoother and creamier when made in a blender rather than a food processor.*

| | | |
|---|---|---|
| 1/2 cup | coarsely chopped fresh parsley leaves | 125 mL |
| 1 cup | 2% cottage cheese | 250 mL |
| 1 tsp | Dijon mustard | 5 mL |
| 1 tsp | each fresh lemon juice, olive oil and 1% milk | 5 mL |
| 1/4 tsp | pepper | 1 mL |

In blender, finely chop parsley. Add cottage cheese, mustard, lemon juice, oil, milk and pepper; blend until well mixed.

*Makes 1 cup (250 mL).*

MAKE AHEAD

Cover and refrigerate for up to three days. (With longer refrigeration the garlic may become very strong.)

## Yogurt Basil Dressing

Prepare Creamy Caesar Dressing omitting Parmesan. Add 2 tbsp (25 mL) chopped fresh basil leaves (or 1/2 tsp/ 2 mL dried leaf basil), a pinch of granulated sugar and 1 tsp (5 mL) fresh lemon juice. The garlic is optional.

PER TBSP:
21 calories
1 g protein
2 g total fat
 trace saturated fat
 1 mg cholesterol
1 g carbohydrate
 0 g dietary fiber
46 mg sodium

# Creamy Caesar Dressing

*A cinch to make, this light creamy dressing is really delicious.*

| | | |
|---|---|---|
| 1/4 cup | 1% plain yogurt | 50 mL |
| 2 tbsp | light mayonnaise | 25 mL |
| 1 tbsp | milk | 15 mL |
| 1 tbsp | freshly grated Parmesan cheese | 15 mL |
| 1 | small clove garlic, minced | 1 |
| Pinch | each salt and pepper | Pinch |

In small bowl, whisk together yogurt, mayonnaise and milk until smooth. Stir in cheese, garlic, salt and pepper.

*Makes 1/2 cup (125 mL).*

**MAKE AHEAD**

Dressing can be covered and refrigerated for up to three days.

# Tomato-French Dressing

*Here is a tomato-based low-calorie, low-fat vinaigrette dressing that turns an ordinary green salad into a treat.*

| 1/2 cup | tomato juice | 125 mL |
|---------|--------------|--------|
| 1 tsp | cornstarch | 5 mL |
| 1 tbsp | red wine vinegar | 15 mL |
| 1 tbsp | olive oil | 15 mL |
| 1/2 tsp | Dijon mustard | 2 mL |
| Half | small clove garlic, minced | Half |
| 1/2 tsp | crushed dried tarragon or basil leaves (or chopped fresh herbs to taste) | 2 mL |
| | Pepper, salt and sugar | |

*Microwave Method*
Use your microwave oven to speed up boiling the tomato juice mixture, whisk in remaining ingedients, then boil for 1 minute, stirring twice.

In small saucepan, whisk together tomato juice and cornstarch. Cook, stirring, over medium heat until boiling and thickened. Boil for 1 minute, stirring constantly.

Remove from heat. Whisk in vinegar, oil, mustard, garlic, tarragon, pepper, salt and sugar to taste. Let cool.

*Makes about 2/3 cup (150 mL).*

**FOR OTHER SALAD DRESSING RECIPES, SEE:**
Balsamic Vinaigrette (page 62)
Creamy Dill Dressing (page 31)
Balsamic-Walnut Vinaigrette (page 63)
Yogurt Dressing (page 64)

**PER TBSP:**
16 calories
trace protein
1 g total fat
  trace saturated fat
  0 mg cholesterol
1 g carbohydrate
  trace dietary fiber
46 mg sodium

## PORTABLE LUNCH MENUS

Whole-wheat pita bread filled with Hummus (page 34) or
Tabbouleh (page 60), leaf lettuce and alfalfa sprouts
Apple
Milk

Refrigerator Applesauce-Spice Bran Muffin (page 178)
Raw vegetables (carrots, sweet green and red peppers,
zucchini, cauliflower) with Creamy Fresh Dill Dip (page 31)
or Parsley Dressing (page 81)
Banana
Milk

Crunchy Green Bean Salad with Asian Dressing (page 75) or
carrot sticks
Whole-wheat bagel with light cream cheese
Best-Ever Date Squares (page 182)
Orange
Milk

Bagel
White Kidney Bean Salad (page 70)
Cantaloupe wedge
Almond Apricot Squares (page 183)
Milk

Chicken sandwich on whole-wheat bread
Fresh grapes or figs
Oatmeal Raisin Cookies (page 186)
Milk

# Poultry

FROM COQ AU VIN TO TANDOORI, CHICKEN is a mainstay of cuisines around the world. Its flavor appeals to children as well as to adults and it lends itself to a wide range of seasonings and sauces.

For the health-conscious cook, chicken has the added benefit of being a low-fat source of animal protein. To keep the fat at a minimum, remove the skin and any visible fat from chicken pieces before cooking; for whole chickens, cut the skin away before eating (whole chickens take longer to cook and would dry out if skin were removed before cooking). Roast chicken with skin has 53 percent calories from fat, while roast chicken without skin has 31 percent calories from fat.

Obviously, frying chicken adds to the fat intake; baking and broiling are far better cooking methods. Dark meat has a little more fat than white meat. When baking chicken, place pieces or the whole bird on a rack so the fat drips off and the chicken doesn't roast in it. Both turkey and chicken are low in fat; however, duck and goose have a much higher fat content.

**MAKE AHEAD**

Unbaked chicken can be covered and refrigerated for up to two hours. Bake as directed. Baked chicken can be covered and refrigerated for up to two days.

In Chicken Dijon the skin is removed to reduce the fat content. Because of the mustard mixture and bread-crumb coating, the chicken stays moist. Make the crumbs from whole-wheat bread; it is higher in fiber and has a more attractive color for crumbs than white bread. They are quick to make using a food processor.

**PER SERVING:**
178 calories
30 g protein
3 g total fat
  1 g saturated fat
  69 mg cholesterol
7 g carbohydrate
  trace dietary fiber
389 mg sodium

## Chicken Dijon

*This is one of my all-time favorite recipes, mainly because it's so easy to make and tastes so good. Crisp and juicy, this chicken can be prepared ahead of time and served hot, warm or cold. I make the bread crumbs in the food processor from at least one-day-old whole-wheat bread.*

| | | |
|---|---|---|
| 1/4 cup | plain yogurt | 50 mL |
| 2 to 3 tbsp | Dijon mustard | 25 to 50 mL |
| 1 cup | fresh whole-wheat bread crumbs | 250 mL |
| 1 tsp | crushed dried thyme leaves | 5 mL |
| 1/4 tsp | each salt and pepper | 1 mL |
| 4 | skinless chicken breasts or legs (boned if desired) | 4 |

In small bowl, combine yogurt and mustard. In shallow bowl, mix bread crumbs, thyme, salt and pepper.

Spread each piece of chicken with mustard mixture, then roll in bread-crumb mixture. Place chicken in single layer on lightly greased baking sheet. Bake in 350°F (180°C) oven for 45 to 50 minutes for bone-in chicken, 30 minutes for boneless, or until golden brown and meat is no longer pink.

*Makes 4 servings.*

# Crispy Herbed Chicken

*I keep a small jar of herb-seasoned flour on hand so I can make this chicken dish quickly — it's one of my children's favorites. To make only enough seasoned flour for one meal, combine 2 tbsp (25 mL) flour with 2 tsp (10 mL) dried herbs such as crushed oregano, thyme, tarragon and/or Italian seasonings, and salt and pepper.*

| 6 | chicken pieces (about 2 lb/1 kg, bone-in) | 6 |
|---|---|---|
| 2 tbsp | Herb-Seasoned Flour* | 25 mL |
| 1/3 cup | (approx) warm water | 75 mL |

Remove skin from chicken; rinse chicken under cold running water and pat dry with paper towels. Place chicken in single layer in lightly greased shallow roasting pan or baking dish. Use small sieve or spoon to sprinkle Herb-Seasoned Flour over chicken. Pour warm water down side of pan, not directly over chicken.

Bake, uncovered, in 375°F (190°C) oven for 40 to 50 minutes or until chicken is no longer pink inside, basting occasionally with liquid in pan to brown top of chicken. Add more water if there's not enough liquid in pan for basting.

*Makes 6 servings.*

*Herb-Seasoned Flour
Use crushed dried leaf form of herbs, not powdered or ground. In small jar with lid, combine 1/2 cup (125 mL) all-purpose flour, 2 tsp (10 mL) each salt, crushed dried basil and thyme leaves, 1 tsp (5 mL) each crushed dried oregano and tarragon leaves and paprika and 1/2 tsp (2 mL) pepper. Cover and shake to mix; store at room temperature. Makes about 2/3 cup (150 mL).

***August Dinner Menu***
Fresh Tomato and Basil Soup (page 41)
Chicken Dijon (page 84)
Herbed Green Beans with Garlic
(page 164)
Bulgur Pilaf with Fresh Basil,
Mushrooms and Tomatoes (page 145)
Melon with Blueberries (page 205)

| COMPARE: | |
|---|---|
| | % calories from fat |
| Roast chicken breast with skin on | 37 |
| Roast chicken breast without skin | 19 |

**PER SERVING:**
111 calories
16 g protein
4 g total fat
  1 g saturated fat
  48 mg cholesterol
2 g carbohydrate
  trace dietary fiber
186 mg sodium

# Lemon Chicken Schnitzel

*Serve this easy-to-make, moist and tender chicken to family and guests. You can use boneless turkey instead of chicken.*

| 1 lb | boneless skinless chicken breasts | 500 g |
|---|---|---|
| | Juice of 1 large lemon | |
| 1/4 cup | all-purpose flour | 50 mL |
| 1/2 tsp | each salt, crushed dried thyme leaves and celery salt | 2 mL |
| 1 | egg | 1 |
| 2 tsp | water | 10 mL |
| 1/2 to 1 cup | fine dry bread crumbs | 125 to 250 mL |

One pound (500 g) of boneless chicken will usually serve four people. Since the chicken in this recipe is cut into thin slices, it looks like a lot more, and you should be able to serve five people instead of four.

Cut chicken horizontally into 1/4-inch (5 mm) thick slices. Place between 2 pieces of waxed paper and pound with flat side of cleaver or bottom of bottle to flatten chicken. Sprinkle with lemon juice; let stand for 10 minutes.

In shallow dish, combine flour, salt, thyme and celery salt. In another shallow dish, lightly beat egg with water. Dip chicken pieces into flour mixture, then into egg mixture, then into bread crumbs. Place on lightly greased baking sheet or in microwaveable dish. Bake in 400°F (200°C) oven for 10 to 15 minutes, or microwave, uncovered, on High for 4 minutes, or until chicken is no longer pink inside.

*Makes 5 servings.*

**PER SERVING:**
184 calories
24 g protein
3 g total fat
 1 g saturated fat
 96 mg cholesterol
14 g carbohydrate
 trace dietary fiber
489 mg sodium

# Sautéed Chicken with Mushrooms and Onions

*A flavorful rich-tasting dish for family or guests, this is a natural partner for broiled tomatoes, a green vegetable and rice. Any kind of mushrooms can be used—domestic, wild or dried. Try shiitake, cèpe, portobello, oyster, or a combination.*

| | | |
|---|---|---|
| 3 | skinless chicken legs (about 1 1/2 lb/750 g) | 3 |
| 1/4 tsp | paprika | 1 mL |
| 2 tsp | butter or olive oil | 10 mL |
| 1 | onion, thinly sliced | 1 |
| 3 cups | thickly sliced mushrooms | 750 mL |
| 1/4 cup | plain yogurt | 50 mL |
| 1 tsp | all-purpose flour | 5 mL |
| | Salt and pepper | |

***Nutrition Bonus***
One serving is a high source of iron.

If using only dried mushrooms, soak 1 or 2 ounces (30 to 60 g) of dried mushrooms in small amount of hot water for 15 to 30 minutes or until soft; drain (saving liquid for a soup or sauce) and slice.

Chicken is cooked when white meat shows no trace of pink and juices of dark meat run clear when chicken is pierced with a fork.

Sprinkle chicken with paprika. In large nonstick skillet, melt butter over medium-high heat; cook chicken until browned all over, about 5 minutes on each side. Reduce heat to medium-low; cover and cook for 10 minutes longer on each side or until juices run clear when chicken is pierced. If necessary to prevent burning, add a spoonful or two of water or mushroom soaking liquid if using dried mushrooms. Remove from pan and keep warm.

Add onion and mushrooms to pan; cook over medium heat, stirring often, for 5 to 10 minutes or until tender.

In small bowl, combine yogurt and flour; stir into onion mixture. Season with salt and pepper to taste. Return chicken to pan and spoon sauce over top; cook over medium-low heat for 1 to 2 minutes or until hot.

*Makes 3 servings.*

**PER SERVING:**
250 calories
34 g protein
9 g total fat
  3 g saturated fat
  131 mg cholesterol
8 g carbohydrate
  2 g dietary fiber
174 mg sodium

## MAKE AHEAD

Refrigerate prepared unbaked chicken for 20 minutes or up to two hours. Cook spinach a few hours in advance; reheat in microwave or on stove, then add lemon juice, butter and salt and pepper. Tarragon and Mushroom Sauce can be covered and refrigerated for up to two days.

*Nutrition Bonus*
One serving provides 89% of an adult's daily requirement of vitamin A and is also a very high source of iron and folacin and a high source of calcium.

**PER SERVING:**
274 calories
37 g protein
8 g total fat
 4 g saturated fat
 135 mg cholesterol
13 g carbohydrate
 3 g dietary fiber
740 mg sodium

Photo:

*Thai Honey Chicken (page 93) Crunchy Green Bean Salad with Asian Dressing (page 75) Orange Sherried Sweet Potatoes (page 171)*

# Breast of Chicken and Spinach with Mushroom Tarragon Sauce

*This recipe may look lengthy but it isn't hard to make. Because most of the preparation can be done in advance, it's ideal for a dinner party. Serve with Two-Cabbage Stir-Fry (page 163) or Tomatoes Provençal (page 157) and brown rice.*

| | | |
|---|---|---|
| 1 lb | fresh spinach | 500 g |
| 1 tsp | fresh lemon juice | 5 mL |
| 1 tsp | butter | 5 mL |
| | Salt and pepper | |
| 1 cup | Tarragon and Mushroom Sauce (page 152) | 250 mL |
| 4 oz | enoki mushrooms (optional)* | 125 g |

*Chicken:*

| | | |
|---|---|---|
| 1/4 cup | all-purpose flour | 50 mL |
| 1 tsp | crushed dried thyme leaves | 5 mL |
| 1/2 tsp | salt | 2 mL |
| | Pepper | |
| 1 | egg, lightly beaten | 1 |
| 1 tbsp | water | 15 mL |
| 1/2 cup | fresh bread crumbs | 125 mL |
| 1/4 cup | freshly grated Parmesan cheese | 50 mL |
| 4 | boneless skinless chicken breasts (about 1 lb/500 g) | 4 |

**Chicken:** On plate, combine flour, thyme, salt, and pepper to taste. In shallow bowl, combine egg and water. On another plate, combine bread crumbs and cheese. Coat chicken pieces with seasoned flour; shake off excess. Dip into egg mixture, then roll in crumb mixture. Set aside.

Trim stems from spinach. Wash and shake off water; place in saucepan with just the water clinging to leaves. Cover and cook over medium-high heat until wilted. Drain thoroughly; squeeze out excess liquid and chop coarsely. Toss with lemon juice, butter, and salt and pepper to taste.

On lightly greased baking sheet or in microwaveable dish, bake chicken in 400°F (200°C) oven for 15 minutes, or microwave, loosely covered with waxed paper, on High for 5 to 6 minutes, or until chicken is no longer pink inside. If microwaving, let stand for 1 to 2 minutes (cooking time will vary, depending on thickness of chicken).

Place chicken on top of spinach. Garnish with a few spoonfuls of Tarragon and Mushroom Sauce. Sprinkle with raw enoki mushrooms (if using).

*Makes 4 servings.*

*Enoki mushrooms have long, thin stems and small, round heads. They add a woodsy flavor to salads and are lovely as a garnish on cooked meats and chicken. They are available in some supermarkets and specialty vegetable stores. Eat them raw or cooked. If you do cook them, they have to be added to the pan during the last few minutes of cooking only, as cooking makes them tough.

| COMPARE: | |
| --- | --- |
| *Per 3 1/2 oz (100 g)* | Grams fat |
| Kentucky-fried chicken (1 piece) | 17 |
| Broiled chicken without skin (1 piece) | 4 |

Photo:
**Navarin of Lamb**
*(pages 112–13)*

# Orange Ginger Chicken with Leeks

*This quickly prepared dish for guests or family can be dressed up with a garnish of fresh mango slices or grapes and cooked snow peas. Serve over Chinese vermicelli or rice.*

| | | |
|---|---|---|
| 1 1/4 lb | boneless skinless chicken breasts | 625 g |
| 2 | large leeks | 2 |
| 1 tbsp | vegetable oil | 15 mL |
| 2 | green onions, chopped | 2 |
| 3 | large cloves garlic, chopped | 3 |
| 1/4 cup | dry white wine or chicken stock | 50 mL |
| 4 tsp | grated fresh gingerroot | 20 mL |
| 1 | tomato, coarsely chopped | 1 |
| | Grated rind of 1 medium orange | |
| 1/2 cup | fresh orange juice | 125 mL |
| 1 tbsp | all-purpose flour | 15 mL |
| 1/4 tsp | granulated sugar | 1 mL |
| | Salt and pepper | |
| 1/4 cup | toasted slivered almonds (optional) | 50 mL |

**Nutrition Bonus**
One serving is a high source of iron, vitamin C and folacin.

Chinese rice vermicelli, or rice sticks, are available in some supermarkets and Chinese grocery stores. They take only a few minutes to cook or, for a special occasion, drop a few noodles at a time into hot oil in a wok and watch them explode to six times their volume.

Cut chicken into 1-inch (2.5 cm) cubes. Cut off and discard tough green part of leeks. Cut leeks in half and wash thoroughly under cold water. Cut into matchstick-size julienne strips.

In large nonstick skillet, heat oil over high heat; stir-fry chicken for 3 minutes or until browned and no longer pink inside; remove to plate. Stir in leeks, onions and garlic; cook for 1 minute or until leeks begin to wilt. Stir in wine, gingerroot and tomato, scraping up any brown bits from bottom of pan. Return chicken to pan.

In measuring cup, combine orange rind, orange juice, flour and sugar until smooth. Pour into pan, stirring constantly. Bring to boil, stirring constantly; simmer 2 to 3 minutes. Season with salt and pepper to taste. Sprinkle with almonds (if using).

*Makes 4 servings.*

**PER SERVING:**
260 calories
35 g protein
6 g total fat
  1 g saturated fat
  82 mg cholesterol
16 g carbohydrate
  2 g dietary fiber
106 mg sodium

**MAKE AHEAD**

Measure and prepare all ingredients a few hours in advance. Cook just before serving.

*Nutrition Bonus*
One serving provides 128% of an adult's daily requirement of vitamin C and is also a high source of iron.

*Step-by-Step Stir-Frying*
Once you have tried a few recipes for stir-frying, you'll find it easy to improvise and make up your own. I make a stir-fried dish for dinner at least once a week, rarely following a recipe. This lets me use up all the small quantities of raw vegetables hiding in the back of the refrigerator. Stir-fries are excellent for stretching a small amount of meat, chicken or seafood and are ideal for low-fat main dishes.

• Have all ingredients cut and measured.
• Heat wok or nonstick skillet over high heat.
• Add oil and when hot (but not smoking), add foods in the order listed in the recipe (or the ones requiring the longest cooking time first).
• Use a long-handled spatula or wooden spoon to continuously stir the foods.
• Add chopped garlic, ginger or onions along with vegetables; add soy sauce, sherry or vinegar at the end for flavor.
• Mix 1 to 2 tsp (5 to 10 mL) cornstarch with 2 tbsp (25 mL) cold water or stock and add to wok to thicken sauce if desired.

**PER SERVING:**
240 calories
29 g protein
5 g total fat
  1 g saturated fat
  66 mg cholesterol
16 g carbohydrate
  3 g dietary fiber
497 mg sodium

# Chicken with Snow Peas

*Keep this stir-fried dish in mind for when you want a special meal but have only a few minutes to prepare it. The hot pepper sauce is optional, so those who like spicy food can add it. Serve over rice or noodles.*

| | | |
|---|---|---|
| 1 lb | boneless skinless chicken breasts | 500 g |
| 3 tbsp | dry sherry | 50 mL |
| 4 tsp | cornstarch | 20 mL |
| 2 tbsp | soy sauce* | 25 mL |
| 1 tsp | granulated sugar | 5 mL |
| 1 tbsp | vegetable oil | 15 mL |
| 4 | cloves garlic, minced (1 tbsp/15 mL) | 4 |
| 1 tbsp | grated fresh gingerroot (or 3/4 tsp/4 mL ground ginger) | 15 mL |
| 2 | onions, sliced | 2 |
| 1 | sweet red pepper, sliced | 1 |
| 8 oz | snow peas, trimmed | 250 g |
| 1/2 cup | water or chicken stock | 125 mL |
| 1 tbsp | sesame oil (optional) | 15 mL |
| 1/4 tsp | hot pepper sauce or chili paste (optional) | 1 mL |

Cut chicken into 1-inch (2.5 cm) cubes. In bowl, combine 2 tbsp (25 mL) of the sherry and 3 tsp (15 mL) of the cornstarch; stir in chicken. Cover and marinate in refrigerator for at least 1 hour.

In small bowl, combine soy sauce, sugar and remaining sherry and cornstarch; set aside.

In large heavy skillet or wok, heat vegetable oil over high heat until hot but not smoking. Add chicken and stir-fry for 2 minutes. Remove from pan and set aside.

Add garlic and ginger to pan; stir well. Add onions, red pepper, snow peas and water; stir-fry for 2 minutes. Return chicken to pan, add soy sauce mixture and stir rapidly over high heat until thickened and hot. Stir in sesame oil and hot pepper sauce (if using).

*Makes 4 servings.*

*Soy sauce is very high in sodium. If possible, use a sodium-reduced soy sauce. If unavailable, look for naturally brewed soy sauce. The highest amount of sodium is found in chemically brewed soy sauce.

**MAKE AHEAD**

Assembled dish can be covered and refrigerated for up to six hours before cooking.

*Nutrition Bonus*
One serving is a very high source of vitamin A.

# Microwave Tarragon Chicken with Julienne Vegetables

*Leeks are particularly good when cooked this way with chicken, but carrots, zucchini or celery, or a combination of these, also work well. The sauce adds a rich flavor, yet it is deceptively low in fat and calories. If you don't have time to make the sauce, spoon cooking juices over the chicken and vegetables.*

| | | |
|---|---|---|
| 1 cup | each julienne strips leeks, carrots, celery and zucchini | 250 mL |
| 1 tbsp | butter, melted | 15 mL |
| 4 | skinless chicken pieces | 4 |
| | Salt and pepper | |
| 1/2 tsp | dried tarragon (or 4 sprigs fresh tarragon or rosemary) | 2 mL |
| 1/2 cup | Yogurt Hollandaise (page 153) or Tarragon and Mushroom Sauce (page 152) | 125 mL |

Toss leeks, carrots, celery and zucchini with butter.

In microwaveable baking dish just large enough to hold chicken in single layer, sprinkle half of the vegetables. Place chicken on top; season with salt and pepper to taste. Top with remaining vegetables. Sprinkle with tarragon.

Cover with plastic wrap, turning back one corner to vent; microwave on High for 7 to 9 minutes if boneless, 10 to 12 minutes bone-in, or until white chicken meat is no longer pink. Spoon Yogurt Hollandaise over top.

*Makes 4 servings.*

**PER SERVING:**
216 calories
30 g protein
6 g total fat
  3 g saturated fat
  144 mg cholesterol
8 g carbohydrate
  2 g dietary fiber
289 mg sodium

92

# Thai Honey Chicken

**MAKE AHEAD**

Chicken can be marinated in refrigerator for up to one day.

*Fast and easy, this dish is similar to Chinese honey-garlic chicken but with a little extra spice.*

| 4 | skinless chicken breasts or legs (1 1/2 lb/750 g) | 4 |
| 3 | cloves garlic, minced | 3 |
| 2 tbsp | liquid honey | 25 mL |
| 2 tbsp | soy sauce | 25 mL |
| 2 tsp | chili paste | 10 mL |

Hot chili paste or sauce made from chili peppers and seasonings is red in color and adds heat to dishes. I use the Indonesian chili paste called sambal oelek; Chinese chili sauce or Thai chili paste are others. They are often available at supermarkets in the Chinese or ethnic section. They keep for months in the refrigerator. If not available, use hot pepper sauce or crushed dried red chili peppers.

Place chicken in single layer in shallow dish. Make a few shallow cuts on meaty side. Combine garlic, honey, soy sauce and chili paste; spread over chicken. Cover and refrigerate for at least 6 hours.

Place chicken on baking sheet; bake in 375°F (190°C) oven, turning once and basting occasionally with juices, for 30 to 40 minutes or until breasts are no longer pink in center or juices run clear when legs are pierced. Strain juices through fine sieve and serve with chicken.

*Makes 4 servings.*

---

*How to Microwave Whole Poultry*

Microwaving is an easy and moist way to cook chicken or turkey when you want to remove the meat from the bone to use in salad, such as Chicken and Melon Salad (page 67), or other dishes such as Turkey and Melon with Curry Sauce (page 94).

Tie wings and legs tightly to body.

Place bird on microwaveable rack in shallow microwaveable dish; cover with waxed paper, but don't tuck in waxed paper or bird will stew.

Microwave chicken on High for 17 to 20 minutes for a 2 1/2 lb (1.25 kg) chicken (about 8 minutes per pound/500 g), turning dish occasionally.

For 14 lb (6.5 kg) turkey, microwave breast-side down on microwaveable rack in microwaveable dish; cover loosely with waxed paper. Microwave on High for 10 minutes, draining liquid once or twice. Microwave at Medium for 3 1/4 hours more or 12 to 15 minutes per pound or until meat thermometer registers 180°F (82°C) when placed in thickest part of thigh. Drain off juices every 15 minutes. Turn turkey 2 or 3 times during cooking.

Transfer bird to carving board; cover with tent of foil; let chicken stand for 10 to 15 minutes, turkey for 20 to 30 minutes, before using. Pour cooking juices into container and refrigerate or freeze. Fat will rise to the surface and solidify; lift fat off and discard. Use remaining liquid for stock or for making sauces or soups.

**PER SERVING:**
182 calories
31 g protein
2 g total fat
  trace saturated fat
  76 mg cholesterol
10 g carbohydrate
  trace dietary fiber
511 mg sodium

MAKE AHEAD

Sauce can be covered and refrigerated for up to two days. Reheat gently, then continue with the recipe.

**Nutrition Bonus**
One serving is a high source of iron.

**Boxing Day Buffet**
Turkey and Melon with Curry Sauce (this page)
Brown and wild rice
Chutney
Steamed snow peas
Tossed green salad
French bread
Orange Sponge Cake (page 190) with Sherry Orange Sauce (page 204) and Frozen Lemon Cream (page 201)

This is a lovely buffet dish. It's easy to eat without a knife and can be prepared in advance. (Add melon to turkey dish just before serving.) It can be easily doubled or tripled for a larger number of guests. You can substitute chicken for the turkey and can also include shrimp. Plan on about 4 oz (125 g) snow peas per person or use less and serve another vegetable as well.

PER SERVING:
259 calories
24 g protein
12 g total fat
  6 g saturated fat
 74 mg cholesterol
14 g carbohydrate
 1 g dietary fiber
587 mg sodium

# Turkey and Melon with Curry Sauce

*Juicy melons, mangoes or peaches add a festive touch and cooling flavor to this quick curry dish. The sauce is also good with shrimp or hard-cooked eggs. If using the sauce for shrimp, use half chicken stock and half clam juice.*

| | | |
|---|---|---|
| 3 cups | large chunks cooked turkey or chicken* | 750 mL |
| 2 cups | melon balls, sliced mango or peaches | 500 mL |

*Curry Sauce:*

| | | |
|---|---|---|
| 1/4 cup | butter | 50 mL |
| 1 | onion, chopped | 1 |
| 1 | clove garlic, minced | 1 |
| 4 tsp | curry powder or paste | 20 mL |
| 1/2 tsp | each chili powder and ground cumin | 2 mL |
| 1/3 cup | all-purpose flour | 75 mL |
| 2 cups | chicken stock | 500 mL |
| 1/2 tsp | salt | 2 mL |
| | Pepper | |

**Curry Sauce:** In saucepan, melt butter over medium-low heat. Add onion, garlic, curry powder, chili powder and cumin; cook, stirring, until onion is tender. Stir in flour, mixing well. Stir in stock; bring to boil, stirring; simmer, uncovered, for 5 minutes. Add salt; season with pepper to taste.

Stir in turkey; cook for 3 minutes. Add melon and cook, stirring, until heated through, 2 to 3 minutes.

*Makes 6 servings.*

*See page 93 for microwave instructions.

---

*Eggs with Curry Sauce*
Here's a delicious dish for an Easter buffet. In large skillet, prepare Curry Sauce. Add nine hard-cooked eggs, peeled and halved, to Curry Sauce and warm over low heat until heated through, about 5 minutes. Serve over rice. Makes 6 servings.

# TO ROAST TURKEY OR CHICKEN

- Truss bird with kitchen twine or string, tying wings and legs close to body (do not use synthetic twine).

- Place bird on rack in roasting pan. This makes it easier to remove the bird and keeps it from cooking in its own juices and fat.

- Cover turkey lightly with foil (shiny side down); remove foil during last hour of roasting to brown top.

- Roast turkey in 325°F (160°C) oven for 3 3/4 to 4 hours for 12 to 16 lb (5.5 to 7 kg) stuffed bird or 3 1/4 to 3 1/2 hours for 12 to 16 lb (5.5 to 7 kg) unstuffed bird.

- Roast chicken in 325°F (160°C) oven for 20 minutes per lb (500 g), about 1 1/2 hours for 4 lb (2 kg) chicken or until meat thermometer inserted in inner thigh registers 185°F (85°C).

- Turkey is cooked when a meat thermometer inserted in inner thigh registers 180°F (82°C) for stuffed bird, 170°F (77°C) for unstuffed bird, drumstick moves easily in socket and juices from thigh run clear when pierced and white meat shows no trace of pink.

- Transfer turkey to platter; let stand for 15 minutes before carving.

*To reduce fat content when roasting chicken or turkey:*

- Avoid recipes for stuffing that use oil or butter.

- If making a bread stuffing, use fairly fresh bread, or moisten stale bread with chicken stock; add chopped onions, celery and apple instead of oil or butter.

- Instead of stuffing poultry, slip garlic slivers, fresh herbs, sliced fresh gingerroot between flesh and skin or place in cavity.

- Instead of stuffing, place apple slices, onion wedges, mushrooms and/or orange sections in cavity.

- Instead of gravy, serve pan juices with fat removed, Blackberry Sauce (page 151) or cranberry sauce (you can add flavor and interest with chutney, port or brandy).

- Discard skin before serving.

# Meat

M EAT CAN BE A HIGH SOURCE OF FAT in our diet. One way of reducing our fat intake is to eat lean cuts of meat and to cut down on the size of the serving. Remember: Cut down. A healthy diet can include meat. Meat is an important source of complete protein; this means it has all the essential amino acids, the building blocks of protein. Meat is also an important source of iron in a form the body can easily use, as well as a good source of B vitamins and minerals. Just 3 1/2 ounces (100 g) of cooked lean beef (such as flank steak) provides 30 g of protein and 3 mg of iron. This constitutes more than half of an adult's average daily requirements for protein and one-third of an adult male's average daily requirement for iron (teenagers and women aged 16 to 49 require up to 13 mg of iron a day).

The problem is that we often don't limit our meat portions to 2 to 3 ounces (50 to 100 g) as recommended in *Canada's Food Guide to Healthy Eating*. We eat fatty marbled as well as lean meat. To help us eat more healthily, the meat industry is producing leaner beef and pork.

To keep the portion size down yet still make it appear satisfying, use meat in mixed dishes such as stir-fries, stews and soups, or in sauces such as spaghetti sauce. If you cut steak in thin slices before serving, a 3-ounce (100 g) portion will look like much more.

**MAKE AHEAD**

Stew can be covered and refrigerated for up to two days. Reheat gently in oven or stovetop or microwave. To freeze, bake for the first 1 1/2 hours, then cool and freeze up to two weeks. Thaw in refrigerator and proceed with recipe.

*Nutrition Bonus*
One serving provides 154% of an adult's daily requirement of vitamin A and is also a very high source of iron and a high source of vitamin C, folacin and dietary fiber.

## Beef and Vegetable Stew

*This savory stew tastes even better the second day when flavors have had a chance to blend. For variety, add mushrooms, parsnips, celery and red wine. Serve with mashed or boiled potatoes or over hot noodles.*

| 1 1/2 lb | stew beef | 750 g |
|---|---|---|
| 2 tsp | vegetable oil | 10 mL |
| 3 tbsp | all-purpose or instant blending flour | 50 mL |
| 2 cups | water or beef stock | 500 mL |
| 1 | can (19 oz/540 mL) tomatoes (undrained), optional | 1 |
| 3 | onions, quartered | 3 |
| 1 | bay leaf | 1 |
| 1 tsp | crushed dried thyme leaves | 5 mL |
| 1 tsp | crushed dried marjoram or oregano leaves | 5 mL |
| 1/4 tsp | (approx) pepper | 1 mL |

Stews are an ideal way to serve a 3-oz (100 g) portion of meat without appearing skimpy. The addition of vegetables not only stretches the meal but increases the fiber; add a potato (boiled with skin) per person and the fiber content is up to 10 g per serving.

When making any kind of stew, make it a day in advance and refrigerate. Any fat will solidify on the surface and can easily be removed.

For a special occasion, substitute 1 cup (250 mL) each dry red wine and beef stock for the 2 cups (500 mL) water.

### Reducing fat content in meat and meat dishes

- Buy lean cuts of meat such as flank, sirloin tip and lean ground beef.
- Trim all visible fat from meat.
- When browning meat or cooking ground meat, use a nonstick pan so you don't need to add any fat, then pour off all fat before adding other ingredients.
- Cook stews and simmer meat dishes a day in advance and refrigerate overnight. The next day you can easily remove hardened fat from the surface.
- Cut off any fat from cooked meat before eating.
- Processed meats such as salami, bologna, hot dogs and sausages are usually high in fat as well as salt, nitrates and nitrites. They should be eaten less often and only in small amounts.
  See Table B (page 228) for fat content of various meats.

**PER SERVING:**
305 calories
29 g protein
10 g total fat
 3 g saturated fat
 55 mg cholesterol
25 g carbohydrate
 6 g dietary fiber
149 mg sodium

| | | |
|---|---|---|
| 1 | strip orange rind (or 1/2 tsp/2 mL grated) | 1 |
| 3 cups | cubed (1/2-inch /1 cm) peeled turnip or rutabaga | 750 mL |
| 3 cups | cubed (3/4-inch/2 cm) carrots | 750 mL |
| 1 cup | frozen peas | 250 mL |
| 1/4 cup | chopped fresh parsley leaves | 50 mL |
| | Salt | |

Cut visible fat from beef; cut beef into about 1-inch (2.5 cm) cubes.

In nonstick pan, heat oil over medium-high heat. Cook beef, a few pieces at a time, stirring, until brown on all sides. Sprinkle with flour.

Pour in water and tomatoes (if using) and bring to boil, scraping up any brown bits on bottom of pan. Add onions, bay leaf, thyme, marjoram, pepper and orange rind. Cover and simmer for 1 1/2 hours.

Add turnip and carrots; simmer, covered, for 40 minutes or until vegetables are tender. Add peas and parsley. Season with salt and more pepper to taste. Simmer until peas are hot. Discard bay leaf and orange rind.

*Makes 6 servings.*

---

### Making the Most of Pan Juices

Pan juices from roasting meats are flavorful and make a wonderful sauce. To remove fat, either use a large spoon and skim from surface, or pour juices through a cup designed with the spout coming from the bottom, leaving the fat that has floated to the top behind. Or refrigerate pan juices, or add a tray of ice cubes to the juices; the fat will cool and harden, and then can easily be removed. Once the fat has been removed, bring the juices to a boil; boil for a few minutes to evaporate extra water and reduce sauce to desired consistency.

Pan juices and brown bits on the bottom of the pan after broiling or sautéing meats, chicken and fish also make a good base for a savory sauce. Simply spoon off the fat, add a large spoonful or two of wine, vinegar or fruit juice and bring to a boil, scraping up all brown bits from bottom of the pan. Add other flavorings, such as garlic, onions, shallots and parsley, if desired. Remove from heat and stir in a little yogurt.

**MAKE AHEAD**

Steak can be marinated in refrigerator for up to three days. If serving cold, cook, cover and refrigerate for up to twenty-four hours; slice just before serving.

# Marinated Flank Steak

*Whether served hot or cold, this is my son John's favorite steak. It's tender, flavorful and one of the leanest cuts of beef.*

| | | |
|---|---|---|
| 1 lb | flank steak | 500 g |
| 1/4 cup | soy sauce* | 50 mL |
| 2 tbsp | white or cider vinegar | 25 mL |
| 2 tbsp | granulated sugar or liquid honey | 25 mL |
| 1 tbsp | vegetable oil | 15 mL |
| 1 tbsp | grated fresh gingerroot (or 1 tsp/5 mL ground) | 15 mL |

*September Dinner*
Balkan Beet Cream Soup (page 36)
Marinated Flank Steak (this page)
Tomatoes Florentine (page 157) or
Tarragon Carrots (page 159)
Barley and Parsley Pilaf (page 146)
Lemon and Fresh Blueberry Tart
(page 208)

Trim any fat from steak. Place meat in shallow dish or plastic bag. Combine soy sauce, vinegar, sugar, oil and ginger; pour over meat. Cover and refrigerate for at least 24 hours, or let stand at room temperature for up to 1 hour, turning occasionally.

Discarding marinade, broil steak for 3 to 4 minutes on each side or until desired doneness. Slice thinly on angle across the grain.

*Makes 4 servings.*

*Soy sauce is very high in sodium. If possible, use a sodium-reduced soy sauce. If unavailable, look for naturally brewed soy sauce. The highest amount of sodium is found in chemically brewed soy sauce.

**PER SERVING:**
214 calories
26 g protein
10 g total fat
　4 g saturated fat
　44 mg cholesterol
4 g carbohydrate
　0 g dietary fiber
469 mg sodium

## MAKE AHEAD

Stuffed unbaked peppers can be covered and refrigerated for up to one day or frozen for up to one month. Cook frozen or thawed peppers in microwave or conventional oven.

*Nutrition Bonus*
One serving is a very high source of vitamin A (providing 98% of an adult's daily requirements), vitamin C (678%) and is a very high source of folacin and a high source of iron. It also contains a very high amount of dietary fiber.

*September Supper*
Stuffed Peppers with Tomato Basil Sauce (this page)
Steamed carrots
Whole-wheat bread
Peach Blueberry Crisp (page 207)

Instead of Tomato Basil Sauce, sprinkle stuffed peppers with grated Parmesan cheese or low-fat mozzarella cheese before baking.

**PER SERVING:**
303 calories
16 g protein
8 g total fat
   3 g saturated fat
   28 mg cholesterol
45 g carbohydrate
   7 g dietary fiber
751 mg sodium

# Stuffed Peppers with Tomato Basil Sauce

*For a truly attractive dish, use a colorful variety of peppers in this flavorful main course that can be tucked away in the freezer. Tiny baby peppers are available in small grocery stores and are a nice choice for a buffet.*

| | | |
|---|---|---|
| 12 | medium sweet red, green, yellow or purple peppers (or 24 baby peppers) | 12 |
| 12 oz | medium ground beef | 375 g |
| 1 | onion, finely chopped | 1 |
| 2 cups | cooked rice (1 cup/250 mL raw) | 500 mL |
| 1 1/2 cups | drained canned or chopped fresh tomatoes | 375 mL |
| 1/2 cup | tomato sauce* | 125 mL |
| 1 tbsp | Worcestershire sauce | 15 mL |
| 1 tsp | salt | 5 mL |
| 1 1/2 cups | Tomato Basil Sauce (page 152) | 375 mL |

Slice top off each pepper; chop tops and reserve for filling. Remove core, seeds and membranes from peppers. Blanch peppers in boiling water for 3 minutes; drain and set aside.

In large nonstick skillet or saucepan, cook beef, onion and chopped pepper until beef is no longer pink and onions are tender. Drain off fat. Stir in rice, tomatoes, tomato sauce, Worcestershire and salt; simmer for 2 minutes. Spoon meat mixture into peppers. Bake in 350°F (180°C) oven for 20 minutes or until hot. Serve with Tomato Basil Sauce to spoon over top.

*Makes 6 servings.*

*Instead of tomato sauce, you can mix 1/4 cup (50 mL) tomato paste with 1/4 cup (50 mL) water, or use 1/2 cup (125 mL) ketchup.

MAKE AHEAD

Chili can be covered and refrigerated for up to three days or frozen for up to six weeks.

*Nutrition Bonus*
One serving of this chili has 6.6 mg iron, which is 50% of an average adult's daily requirement, and over 50% of an adult's daily fiber needs. It's also a very high source of folacin and a high source of vitamins A and C.

For information on soaking and cooking dried beans, see page 74.

**PER SERVING:**
357 calories
29 g protein
7 g total fat
  2 g saturated fat
  39 mg cholesterol
49 g carbohydrate
  15 g dietary fiber
623 mg sodium

# Tex-Mex Chili

*This is the best chili I've tasted and needless to say one of my favorite recipes. I often add a can of cooked brown beans or any other type of beans.*

| | | |
|---|---|---|
| 1 lb | extra lean ground beef | 500 g |
| 2 | large onions, coarsely chopped | 2 |
| 2 | large cloves garlic, minced | 2 |
| 2 tbsp | (approx) chili powder | 25 mL |
| 1 tsp | ground cumin | 5 mL |
| 1/2 tsp | crushed dried oregano leaves | 2 mL |
| 1/2 tsp | crushed hot red pepper flakes | 2 mL |
| 1 | can (28 oz/796 mL) tomatoes | 1 |
| 4 cups | cooked red kidney beans (or 2 cans (19 oz/540 mL each), drained and rinsed) | 1 L |
| 1/2 tsp | salt | 2 mL |
| 1 1/2 cups | corn kernels (canned, frozen or fresh) | 375 mL |

In large heavy saucepan or nonstick skillet, cook beef over medium-high heat for about 5 minutes or until no longer pink. Pour off any fat. Add onions, garlic, chili powder, cumin, oregano and hot red pepper flakes; cook, stirring, over medium-low heat for 5 minutes or until onions are tender.

Stir in tomatoes, breaking up with back of spoon, kidney beans and salt; bring to boil. Reduce heat and simmer over medium-low heat, stirring often, for 20 minutes or until desired consistency. Add corn; cook until heated through.
*Makes 6 servings, 1 1/2 cups (375 mL) each.*

MAKE AHEAD

Cover and refrigerate up to six hours. Bake as directed.

*Nutrition Bonus*
One serving is a very high source of zinc and a high source of iron.

# Old-Fashioned Meatloaf

*Adding bran to a family favorite is an easy way to add a little fiber to your meals. Serve this traditional meatloaf with baked potatoes and a green vegetable.*

| | | |
|---|---|---|
| 1 lb | lean ground beef | 500 g |
| 1 | large onion, finely chopped | 1 |
| 1/4 cup | wheat bran | 50 mL |
| 2 | slices whole-wheat bread, crumbled | 2 |
| 2 tsp | Worcestershire sauce | 10 mL |

| | | |
|---|---|---|
| 1 1/2 tsp | crushed dried thyme leaves | 7 mL |
| 1/2 tsp | salt | 2 mL |
| 1/4 tsp | pepper | 1 mL |
| 1 cup | tomato sauce* | 250 mL |
| 1 | egg, lightly beaten | 1 |
| 1 tbsp | chopped fresh herbs (thyme, rosemary, savory, sage), optional | 15 mL |
| 2 tbsp | chopped fresh parsley leaves (or 1 tsp/5 mL dried) | 25 mL |

In bowl, combine beef, onion, bran, bread crumbs, Worcestershire sauce, thyme, salt and pepper. Stir in 1/2 cup (125 mL) of the tomato sauce, the egg, and dried herbs (if using); mix lightly. Turn into 9- x 5-inch (2 L) loaf pan or baking dish.

Spread remaining tomato sauce over meatloaf. Sprinkle with parsley. Bake in 350°F (180°C) oven for 45 minutes or until firm to the touch and meat thermometer registers 170°F (75°C). Pour off fat. Let stand a few minutes before serving.

*Makes 5 servings.*

*Instead of tomato sauce, you can substitute 1/4 cup (50 mL) tomato ketchup or tomato paste plus 1/4 cup (50 mL) water. Omit topping.

*Leftovers*

Any leftovers of this dish can be covered and refrigerated for up to two days. Reheat, covered, in microwave. (For one serving, microwave at High for 1 minute.) Or serve cold as a sandwich filling.

If salt is a concern, omit salt and instead of tomato sauce use 1/4 cup (50 mL) each tomato paste and water; omit topping. Sodium will then be 140 mg per serving.

*Extra Lean, Lean, Medium or Regular*

Extra lean ground beef contains not more than 10% fat by weight
Lean ground beef contains not more than 17% fat by weight
Medium ground beef contains not more than 23% fat by weight
Regular ground beef contains not more than 30% fat by weight

- Use medium or regular ground beef when you can pour fat from pan after browning the meat and when it is much less expensive than lean or extra lean.
- Use lean or medium ground beef where some fat is needed for tenderness and juiciness (hamburgers).
- Use extra lean ground beef when you can't pour off the fat (shepherd's pie, or stuffing for pasta), or where other fats are in same dish.

**PER SERVING:**
238 calories
21 g protein
11 g total fat
  4 g saturated fat
  89 mg cholesterol
14 g carbohydrate
  4 g dietary fiber
657 mg sodium

**COMPARE:**

| mg sodium per 1/4 cup (50 mL) | |
|---|---|
| Tomato sauce | 315 |
| Tomato paste | 43 |

**COMPARE:**

| | g fat/serving |
|---|---|
| *Meatloaf made with:* | |
| • extra lean beef | 10.7 |
| • lean beef | 11.4 |
| • medium beef | 14.0 |
| • regular beef | 14.9 |

**MAKE AHEAD**

Uncooked patties with peppercorns can be covered and refrigerated for up to six hours.

# Hamburgers au Poivre

*These peppery hamburgers are drizzled with a shallot-yogurt sauce that turns an ordinary meal into a dressed-up plate.*

| | | |
|---|---|---|
| 1 lb | lean ground beef | 500 g |
| 1 to 2 tsp | peppercorns | 5 to 10 mL |
| 1 tsp | vegetable oil | 5 mL |
| 1 tbsp | finely chopped shallots* | 15 mL |
| 1 tbsp | red wine vinegar | 15 mL |
| 1/4 cup | 2% yogurt or sour cream | 50 mL |
| 1 tsp | all-purpose flour | 5 mL |
| 1 tbsp | chopped fresh parsley and/or coriander (cilantro) leaves | 15 mL |

*Nutrition Bonus*
One serving is a high source of iron.

Divide meat into 4 portions and shape into hamburger patties.

Put peppercorns on large piece of waxed paper, foil or plastic bag. Using bottom of heavy skillet or pan or with side of cleaver or in mini-chopper, crack peppercorns coarsely. Spread peppercorns out. Press patties onto peppercorns; turn patties over and sprinkle any remaining peppercorns over top, pressing to adhere.

In nonstick skillet, heat oil over high heat. Add patties and cook for 2 to 3 minutes or until browned; turn and cook for 1 to 2 minutes or until no longer pink inside, reducing heat if necessary to prevent burning. Transfer to plate and keep warm.

Pour off any fat in pan; reduce heat to medium. Add shallots, cook for 1 minute. Add vinegar; cook for 1 minute, scraping up brown bits from bottom of pan. Remove from heat.

Mix yogurt with flour; stir into skillet, mixing well. Stir in parsley and/or coriander. Place patties on individual plates; spoon sauce over patties.

*Makes 4 servings.*

*If shallots are unavailable, use cooking onions.

**PER SERVING:**
209 calories
22 g protein
12 g total fat
  4 g saturated fat
  57 mg cholesterol
3 g carbohydrate
  trace dietary fiber
72 mg sodium

*Nutrition Bonus*
One serving provides a high source of vitamin A (92% of an adult's daily requirement) and a high source of iron.

## Stir-Frying

Stir-frying is a quick and easy way to cook meats, poultry, seafood and vegetables. By frying in a small amount of oil over high heat and stirring continuously and vigorously, foods are seared and quickly cooked. Vegetables are crisp, and meats are very tender. You can control the temperature by moving the pan on and off the heat.

- Use a nonstick wok or skillet. Heat the oil before adding the ingredients; otherwise, the food will absorb the oil.
- Because stir-frying is so fast, have all your food chopped and measured before you start to cook. The food should be evenly shredded, diced or cut into thin slices so it will cook in a short time. By cutting meats and vegetables on the diagonal, meats will be tenderized, and the largest possible surface area of the food is exposed to the heat.
- To add flavor and tenderize the meat, marinate it in advance; using cornstarch in the marinade helps to tenderize the meat and thicken the sauce.
- When using vegetables that require a longer cooking time, add a little water, chicken stock or rice vinegar, then cover and steam for a few minutes. When preparing a large quantity of stir-fried vegetables, blanch (cook in boiling water for a short time) the longer-cooking vegetables first (blanch cut vegetables in boiling water, then cool under cold running water, to prevent further cooking).

**PER SERVING:**
179 calories
21 g protein
5 g total fat
  1 g saturated fat
  37 mg cholesterol
14 g carbohydrate
  3 g dietary fiber
372 mg sodium

# Stir-Fry Beef Curry

*Here we combine the wonderful flavors of curry and the quick cooking of a beef and vegetable stir-fry to make an easy, delicious dinner. Serve over mashed potatoes or rice.*

| | | |
|---|---|---|
| 12 oz | beef top round steak | 375 g |
| 1 tbsp | minced fresh gingerroot | 15 mL |
| 2 tsp | vegetable oil | 10 mL |
| 1 tsp | medium curry powder or paste | 5 mL |
| 1/2 tsp | ground cinnamon | 2 mL |
| 1/2 tsp | ground coriander | 2 mL |
| 2 | carrots, thinly sliced on diagonal | 2 |
| 3 cups | sliced cabbage | 750 mL |
| 1 | apple, cored and cut in chunks | 1 |
| 3/4 cup | water | 175 mL |
| 1 tbsp | fresh lemon juice | 15 mL |
| 1/2 tsp | cornstarch | 2 mL |
| 1/4 cup | chopped green onions | 50 mL |
| 1/2 tsp | each salt and granulated sugar | 2 mL |
| 1/4 tsp | pepper | 1 mL |

Slice meat diagonally across the grain into thin strips; set aside.

In small bowl, combine gingerroot, oil, curry powder, cinnamon and coriander. In large nonstick skillet, cook half of the spice mixture over medium heat, stirring, for 1 minute. Increase heat to high. Add beef; stir-fry for 2 minutes or until browned yet still pink inside. Transfer to plate.

Reduce heat to medium. Add remaining spice mixture, carrots, cabbage and apple; cook, stirring, for 1 minute. Add water, mixing well; cover and simmer for 3 minutes.

Mix lemon juice with cornstarch; stir into pan along with green onions, salt, sugar and pepper. Simmer, stirring constantly, for 2 to 3 minutes or until vegetables are tender. Stir in beef and any accumulated juices until heated through.

*Makes 4 servings.*

**MAKE AHEAD**

Stew can be covered and refrigerated for up to two days.

*Nutrition Bonus*
One serving provides a very high source of vitamin A (114% of an adult's daily requirement), and iron and a high source of vitamin C and folacin.

*Crock Pot Method for Pot-Au-Feu*
For a medium-size Crock Pot, cut recipe in half. Reduce liquid to 2 cups (500 mL) and use low-sodium beef stock. Add all vegetables except cabbage. Cover and cook on low for 8 to 9 hours. Add cabbage, cook for 1 hour. Add salt and pepper.

# Pot-Au-Feu

*This French savory classic consists of a pot roast of beef and vegetables slowly simmered together. Serve meat and vegetables along with mashed or boiled potatoes in individual large shallow bowls and pour cooking broth over top. It's best to make this a day in advance and refrigerate it overnight so the fat will solidify on top for easy removal. Serve with horseradish.*

| | | |
|---|---|---|
| 2 lb | boneless rib, blade or sirloin tip roast of beef | 1 kg |
| 6 cups | water | 1.5 L |
| 1 tsp | crushed dried thyme leaves | 5 mL |
| 1 | bay leaf | 1 |
| 6 | peppercorns | 6 |
| 2 | large carrots, cut in chunks | 2 |
| 2 | medium onions, quartered | 2 |
| 1 | small white turnip (or 1/4 yellow rutabaga), peeled and cut in 1/2-inch (1 cm) cubes | 1 |
| 2 | stalks celery, sliced | 2 |
| Quarter | small cabbage, cut in wedges | Quarter |
| 1/4 tsp | each salt and pepper | 1 mL |

Be sure roast is securely tied. Place in large deep saucepan or flameproof casserole and add water. Bring to boil over medium heat; remove any scum. Add thyme, bay leaf and peppercorns; simmer for 3 hours or until tender. Skim off fat, or refrigerate overnight then remove fat.

Add carrots, onions and turnip to hot stock; cover and simmer for 30 to 40 minutes or until vegetables are nearly tender. Add celery and cabbage; cook for 15 minutes or until vegetables are fork-tender. Season with salt and pepper. Remove meat to platter; let stand for 10 minutes before carving. Discard bay leaf. Keep vegetables warm; serve with meat and pour broth over top.

*Makes 8 servings.*

**PER SERVING:**
422 calories
49 g protein
18 g total fat
 7 g saturated fat
 110 mg cholesterol
14 g carbohydrate
 4 g dietary fiber
348 mg sodium

**MAKE AHEAD**

Stew can be covered and refrigerated for up to two days.

# Mexican Pork Stew

*My sons Jeff and John really like this stew. Cubed pork cooks much faster than chops or a roast, making this ideal for a quick family dinner. Add crushed hot pepper flakes to taste and any other vegetables in season, such as eggplant or zucchini. Serve with boiled potatoes or over hot noodles.*

| | | |
|---|---|---|
| 1 lb | boneless pork (butt, shoulder) | 500 g |
| 1 tsp | vegetable oil | 5 mL |
| 1 | large onion, coarsely chopped | 1 |
| 1 | clove garlic, minced | 1 |
| 1 1/2 tsp | chili powder | 7 mL |
| 1/2 tsp | ground cumin | 2 mL |
| 1 | can (19 oz/540 mL) tomatoes | 1 |
| 1 | small sweet green pepper, coarsely chopped | 1 |
| 2 tbsp | chopped fresh parsley leaves | 25 mL |
| 1/2 tsp | each crumbled dried oregano and thyme leaves | 2 mL |
| 1/4 tsp | each salt, pepper and granulated sugar | 1 mL |

*Nutrition Bonus*
One serving is a very high source of vitamin C and a high source of iron.

*Shopping Tip*
Various boneless pork cuts including pork shoulders are often featured in supermarket specials. Cut the meat into cubes or strips, discarding fat, and use in stews and stir-fries or on skewers. Package them in 1 lb (500 g) portions (or a size to suit your household) and freeze until needed.

Cut off any visible fat from pork; cut into 1-inch (2.5 cm) cubes. In nonstick skillet, heat oil over medium-high heat. Add pork a few pieces at a time and cook until lightly browned on all sides. Add onion and garlic; cook, stirring, for 5 minutes or until onion is tender. Stir in chili powder and cumin; cook for 1 minute.

Stir in tomatoes, breaking up with back of spoon, green pepper, parsley, oregano, thyme, salt, pepper and sugar; bring to boil. Reduce heat and simmer, covered, for 15 minutes.

*Makes 4 servings.*

**PER SERVING:**
186 calories
21 g protein
7 g total fat
  2 g saturated fat
  52 mg cholesterol
12 g carbohydrate
  3 g dietary fiber
447 mg sodium

**MAKE AHEAD**

Ingredients can be prepared, covered and refrigerated up to eight hours before cooking.

# Chinese Pork and Vegetables

*When my children were little they liked this without the hot red pepper flakes. Now that they are young adults they probably wish I would double the hotness. You may want to add sherry, hot pepper sauce or chili paste, or perhaps more ginger or hot red pepper flakes to taste. Serve on a bed of hot fluffy rice.*

| | | |
|---|---|---|
| 1 tbsp | vegetable oil | 15 mL |
| 1 lb | lean boneless pork, cut in thin strips | 500 g |
| 4 | cloves garlic, minced | 4 |
| 1 | onion, sliced | 1 |
| 5 | stalks celery, diagonally sliced | 5 |
| 4 | carrots, diagonally sliced | 4 |
| 2 tbsp | chopped fresh gingerroot | 25 mL |
| 4 cups | thinly sliced cabbage | 1 L |
| 1/2 cup | hot chicken stock | 125 mL |
| 2 tbsp | soy sauce | 25 mL |
| 1/4 tsp | crushed hot red pepper flakes | 1 mL |
| 1 tbsp | cornstarch | 15 mL |
| 2 tbsp | cold water | 25 mL |

In large nonstick skillet, heat oil over high heat. Add pork and stir-fry until pork is no longer pink. Add garlic, onion, celery, carrots and gingerroot; stir-fry until onion is tender.

Stir in cabbage, stock, soy sauce and hot red pepper flakes; cook, covered, for 3 to 4 minutes or until vegetables are tender-crisp. Blend cornstarch with cold water; add to skillet; cook, stirring constantly, until sauce thickens.

*Makes 4 servings.*

*Nutrition Bonus*
One serving provides a very high source of vitamin A (184% of an adult's daily requirement) and a high source of iron, vitamin C, dietary fiber and folacin.

**PER SERVING:**
274 calories
27 g protein
10 g total fat
  2 g saturated fat
  64 mg cholesterol
20 g carbohydrate
  4 g dietary fiber
691 mg sodium

*Fresh Gingerroot*
Whenever possible, use fresh, not ground, ginger in recipes calling for fresh — the flavor is far superior. Fresh ginger can elevate an ordinary dish into something really delicious. Use it in stir-fries, in curries, with vegetables and in stuffings, stews and other savory dishes. This brown, knobby root is available in the vegetable section of most supermarkets and fruit and vegetable stores.

To buy: Buy young ginger with smooth pale brown skin. Shriveled skin is a sign of age. Avoid buying ginger with cracks, mold or a musty smell.

To store: I use it so often I store it along with garlic in a wire basket or garlic keeper. Or, wrap in paper towel and store in refrigerator; depending on degree of freshness when bought, it will usually keep two to three weeks. For longer storage, wrap in plastic wrap and freeze.

To use: With a vegetable peeler or knife, peel skin from portion of root you plan to use. Depending on the recipe, either grate or chop it before adding to the dish. Sometimes a slice of fresh ginger is added to a marinade or stew, then discarded before serving.

# Pork Tenderloin with Rosemary and Thyme

*This is another of my favorite, quick and easy-to-make recipes. Pork tenderloin is ideal for a dinner party any time of year. In fall, serve with squash or sweet peppers, in summer with Tomatoes Provençal (page 157), in spring with Asparagus with Red Pepper Purée (page 158) and in winter with Braised Red Cabbage (page 160). In good weather, barbecue for 10 to 20 minutes instead of roasting.*

**Nutrition Bonus**
One serving is a high source of iron.

Pork tenderloin is the leanest cut of pork. Tenderloins range in size from 8 oz to 1 lb (250 to 500 g). Plan on buying 5 to 6 oz (150 to 175 g) per person when entertaining. Pork is quite safe when cooked until just a hint of pink remains inside; if overcooked, it will be dry and tougher.

| | | |
|---|---|---|
| 2 tbsp | Dijon mustard | 25 mL |
| 1 tsp | dried rosemary leaves (or 1 tbsp/15 mL fresh) | 5 mL |
| 1/2 tsp | crushed dried thyme leaves (or 1 tbsp/15 mL fresh) | 2 mL |
| 1/4 tsp | whole black peppercorns, crushed | 1 mL |
| 1 lb | pork tenderloin | 500 g |
| | Fresh rosemary sprigs | |

*To reduce fat*
• Buy lean cuts of pork
• Trim visible fat before cooking
• Don't add extra fat when cooking

In small bowl, combine mustard, rosemary, thyme and peppercorns; spread over pork. Place in roasting pan. Roast in 350°F (180°C) oven for 30 to 40 minutes or until just slightly pink inside. To serve, cut into thin slices. Garnish with fresh rosemary.

*Makes 3 servings.*

**PER SERVING:**
194 calories
32 g protein
6 g total fat
  2 g saturated fat
  76 mg cholesterol
1 g carbohydrate
  trace dietary fiber
209 mg sodium

**COMPARE:**

| *Per 3 1/2 oz (100 grams) serving:* | **g fat** |
|---|---|
| • pork, loincut, lean and fat, fried | 28 |
| • spareribs, braised, lean and fat | 25 |
| • pork loin, center cut, lean and fat, broiled | 20 |
| • pork loincut, lean only, roasted | 12 |
| • pork loin, center cut, lean only, broiled | 9 |
| • pork tenderloin, lean only | 5 |

**MAKE AHEAD**

Best served hot or warm, but ham can be cooked, covered and refrigerated for up to two days.

# Sherry-Braised Ham

*This is one of my favorite entertaining dishes for a large group. I like to serve it with Curried Fruit (page 147) and rice. If you remove the fat before cooking, there will be less salt as well as less fat. Cooking ham in liquid makes it very juicy and tender.*

| | | |
|---|---|---|
| 9 lb | cooked ham | 4 kg |
| 1 | large onion, sliced | 1 |
| 2 | carrots, sliced | 2 |
| 2 1/2 cups | beef stock | 625 mL |
| 1/2 cup | sherry | 125 mL |
| 1 | bay leaf | 1 |
| 1/2 tsp | crushed dried thyme leaves | 2 mL |
| 1 | bunch watercress | 1 |

***Easter Dinner or Buffet***
Crudités with Creamy Fresh Dill Dip
(page 31)
Sherry-Braised Ham (this page)
Curried Fruit (page 147)
Rice
Green beans
Rhubarb Crumb Pie (page 216) or
Strawberry Meringue Torte (page 210)

Remove skin and all but very thin layer of fat covering ham. Arrange onion and carrots in roasting pan; place ham on top. Pour beef stock and sherry over ham; add bay leaf and thyme. Cover and bake in 325°F (160°C) oven for 2 1/2 hours, basting 3 or 4 times. Uncover and cook for 15 minutes longer. Transfer ham to platter, discarding vegetables; tent with foil and let stand for at least 15 minutes before carving into thin slices. Garnish platter with watercress or include a sprig on each plate.

*Makes about 18 servings.*

**PER SERVING:**
177 calories
28 g protein
6 g total fat
 2 g saturated fat
 62 mg cholesterol
trace carbohydrate
 trace dietary fiber
1489 mg sodium

**MAKE AHEAD**

Lamb can be stuffed, covered and refrigerated for up to six hours. Remove from refrigerator one hour before roasting.

# Ginger Apricot Stuffed Lamb

*This is a tasty dish any time of year. If you make it in the spring when bright orange grape-sized fresh kumquats are available, they make a most attractive and interesting edible garnish.*

| | | |
|---|---|---|
| 3 lb | boneless leg or shoulder of lamb, ready for stuffing (about 5 lb/2.2 kg, bone-in) | 1.5 kg |

### *Stuffing:*

| | | |
|---|---|---|
| 1 tsp | butter or olive oil | 5 mL |
| 1 | small onion, chopped | 1 |
| 2/3 cup | coarsely chopped dried apricots | 150 mL |
| 1 tbsp | minced fresh gingerroot | 15 mL |
| 1 tsp | grated lemon rind | 5 mL |
| | Salt and pepper | |

### *Glaze:*

| | | |
|---|---|---|
| 2 tbsp | apricot jam | 25 mL |
| 2 tbsp | Dijon mustard | 25 mL |
| 1 tsp | ground ginger | 5 mL |

### *Garnish:*

| | | |
|---|---|---|
| 8 | apricots (fresh or canned), halved and pitted | 8 |
| 8 | sprigs fresh rosemary or watercress | 8 |
| 8 | small ripe kumquats (optional) | 8 |

*Nutrition Bonus*
One serving is a high source of iron and vitamin A.

*About kumquats*
Tiny, orange kumquats are the smallest of the citrus fruits. They are usually eaten unpeeled and are often blanched and added to salads. For a garnish leave the stems and small leaves attached.

**Stuffing:** In nonstick skillet, melt butter over medium heat. Add onion; cook until softened. Stir in apricots, gingerroot, lemon rind, and salt and pepper to taste. Place stuffing in lamb cavity and sew or tie together. Place on rack in roasting pan. Roast in 325°F (160°C) oven for 1 1/2 hours.

**Glaze:** Combine jam, mustard and ginger; brush over lamb. Roast for 15 minutes longer or until lamb is brown outside and pink inside. Transfer to serving platter; tent with foil and let stand for 15 minutes before carving. Arrange apricots, rosemary, and kumquats (if using) around lamb.

*Makes 8 servings.*

**PER SERVING:**
263 calories
31 g protein
8 g total fat
  4 g saturated fat
  108 mg cholesterol
16 g carbohydrate
  2 g dietary fiber
106 mg sodium

**MAKE AHEAD**

Lamb can be marinated in refrigerator for up to 48 hours.

# Marinated Leg of Lamb with Coriander

*Boneless butterflied legs of lamb are available in the frozen-food sections of many supermarkets or fresh at butcher stores. This marinade is also delicious with lamb chops and rack of lamb. An easy dish to prepare in advance, marinated leg of lamb is also easy to transport (in a plastic bag) to the cottage or camp.*

| | | |
|---|---|---|
| 1 | boneless butterflied leg of lamb (about 3 1/2 lb/1.7 kg boned) | 1 |
| | Salt and pepper | |
| | Dijon mustard or horseradish | |

*Nutrition Bonus*
One serving is a high source of iron.

*Should lamb be rare or well-done?*
As with beef, this is a matter of personal taste. However, if it is too rare, it can be tough. If overcooked, it will be dry. The safest is medium-rare, which is tender, juicy and pink on the inside.

If using frozen lamb to retain the most meat juices, let defrost slowly in the refrigerator.

| | *Marinade:* | |
|---|---|---|
| 1 tbsp | coriander seeds | 15 mL |
| 1/2 cup | fresh lemon juice | 125 mL |
| 2 tbsp | olive or vegetable oil | 25 mL |
| 1 | small onion, chopped | 1 |
| 1 tbsp | grated fresh gingerroot | 15 mL |
| 2 | cloves garlic, chopped | 2 |
| 1 tsp | black peppercorns, crushed | 5 mL |

**Marinade:** In skillet, toast coriander seeds over medium heat for 5 minutes, shaking pan occasionally. Let cool, then crush seeds. Combine crushed seeds, lemon juice, oil, onion, gingerroot, garlic and peppercorns.

Cut off any fat from lamb and discard. If meat is not of even thickness, slash thickest section and open up, book fashion. Place lamb in plastic bag and coat both sides with marinade. Tie bag closed; refrigerate for 24 to 48 hours, turning occasionally. Remove lamb from refrigerator about 1 hour before cooking.

Remove lamb from bag, leaving as many seeds or ginger bits as possible clinging to roast. Place on grill or broiler rack; broil about 6 inches (15 cm) from heat for about 12 minutes on each side for medium-rare, 15 to 20 minutes on each side for well-done. Meat thermometer should register 140°F (60°C) for rare, 160°F (70°C) for medium and 170°F (75°C) for well-done. Transfer to cutting board; tent with foil and let stand for 5 minutes. Season with salt and pepper to taste. Slice thinly across the grain. Serve with mustard or horseradish.

*Makes 8 servings.*

**PER SERVING:**
254 calories
35 g protein
11 g total fat
  4 g saturated fat
  124 mg cholesterol
2 g carbohydrate
  trace dietary fiber
57 mg sodium

MAKE AHEAD

Lamb in lemon juice mixture can be covered and refrigerated for up to 24 hours. Assembled skewers can be covered and refrigerated for up to two hours.

# Souvlakia of Lamb

*Greece is famous for its souvlakia or skewered lamb, which is seasoned with lemon juice and oregano. The Greeks don't usually have vegetables on the skewers, but it's more colorful when you include them and they add extra flavor. Boneless lamb loins are available in the frozen-food sections of supermarkets if you can't find fresh lamb. Serve the skewers on hot rice.*

| | | |
|---|---|---|
| 1 lb | boneless lamb loin or leg | 500 g |
| 2 tbsp | fresh lemon juice | 25 mL |
| 1 tsp | crumbled dried oregano leaves | 5 mL |
| | Salt and pepper | |
| 8 | small onions | 8 |
| 1 | small sweet red pepper | 1 |
| 1 | small sweet yellow or green pepper | 1 |

*Nutrition Bonus*
One serving provides a very high source of vitamin C (108% of an adult's daily requirement) and a high source of iron.

Cut lamb into 1-inch (2.5 cm) cubes. Place in glass dish or plate; sprinkle with lemon juice, oregano, and salt and pepper to taste. Blanch onions in boiling water for 10 to 15 minutes or until almost tender; drain and let cool enough to handle. Cut off root ends; squeeze off skins. Seed red and yellow peppers; cut into 1 1/2-inch (4 cm) pieces.

Alternately thread lamb and vegetables onto metal skewers or wooden skewers that have been soaked in water.

Place skewers on broiler rack or grill about 5 inches (12 cm) from heat; cook, turning once or twice, for 8 to 12 minutes or until meat is brown outside but still pink inside.

*Makes 4 servings.*

PER SERVING:
226 calories
26 g protein
7 g total fat
 3 g saturated fat
 92 mg cholesterol
15 g carbohydrate
 3 g dietary fiber
50 mg sodium

## MAKE AHEAD

Lamb can be baked, covered and refrigerated for up to one day. Gently reheat before adding vegetables.

*Nutrition Bonus*
One serving provides a high source of vitamin A (115% of an adult's daily requirement) and a high source of iron and folacin.

*Winter Dinner Party*
Cream of Broccoli Soup (page 40)
Navarin of Lamb (this page)
Tiny boiled potatoes
Arugula and Radicchio Salad with Balsamic Vinaigrette (page 62)
Apple Cinnamon Sorbet (page 200) or Grapefruit Ice (page 202)
Oatmeal Raisin Cookies (page 186)

*Spring Dinner Buffet*
Asparagus with Orange Vinaigrette (page 80)
Navarin of Lamb (this page)
Tiny boiled potatoes
Tossed green salad with Watercress Dressing (page 81)
Rhubarb Crumb Pie (page 216)

**PER SERVING:**
262 calories
28 g protein
7 g total fat
  2 g saturated fat
  83 mg cholesterol
23 g carbohydrate
  4 g dietary fiber
322 mg sodium

# Navarin of Lamb

*Adapted from Lucy Waverman's beautifully flavored navarin of lamb and wild rice, this has sweet mild garlic and the special flavor of rosemary. Serve with rice, noodles or potatoes.*

| | | |
|---|---|---|
| 2 lb | lean boneless lamb (e.g., leg) | 1 kg |
| 1 tsp | granulated sugar | 5 mL |
| | Salt and pepper | |
| 1 tbsp | vegetable oil | 15 mL |
| 2 tbsp | all-purpose flour | 25 mL |
| 2 cups | beef or lamb stock | 500 mL |
| 1 | clove garlic, minced | 1 |
| 1 tbsp | tomato paste | 15 mL |
| | Bouquet garni* | |
| 1 | long strip orange rind (orange part only) | 1 |
| 1 tbsp | fresh rosemary leaves (or 1 tsp/5 mL dried) | 15 mL |

| *Vegetables:* | | |
|---|---|---|
| 5 | carrots | 5 |
| 3 | small white turnips or 1 yellow rutabaga (about 1 lb/500 g) | 3 |
| 10 | small onions (or 1 cup/250 mL pearl onions) | 10 |

| *Garlic Garnish:* | | |
|---|---|---|
| 4 | heads garlic | 4 |
| 1/2 cup | low-fat milk | 125 mL |

Trim any fat from lamb; cut into bite-size cubes. Sprinkle with sugar, and salt and pepper to taste. In large heavy Dutch oven or nonstick pan, heat oil over medium heat. Add meat a few pieces at a time and brown well.

Remove meat from pan and pour off all fat; return meat to pan. Sprinkle with flour; cook over medium heat, stirring constantly, for 1 minute or until flour has browned. Add stock, garlic, tomato paste, bouquet garni and orange rind; bring to boil, stirring to scrape up brown bits from bottom of pan. Cover and bake in 325°F (160°C) oven for 1 hour. Let cool, then refrigerate until cold. Remove fat from surface of stew; discard orange rind and bouquet garni.

**Vegetables:** Peel carrots and turnips; cut into 3/4-inch (2 cm) pieces. Peel onions. (If using pearl onions, blanch in boiling water for 1 minute; drain, cut off root end and gently squeeze to remove skin.)

**Garlic Garnish:** Separate garlic heads into cloves. Place in small saucepan along with milk; bring to boil and boil for 2 minutes. Reduce heat to low; cover and simmer until soft. Drain and let cool; gently squeeze to remove skins. Set aside.

About 45 minutes before serving, gently reheat lamb mixture, stirring to prevent scorching. Add vegetables and simmer, covered, for 30 to 40 minutes or until vegetables are tender, adding water if necessary. (For a thicker gravy, add 2 tbsp/25 mL flour mixed with 1/2 cup/125 mL water or stock; bring to boil and cook, stirring, until thickened slightly.) Add rosemary and garnish with garlic cloves.

*Makes 8 servings.*

*Bouquet Garni: Tie 2 sprigs fresh parsley, 1 sprig fresh thyme and 1 bay leaf in hollow of 1 stalk of celery or place in cheesecloth bag (if you don't have fresh thyme, use 1/2 tsp/2 mL dried).

# Fish and Seafood

WHEN IT COMES TO FISH AND SEAFOOD, Canadians on the east and west coasts don't know how lucky they are. I grew up in Vancouver, and it wasn't until I moved to Ontario that I realized inexpensive fresh fish was a rare commodity to many people. And when I say fresh, I mean no more than a day or two out of the water. Be careful with the meaning of the word fresh. Sometimes we say fresh to mean not frozen, but just because a fish has not yet been frozen, it's not necessarily fresh — it may have been out of the water for days.

The best test of a fresh fish or seafood is its smell. It should be very mildly fishy, nothing stronger. Don't hesitate to ask to smell the fish; a reputable store will encourage your scrutiny, and you'll discover it pays to find a store you can rely on.

If you can't get good fresh fish, don't let that prevent you from enjoying it anyway. Frozen fish is available right across the country. Part of the trick of cooking frozen fish is defrosting it properly. Don't put it out on the counter hours before you plan to cook it. It's important to keep fish cold so the outside portions don't deteriorate while the inside is still frozen. The best method of defrosting is to place it in the refrigerator. Often we don't have the time, so the next best way is to immerse the package in cold water for about 1 1/2 hours. That way, the outside thawed portion stays cold while the center is still defrosting. Before cooking, separate the fish into fillets if it has been frozen in a block; it looks more appealing that way.

There is an unnecessary mystique about cooking fish. Too many people are afraid to take the plunge, when in fact fish is one of the easiest foods to cook. With fish, the simpler the better. Most fish has a delicate flavor that you don't want to mask with strong seasonings or heavy sauces. A sprinkling of lemon juice and chopped fresh parsley is a classic, delicious preparation. Just try Sole Fillets with Lemon and Parsley (page 115).

And thanks to the Department of Fisheries and Oceans, the Canadian method of cooking fish (as the Americans call it) means we no longer have to guess how long to cook a piece of fish. It's very simple: measure the thickness of the fish at the thickest part; for each inch (2.5 cm) of thickness, allow 10 minutes of cooking time at 400°F (200°C); add 5 minutes if the fish is wrapped in foil and double the time if the fish is still frozen. Perfectly cooked fish is opaque and flakes slightly when tested with a fork. Avoid overcooking; it dries the fish out.

Best of all, fish is healthy: it's low in fat and calories and high in protein. And for cooks on the run, it's one of the fastest foods around.

# Sole Fillets with Lemon and Parsley

*This really simple recipe is one of the very best ways to make tender, moist fish fillets. If using frozen fillets, try to thaw and separate them before cooking for best results.*

| | | |
|---|---|---|
| 1 lb | sole fillets* | 500 g |
| | Salt and pepper | |
| 2 tbsp | chopped fresh parsley | 25 mL |
| 1 tbsp | fresh lemon juice | 15 mL |
| 2 tsp | butter, melted, or olive oil | 10 mL |

Fish is an excellent source of protein and is low in fat and calories.

Place fillets in lightly greased baking or microwaveable dish just large enough to hold them in single layer. Sprinkle with salt and pepper to taste. Combine parsley, lemon juice and butter; drizzle over fish.

Bake, uncovered, in 450°F (230°C) oven for 8 to 10 minutes or until fish is opaque and flakes easily when tested with fork. Or cover with vented plastic wrap and microwave on High for 3 1/2 to 4 minutes.

*Makes 4 servings.*

*Pacific perch, snapper or cod may be substituted for the sole.

**PER SERVING:**
122 calories
21 g protein
3 g total fat
  2 g saturated fat
  65 mg cholesterol
trace carbohydrate
  trace dietary fiber
113 mg sodium

MAKE AHEAD

Dish can be assembled, covered and refrigerated for up to three hours. Let stand at room temperature for 20 minutes; add 5 to 10 minutes to cooking time.

# Sole Florentine

*This colorful dish is a little fancier than Sole Fillets with Lemon and Parsley and makes for easy entertaining since you can prepare it in advance. Serve with Braised Red Peppers and Leeks (page 165), rice or Mashed Potatoes with Garlic and Onions (page 169).*

| | | |
|---|---|---|
| 1 lb | fresh spinach | 500 g |
| 1 1/4 lb | sole fillets | 625 g |
| 1 | onion, chopped | 1 |
| Half | bay leaf | Half |
| 2 tbsp | fresh lemon juice | 25 mL |
| 3 | peppercorns | 3 |
| 1/2 tsp | salt | 2 mL |
| 3/4 cup | dry white wine | 175 mL |
| 1 tbsp | butter | 15 mL |
| 2 tbsp | all-purpose flour | 25 mL |
| 1/2 cup | 1% milk | 125 mL |
| 1/4 tsp | each salt and pepper | 1 mL |
| 2 tbsp | grated Parmesan cheese | 25 mL |

*Nutrition Bonus*
One serving is a very high source of vitamin A (providing 88% of an adult's daily requirement) as well as being a very high source of iron and folacin and a high source of calcium.

Trim stems from spinach. Wash and shake off water; place in saucepan with just the water clinging to leaves. Cover and cook until wilted. Drain and squeeze out excess water; chop finely. Set aside.

Roll up each fillet and secure with toothpick. Arrange rolls in skillet or pan just large enough to hold them in single layer; add onion, bay leaf, lemon juice, peppercorns and salt. Pour in wine; bring to boil. Cover, reduce heat and simmer for 5 minutes. Remove fillets from liquid, reserving liquid.

Arrange spinach over bottom of shallow greased dish just large enough to hold fish rolls in single layer. Removing toothpicks from fish, place fish rolls on top of spinach. Cover dish.

Strain reserved poaching liquid into measure to make 1 cup (250 mL), adding water if necessary. In small saucepan, melt butter over low heat; add flour and stir for 1 minute. Whisk in poaching liquid; bring to boil, stirring constantly. Stir in milk, salt and pepper. Remove from heat.

Pour sauce over fish. Sprinkle with Parmesan cheese. Bake, uncovered, in 375° F (190° C) oven for 10 minutes or until bubbly.

*Makes 4 servings.*

PER SERVING:
233 calories
33 g protein
6 g total fat
  3 g saturated fat
  79 mg cholesterol
9 g carbohydrate
  3 g dietary fiber
720 mg sodium

# Sole Poached with Tomatoes, Artichokes and Mushrooms

*You can use any type of white fish fillets or steaks, such as cod, halibut or haddock, in this moist and savory fish dish. Serve over pasta or rice.*

| | | |
|---|---|---|
| 1 tbsp | olive oil | 15 mL |
| 1 1/2 cups | thickly sliced mushrooms | 375 mL |
| 1 | clove garlic, minced | 1 |
| 3 | tomatoes, seeded and cut in chunks | 3 |
| 1/2 tsp | crushed dried basil leaves (or 1/4 cup/50 mL chopped fresh) | 2 mL |
| Pinch | crushed dried thyme leaves | Pinch |
| 1 lb | sole fillets | 500 g |
| 1 | can (14 oz/398 mL) artichoke hearts, drained and halved | 1 |
| | Salt and pepper | |
| Pinch | Granulated sugar (optional) | Pinch |

*Nutrition Bonus*
One serving is a high source of vitamin C, folacin and dietary fiber.

In heavy saucepan or nonstick skillet, heat oil over medium-high heat. Add mushrooms and garlic; cook, stirring often, until mushrooms are tender.

Add tomatoes, basil (if using dried) and thyme; bring to simmer. Add sole and artichokes; cover and simmer for 3 minutes. Uncover and cook for 5 minutes longer or until fish is opaque. Sprinkle with fresh basil (if using). Season with salt and pepper to taste; add sugar if tomatoes are too acidic.

*Makes 4 servings.*

**PER SERVING:**
186 calories
25 g protein
5 g total fat
  1 g saturated fat
  54 mg cholesterol
12 g carbohydrate
  5 g dietary fiber
300 mg sodium

**MAKE AHEAD**

Can be assembled, except for topping, covered and refrigerated for up to four hours.

# Microwave Fillets Provençal

*Use any lean fish fillets — red snapper, rockfish, Pacific Ocean perch, sole, cod, flounder, haddock or monkfish. If using frozen fillets, it's best to thaw before using. Use chunky or diced or regular canned tomatoes but not crushed.*

| | | |
|---|---|---|
| 1 | can (19 oz/540 mL) tomatoes | 1 |
| 1 lb | fish fillets | 500 g |
| | Salt and pepper | |
| 1/2 cup | chopped fresh parsley leaves | 125 mL |
| 1/2 cup | fresh bread crumbs | 125 mL |
| 2 tbsp | minced green onions (including tops) | 25 mL |
| 1 tbsp | extra virgin olive oil | 15 mL |
| 2 | cloves garlic, minced | 2 |

To cook Fillets Provençal in conventional oven, bake in 450°F (230°C) oven for 20 minutes for fresh, 40 minutes for frozen, or until opaque.

Drain and coarsely chop tomatoes; spoon half into shallow microwaveable dish just large enough to hold fillets in single layer. Arrange fillets on top; sprinkle with salt and pepper to taste. Top with remaining tomatoes.

In small bowl, combine parsley, bread crumbs, onions, oil and garlic; sprinkle over tomatoes. Partially cover and microwave on High for 7 to 12 minutes or until fish is opaque. (Cooking times will vary depending on thickness of fish.) Let stand for 3 minutes before serving.

*Makes 4 servings.*

*Dinner Party for Six*
Fresh Tomato and Basil Soup (page 41)
Baked Salmon with Herbs (page 119)
Rice or tiny potatoes in skins
Herbed Green Beans with Garlic
(page 164)
Frozen Lemon Cream (page 201) with
Raspberry Coulis (page 199)

**PER SERVING:**
182 calories
25 g protein
5 g total fat
   1 g saturated fat
   42 mg cholesterol
8 g carbohydrate
   1 g dietary fiber
252 mg sodium

MAKE AHEAD

To serve cold: While salmon is still warm, discard skin and scrape off any dark fat. Brush salmon lightly with oil and cover with foil. Refrigerate for up to six hours.

*Nutrition Bonus*
One serving is a high source of folacin.

When buying a whole fish, ask the fishmonger to clean and scale it. If you don't want the head left on, ask him to cut it off. If you want fillets, the fishmonger will usually fillet the fish for you, and sometimes will even remove the backbone and yet leave the fish whole. (Fillets are boneless pieces of fish cut from either side of the backbone; steaks are cut crosswise and include some bone.)

*Alternative method*
I also often bake salmon unwrapped on a foil-lined baking sheet; the skin on the salmon keeps it moist.

# Baked Salmon with Herbs

*One of my favorite dinner party main courses is a baked whole salmon. It's elegant, delicious and about the easiest dish to prepare. When serving four to six people, arrange hot cooked vegetables such as green beans or snow peas on a platter alongside the salmon. Serve with Yogurt Hollandaise (page 153), Creamy Fresh Dill Dip (page 31) or lemon wedges. It will look like a sumptuous feast.*

| | | |
|---|---|---|
| 1 | whole salmon or piece about 2 1/2 lb (1.25 kg)* | 1 |
| 1/2 cup | chopped fresh parsley leaves | 125 mL |
| 2 tbsp | mixed chopped fresh herbs (dill, chives, chervil, basil, sage), optional | 25 mL |
| | Salt and pepper | |
| 1 tbsp | water | 15 mL |
| 1 tbsp | fresh lemon juice | 15 mL |

*Garnish (optional):*
Cucumber slices, fresh parsley, dill or watercress

Place salmon on foil; measure at thickest part. Sprinkle parsley, mixed herbs (if using), and salt and pepper to taste inside cavity. Mix water with lemon juice; sprinkle over outside of salmon. Fold foil and seal.

Place on baking sheet; bake in 450°F (230°C) oven for 10 minutes per 1 inch (2.5 cm) thickness of fish, plus additional 10 minutes because it's wrapped in foil (35 to 40 minutes total), or until salmon is opaque. Unwrap salmon and discard skin (most of it should stick to foil). Place salmon on warmed platter. Garnish with cucumber, parsley, dill or watercress (if using).

*Makes about 4 servings.*

*Plan on about 1/2 lb (250 g) per person for a whole salmon under 4 lb (2 kg); or about 1/3 lb (170 g) per person for a salmon over 4 lb (2 kg) or a chunk piece. Sockeye salmon is the reddest in color, and thus best for mousse recipes. The fat content of salmon will vary considerably depending on many factors including the time of year and species of salmon. As with chicken, remove skin before eating. The fat in salmon is a good source of omega 3 fatty acids, which may reduce our risk of heart disease.

PER SERVING:
269 calories
37 g protein
12 g total fat
  2 g saturated fat
  103 mg cholesterol
1 g carbohydrate
  trace dietary fiber
85 mg sodium

**MAKE AHEAD**

Ingredients can be prepared and refrigerated early in day. Dish can be assembled up to point of adding seafood, then covered and refrigerated for up to one hour.

# Scallops and Shrimp in Thai Lemon Cream with Julienne Vegetables

*Serve this elegant, wonderfully flavored dish for a special dinner. It's the only recipe in this book with coconut milk or whipping cream. The milk or cream is optional; however, I really love the delicious smoothness and rich flavor that coconut milk adds. Luckily, the rest of the ingredients are low in fat so that even with whipping cream this easily fits into a healthful diet.*

*Nutrition Bonus*
One serving is a very high source of vitamin A (providing 115% of an adult's daily requirement), and a very high source of vitamin C (130% of an adult's daily requirement); it is also a very high source of iron and folacin and a high source of dietary fiber.

| | | |
|---|---|---|
| 12 oz | large raw shrimp | 375 g |
| 1 lb | mussels (optional) | 500 g |
| 8 oz | scallops | 250 g |
| 2 | leeks (white part only) | 2 |
| 2 | medium carrots, peeled | 2 |
| 1 | sweet red pepper, seeded | 1 |
| 1 | small zucchini | 1 |
| 1 tbsp | vegetable oil | 15 mL |
| 1/4 cup | finely chopped onions or shallots | 50 mL |
| 4 | large cloves garlic, minced | 4 |
| 1/4 cup | finely chopped fresh gingerroot | 50 mL |
| 1/2 cup | white wine | 125 mL |
| 1/2 cup | whipping cream or unsweetened coconut milk (optional) | 125 mL |
| 1/4 cup | fresh lemon juice | 50 mL |
| 1/4 tsp | crushed hot red pepper flakes | 1 mL |
| 1 cup | chopped fresh parsley leaves | 250 mL |
| 1/2 tsp | grated lemon rind | 2 mL |
| | Salt and pepper | |
| 3 cups | hot cooked basmati or long grain rice | 750 mL |
| 1/4 cup | chopped fresh coriander leaves | 50 mL |

*Scallops*
Scallops are very low in both fat and cholesterol. I buy the regular size scallops because I prefer their flavor and texture rather than the tiny Bay scallops, which can cook too quickly. If the available scallops are really huge I cut them in half for use in this recipe.

Be very careful not to overcook scallops. They cook very fast and can change from tender to tough and rubbery in just a minute. Cook them just until they become opaque.

Peel shell from shrimp; remove dark intestinal tract running down back. Wash mussels (if using), discarding any that do not close when tapped; cut off hairy beards. Cut scallops in half if large. Cut leeks lengthwise; wash under cold running water. Cut leeks, carrots, red pepper and zucchini into julienne (matchstick-size) strips.

**PER SERVING:**
435 calories
29 g protein
6 g total fat
  1 g saturated fat
  116 mg cholesterol
64 g carbohydrate
  5 g dietary fiber
231 mg sodium

120

Crushed dried hot red pepper flakes come in a small jar in the spice section of the supermarket. They are added to recipes to add hotness. You can substitute hot pepper sauce or bottled fresh chili paste or sauce (see page 55) in amounts to taste depending on how hot and spicy you like your food.

In large nonstick saucepan or skillet, heat oil over medium heat. Add onions and garlic; cook, stirring, for 3 to 5 minutes or until tender. Add gingerroot, julienned vegetables and 1/4 cup (50 mL) water; cover and cook for 5 minutes or until vegetables are tender.

Add wine, cream or milk (if using), lemon juice and hot pepper flakes; bring to boil. Add shrimp, mussels (if using) and scallops; cover and simmer for 3 to 5 minutes or just until shrimp are pink and scallops are opaque. Discard any mussels that do not open. (Be careful not to overcook or seafood will be tough.)

Stir in parsley and lemon rind. Season with salt and pepper to taste. Spoon over hot rice on plates or shallow bowls; sprinkle with coriander.

*Makes 4 servings.*

***Special Spring Dinner***
Asparagus with Red Pepper Purée
(page 158)
Scallops and Shrimp in Thai Lemon Cream with Julienne Vegetables
(this page)
or Sole Florentine (page 116)
Strawberries with Raspberry Rhubarb Sauce (page 195)

**COMPARE:**

*Per serving:*

|  | g fat | calories | % calories from fat |
|---|---|---|---|
| Made with whipping cream | 16 | 532 | 27 |
| Made with canned coconut milk | 12 | 490 | 22 |

**MAKE AHEAD**

Shrimp and salmon can be marinated in refrigerator for up to eight hours. Skewers can be covered and refrigerated for up to two hours; brush occasionally with marinade.

*Nutrition Bonus*
One serving is a high source of iron and folacin.

*Lemon-Garlic Salmon and Shrimp Brochettes*
Instead of Teriyaki Marinade, mix 2 tbsp (25 mL) fresh lemon or lime juice, 1 tbsp (15 mL) sesame or vegetable oil, 2 cloves minced garlic, 1/4 tsp (1 mL) each salt and pepper; marinate salmon and shrimp for 15 minutes. Thread onto skewers with vegetables, brush lemon mixture over and broil as directed. Serve with Creamy Fresh Dill Dip (page 31).

To prevent scorching, soak wooden skewers in water for at least 30 minutes before threading with food.

# Teriyaki Salmon and Shrimp Brochettes

*Serve these skewers of salmon and shrimp over a bed of fragrant Thai or basmati rice.*

| 8 oz | extra-large raw shrimp | 250 g |
|---|---|---|
| 12 oz | skinless salmon, cut in 3/4-inch (2 cm) cubes | 375 g |
| 4 | stalks asparagus (or 8 cherry tomatoes) | 4 |
| 8 | large mushrooms | 8 |
| 8 | large seedless green grapes | 8 |

*Teriyaki Marinade:*

| 2 tbsp | soy sauce | 25 mL |
|---|---|---|
| 2 tbsp | sherry | 25 mL |
| 1 tbsp | sesame or vegetable oil | 15 mL |
| 1 tbsp | grated fresh gingerroot | 15 mL |
| 2 tsp | granulated sugar | 10 mL |

**Teriyaki Marinade:** In large bowl, combine soy sauce, sherry, oil, gingerroot and sugar, mixing to dissolve sugar. Peel and remove black veins from shrimp; add to bowl along with salmon, stirring to coat well. Cover and refrigerate for 30 minutes.

Snap off tough ends of asparagus; peel stalks if desired. Blanch in boiling water for 3 minutes; drain and plunge into cold water. Drain and cut into 1 1/2-inch (4 cm) lengths.

On thin 8-inch (20 cm) long wooden skewers alternately thread salmon, asparagus, shrimp, mushrooms and grapes. Brush with marinade.

Preheat broiler. Place skewers on broiler pan or grill; cook for 3 to 5 minutes, turning once, or until fish is opaque.

*Makes 4 main-course or 8 appetizer servings.*

PER MAIN-COURSE SERVING:
228 calories
27 g protein
9 g total fat
 1 g saturated fat
 111 mg cholesterol
8 g carbohydrate
 1 g dietary fiber
436 mg sodium

# Linguine with Shrimp and Tomato

*The idea for this recipe came from Toronto caterer Dinah Koo. The shrimp and tomato should be quickly cooked over high heat to preserve flavor and texture. If using fresh pasta, make sauce first, because the pasta cooks so quickly.*

### Nutrition Bonus

One serving is a very high source of iron, vitamin A and vitamin C and a high source of folacin and dietary fiber.

### Cooking Pasta

Cook pasta in a large pot of boiling water, using about 16 cups (4 L) of water for every pound (500 g) of pasta. Add pasta all at once, stirring to make sure noodles don't stick together. Boil, uncovered, stirring occasionally.

Fresh pasta cooks quickly, sometimes in as little time as 2 minutes. Dried pasta takes longer, usually at least 7 minutes, sometimes 10 to 12 minutes. Begin tasting to see whether pasta is done before the suggested cooking time; pasta is cooked when it's al dente (tender but firm, not mushy) and has lost its raw starch taste. Drain in a colander, then toss immediately with sauce, butter or oil as specified in recipe to prevent pasta from sticking together. Because pasta cools quickly, it's important to warm the serving platter or individual plates. When using cooked pasta in salads, rinse under cold running water to prevent sticking; drain well.

Be sure to have the sauce ready before the pasta is finished cooking (overcooked, soft, gluey pasta isn't appealing); then toss pasta with sauce and serve immediately.

| 4 oz | linguine or whole-wheat noodles | 125 g |
|---|---|---|
| 2 tsp | olive oil | 10 mL |
| 1 | large clove garlic, minced | 1 |
| 2 tbsp | finely chopped shallots or onion | 25 mL |
| 2 | large tomatoes, coarsely chopped | 2 |
| 1 tsp | crushed dried basil leaves (or 1/4 cup/50 mL chopped fresh) | 5 mL |
| 8 oz | medium shrimp (raw or cooked) | 250 g |
| 1 or 2 | green onions, chopped | 1 or 2 |
| | Salt and pepper | |
| 2 tbsp | freshly grated Parmesan cheese | 25 mL |

In large pot of boiling water, cook linguine until al dente (tender but firm); drain.

Meanwhile, in heavy skillet, heat oil over high heat. Add garlic and shallots; cook, stirring, for about 30 seconds. Add tomatoes and basil; cook, stirring, for about 1 minute. Add shrimp; cook, stirring, until hot and, if using raw, pink. Sprinkle with green onions; season with salt and pepper to taste. Spoon over hot linguine. Sprinkle with Parmesan cheese.

*Makes 2 servings.*

### PER SERVING:

447 calories
35 g protein
10 g total fat
  2 g saturated fat
  177 mg cholesterol
54 g carbohydrate
  5 g dietary fiber
453 mg sodium

MAKE AHEAD

Red peppers and sauce can be prepared, covered and refrigerated for up to two hours.

# Capellini with Clam Sauce and Sweet Red Peppers

*Capellini are the thinnest of pasta noodles, but this recipe works well with any kind of noodle. Whole-wheat noodles are good because of their higher fiber content. Serve this extremely easy-to-make dish with steamed snow peas or a tossed spinach salad. It's a great dish for company when you don't have much preparation time.*

*Nutrition Bonus*
One serving is a very high source of vitamin C (providing 182% of an adult's daily requirement), as well as a very high source of vitamin A and iron and a high source of calcium and folacin.

| | | |
|---|---|---|
| 2 | sweet red peppers | 2 |
| 2 tbsp | extra virgin olive oil | 25 mL |
| 4 | cloves garlic, minced | 4 |
| | Salt and pepper | |
| 1 cup | dry white wine | 250 mL |
| 2 | cans (5 oz/142 g each) clams, drained | 2 |
| 1 tsp | chopped fresh thyme leaves (or 1/2 tsp/2 mL crushed dried) | 5 mL |
| Pinch | hot red pepper flakes | Pinch |
| 1/2 cup | minced fresh parsley leaves | 125 mL |
| 8 oz | pasta such as capellini | 250 g |
| 1/2 cup | grated Parmesan cheese | 125 mL |

Core and seed red peppers; cut into thin strips.

In heavy nonstick skillet, heat half of the oil over medium heat. Add red peppers and half of the minced garlic; cook, stirring often, until peppers are tender, about 10 minutes. Season with salt and pepper to taste.

Meanwhile, in saucepan, heat remaining oil over medium heat. Add remaining garlic; cook, stirring, for 1 minute. Add wine, clams, thyme and hot pepper flakes; simmer for 5 minutes. Add parsley, and salt and pepper to taste.

Meanwhile, in large pot of boiling water, cook capellini until al dente (tender but firm); drain and arrange on warm plates. Pour sauce over pasta; surround with sautéed red peppers. Sprinkle pasta with Parmesan cheese.

*Makes 4 main-course or 8 appetizer servings.*

PER MAIN-COURSE SERVING:
420 calories
20 g protein
12 g total fat
  4 g saturated fat
  28 mg cholesterol
50 g carbohydrate
  4 g dietary fiber
272 mg sodium

# Mussels Sicilian Style

*This is one of my favorite fast and easy suppers that needs only a salad and fresh bread to sop up the wonderful broth. Cultured mussels take only minutes to clean and supper can be ready in 15 minutes.*

| | | |
|---|---|---:|
| 2 lb | fresh mussels (about 36) | 1 kg |
| 1 tsp | olive oil | 5 mL |
| 1 | small onion, finely chopped | 1 |
| 2 | large cloves garlic, minced | 2 |
| 1/4 tsp | each crushed dried thyme and oregano leaves | 1 mL |
| 1 | can (14 oz/398 mL) tomatoes (or 2 fresh, coarsely chopped) | 1 |
| 1/4 cup | dry white wine | 50 mL |
| 1/4 cup | chopped fresh parsley leaves | 50 mL |

*Nutrition Bonus*
One serving is a very high source of iron, vitamin C and folacin and a high source of vitamin A.

Mussels contain a very high amount of iron.

For other fish and seafood dishes see:
Crab-Cucumber Rounds (page 26)
Crab-Stuffed Mini-Pitas (page 25)
Easy Fish Chowder (page 50)
Nova Scotia Seafood Chowder (page 48)
Salmon Mousse with Dill (page 32)
Teriyaki Shrimp Wrapped with Snow Peas (page 24)

Scrub mussels under cold water; pull off hairy beards. Discard any that do not close when tapped. Set aside.

In large heavy saucepan, heat oil over medium heat. Add onion and garlic; cook for 2 to 3 minutes or until tender. Stir in thyme and oregano. Add tomatoes, breaking up canned tomatoes with back of spoon. Bring to boil; boil for about 2 minutes to reduce liquid. Add wine; return to boil. Add mussels; cover and cook for 5 minutes or until shells open. Discard any mussels that don't open.

Ladle mussels into large soup bowls, spooning tomato mixture and broth over top. Sprinkle with parsley. Serve with fork to pull mussels out of shells, and spoon for broth.

*Makes 2 servings.*

**PER SERVING:**
205 calories
18 g protein
6 g total fat
 1 g saturated fat
 37 mg cholesterol
18 g carbohydrate
 3 g dietary fiber
576 mg sodium

---

*How to Buy and Store Mussels*
It's unbelievable that shellfish as tender and delicious as mussels are so inexpensive. Buy medium-size (about 18 to the pound/500 g) cultured mussels: they're much easier to clean and have more meat than the wild ones. Only buy mussels that have closed shells. The fresher the mussels, the better they taste. Store fresh mussels in the refrigerator in a bowl covered with slightly wet paper towel or with newpaper that has some ice on top. Don't store in a plastic bag. The important thing is to keep them damp. They should be used preferably within 24 hours, at the latest by the second day. Serve as a first course or a main course.

## SOME FACTS ABOUT THE FAT CONTENT OF FISH

Most kinds of fish are low in fat — even the higher-fat varieties are on a par with extra-lean ground beef when it comes to fat content. This means you don't have to worry about fat when choosing the kind of fish to buy and can have it two to three times a week. The important thing to remember is to serve a variety of fish in moderate-sized portions and use little or no extra fat when you prepare it.

### Buying and Storing Fish

**Buying fresh fish**
When possible buy fish the day you want to cook it. The best test for freshness is to use your nose — the fish should have a mild fishy or seawater odor. Anything stronger means the fish has been out of the water too long.
Look for:
• mild smell
• glistening, firm flesh that springs back when touched
• very firmly attached scales
• clear, bright, convex (not sunken) eyes

**Storing fresh fish**
• If not cleaned, clean as soon as possible.
• Wipe with a damp cloth, wrap in waxed paper and place in covered container.
• Store in coldest part of the refrigerator.
• Cook as soon as possible (same day for store-bought, within 4 days if freshly caught).

**Buying frozen fish**
Look for:
• glazed fish coated with ice
• shiny, solidly frozen flesh with no signs of drying or freezer burn (white spots)
• tightly wrapped package with no sign of frost or ice crystals inside

**Storing frozen fish**
• Keep fish at 0°F (-18°C) or lower for ideal storage.
• Store fatty fish (salmon, mackerel, lake trout) for a maximum of 2 months.
• Store lean fish (cod, haddock, ocean perch, pike, sole) for a maximum of 6 months.

### How Long to Cook Fish

• Measure fish at the thickest part (stuffed or not).
• Allow 10 minutes' cooking time per inch (2.5 cm) of thickness for fresh fish; add 2 to 3 minutes extra for frozen fillets, double the time for fish frozen in a block. If wrapped in foil, add 5 minutes for fresh, 10 minutes for a frozen block. This applies to all fish and all cooking methods (if in oven, cook at 450°F/230°C).

Fish is cooked when flesh is opaque and it flakes and separates into solid moist sections when firmly prodded with a fork.

## *Methods of Cooking Fish*

### Steaming (top of stove)
Pour 2 inches (5 cm) of water in a steamer and bring to a boil. Season and wrap fish securely in cheesecloth. Place on a rack over boiling water. Cover and begin timing (see above).

### Baking
Place whole fish, with skin, on baking pan (line with foil if desired); season to taste with salt, pepper, sprinkle of lemon juice and/or herbs. Bake in preheated 450°F (230°C) oven for required time.

### Oven steaming
Place fresh or frozen fish on lightly greased foil on baking sheet. Season to taste with salt, pepper and herbs (parsley, dill, chives or basil). Sprinkle with lemon juice or white wine. Wrap securely in foil. Bake in preheated 450°F (230°C) oven for required time, adding 5 minutes for fresh and 10 minutes for frozen fish because of being wrapped in foil.

### Poaching
Place fish on greased heavy-duty foil. Season to taste with salt and pepper, add chopped onion and celery. Wrap, using double folds to make package watertight. Place in rapidly boiling water and simmer for required cooking time. (Fish may also be wrapped in cheesecloth and poached in court bouillon or fish stock.)

### To microwave fish
Place fish in microwaveable dish. Season to taste with salt and pepper. Cover with plastic wrap and turn back corner to allow steam to escape. Estimate cooking time at 3 to 4 minutes per pound (500 g), plus 2 to 3 minutes standing time. Microwave on High or according to appliance manual.

### To grill fish
Place fish (for fillets, skin side down) on lightly greased grill. Close cover and grill over medium or low heat, turning once, until fish is opaque and flakes. Cooking time will vary depending on the thickness of fish and distance from coals; 1-inch (2.5 cm) thick salmon steaks will take 8 to 10 minutes over medium heat.

### Skillet cooked fish
If fish is washed or marinated, pat dry. Lightly oil (1/2 tsp/2 mL olive oil) a nonstick skillet. Add fish and cook over medium-high heat, turning once. Fish fillets or steaks about 3/4 inch (2 cm) thick will take 2 to 3 minutes per side.

# Vegetarian and Grain Dishes

M EATLESS ENTRÉES ARE NOTHING NEW. Macaroni and cheese and scrambled eggs have been family favorites for generations, and people who would never call themselves vegetarians often enjoy pizza without pepperoni.

It's becoming increasingly apparent that from both a health and cost point of view, vegetarian meals can be very beneficial. They can also include a surprising variety of foods — everything from vegetables and pasta to eggs and cheese, depending on the type of vegetarian. For the inventive cook, the tasty combinations are endless. For the health-conscious, vegetarian meals often offer lower fat and higher fiber and vitamin content than meat dishes, and, after all, that kind of eating is what this book is about. For other vegetarian main-course recipes, be sure to check our soup, salad and vegetable suggestions.

***Nutrition Bonus***
One serving is a very high source of vitamin C (providing 98% of an adult's daily requirement), a very high source of folacin and a high source of vitamin A.

Broccoli is an excellent source of vitamins A and C and fiber.

***Light Supper for a Winter's Day***
Broccoli Frittata (this page)
Danish Cucumber Salad (page 61)
Olive and Rosemary Soda Bread (page 181)
Baked apples

**PER SERVING:**
155 calories
11 g protein
9 g total fat
  3 g saturated fat
  220 mg cholesterol
8 g carbohydrate
  2 g dietary fiber
516 mg sodium

## Broccoli Frittata

*This Italian open-faced omelet is delicious for supper or brunch. Unlike a French omelet, which is cooked quickly over high heat and is creamy in the center, a frittata is cooked slowly and is set or firm in the middle.*

| | | |
|---|---|---|
| 1 | bunch broccoli (1 lb/500 g) | 1 |
| 1 tbsp | olive or canola oil | 15 mL |
| 1 cup | sliced onions | 250 mL |
| 2 or 3 | cloves garlic, minced | 2 or 3 |
| 6 | eggs, lightly beaten | 6 |
| 2 tbsp | finely chopped fresh parsley leaves | 25 mL |
| 1 tsp | salt | 5 mL |
| 1/4 tsp | each ground nutmeg and pepper | 1 mL |
| 1/2 cup | grated part-skim mozzarella cheese | 125 mL |

Trim tough ends from broccoli; peel stems. Cut stems and florets into 3/4-inch (2 cm) pieces to make about 4 cups (1 L). Steam or cook in boiling water for 5 minutes or until crisp-tender; drain thoroughly.

In 10- to 12-inch (25 to 30 cm) nonstick skillet, heat oil over medium heat. Add onions and garlic; cook until onion is tender. Stir in broccoli.

Beat together eggs, parsley, salt, nutmeg and pepper; pour over broccoli mixture and sprinkle with cheese. Cover and cook over medium-low heat for 5 to 10 minutes or until set but still slightly moist on top. Place pan under broiler for 2 to 3 minutes to lightly brown top. (If skillet handle isn't ovenproof, wrap it in foil. Since the oven door is open slightly most of the handle will not be directly under the heat.) Loosen edges of frittata; cut into pie-shaped wedges.

*Makes 6 servings.*

### MAKE AHEAD

Eggs can be poached, cooled in ice water to prevent further cooking and refrigerated in bowl of water for up to one day; reheat in simmering water for about 30 seconds. Spinach can be cooked, then cooled under cold running water, drained and set aside for up to 2 hours, or covered and refrigerated for up to 24 hours. Chop and reheat before continuing. Yogurt Hollandaise, see Make Ahead, page 153.

### *Nutrition Bonus*

One serving is a very high source of vitamin A (providing 82% of an adult's daily requirement), a very high source of folacin and iron and a high source of calcium.

### *Asparagus with Poached Eggs*

In spring, substitute cooked drained asparagus for the spinach in Eggs Florentine. Arrange hot asparagus spears on warmed individual plates or serving dish; sprinkle with lemon juice, salt and pepper. Top with poached egg and grated Parmesan cheese or Yogurt Hollandaise. If desired, broil for a minute to brown.

### PER SERVING:

133 calories
11 g protein
8 g total fat
  3 g saturated fat
  284 mg cholesterol
6 g carbohydrate
  2 g dietary fiber
265 mg sodium

# Eggs Florentine

*This is perfect for entertaining at brunch, lunch or a light supper because the eggs, spinach and sauce can all be prepared in advance and gently reheated.*

| | | |
|---|---|---:|
| 2 | pkg (10 oz/284 g each) fresh spinach | 2 |
| 1 tsp | butter | 5 mL |
| | Salt, pepper and grated nutmeg | |
| 2 tbsp | white vinegar | 25 mL |
| 6 | eggs | 6 |
| 3/4 cup | Yogurt Hollandaise (page 153), warmed | 175 mL |

Trim stems from spinach. Wash and shake off excess water; place in saucepan with just the water clinging to leaves. Cover and cook over medium-high heat until wilted. Drain thoroughly; squeeze out excess liquid and chop coarsely. Toss with butter, and salt, pepper and nutmeg to taste. Return to saucepan; cover and keep warm.

Nearly fill large shallow pan or skillet with water and bring to boil; add vinegar. Reduce to simmer and break egg shells over pan, gently dropping eggs into water. Reduce heat until water is barely simmering; cook eggs for 3 to 5 minutes or until whites are firm and yolks are still soft, spooning water over yolks occasionally to cook slightly.

Spoon spinach onto warmed plates or serving dish. With slotted spoon, place 1 egg over each serving. Spoon about 2 tbsp (25 mL) Yogurt Hollandaise over each.

*Makes 6 servings.*

---

*Brunch or Lunch Menu*
Grapefruit Juice Spritzer (below)
Eggs Florentine (this page)
Tomatoes Provençal (page 157)
Tossed green salad with Buttermilk Herb Dressing (page 78)
Toasted English muffins
Raspberry Meringue Torte (page 210) or Pear Crisp with Ginger (page 212)

*Grapefruit Juice Spritzer*
For a refreshing nonalcoholic drink that's perfect before lunch or brunch, combine equal parts of grapefruit juice and soda water. Serve over ice cubes and garnish with thin slices of lime.

---

# Omelet à la Jardinière

*Don't relegate eggs only to breakfast. Serve with toasted whole-wheat bread and a spinach salad for an instant dinner or lunch. For variety, add sliced mushrooms or chopped tomatoes and cook them along with the carrots.*

### Nutrition Bonus

One serving is an excellent source of vitamin A, folacin and vitamin B12.

A 2-egg omelet is easier to make than a 4-egg or larger omelet. Also, it's important to use the correct size of pan. For a 2- to 3-egg omelet, use an omelet pan that's 7 inches (18 cm) in diameter at the bottom; for a 4-egg omelet, use an 8- to 9-inch (20 to 23 cm) pan.

Egg yolks contribute protein, iron, vitamin A and vitamin E to our diet. A large egg yolk has about 5 grams of fat. Egg yolks are high in cholesterol and should be consumed in moderation. Moderation can mean up to 4 or 6 eggs per week. If you have high blood cholesterol, check with your doctor or a registered dietitian about limiting your intake of fat and cholesterol.

To halve the amount of cholesterol in this recipe, use 2 whole eggs and 3 egg whites.

| | | |
|---|---|---:|
| 1 tsp | vegetable oil | 5 mL |
| 1 | small onion, finely chopped | 1 |
| 1 | clove garlic, minced | 1 |
| 1/3 cup | grated carrot | 75 mL |
| 1/4 cup | chopped sweet green pepper | 50 mL |
| | Salt and pepper | |
| 4 | eggs | 4 |
| 1 tbsp | water | 15 mL |
| 1 tsp | butter | 5 mL |

In nonstick skillet, heat oil over medium heat; sauté onion and garlic, stirring, until tender. Stir in carrot and green pepper; cook, stirring, for 2 to 3 minutes or until carrot is wilted. Season with salt and pepper to taste.

In bowl, beat eggs with water until blended. Heat 8- to 9-inch (20 to 23 cm) nonstick omelet pan or skillet over very high heat; heat butter until sizzling but not browned. Pour in eggs; cook, continuously shaking pan back and forth while stirring eggs quickly with fork to spread evenly over pan until eggs are thickened and almost set.

Spoon carrot mixture over eggs. Tilt pan and roll up omelet, or simply fold in half. Slide onto plate.

*Makes 2 servings.*

### PER SERVING:
208 calories
13 g protein
14 g total fat
  4 g saturated fat
  377 mg cholesterol
7 g carbohydrate
  1 g dietary fiber
154 mg sodium

# Fettuccine with Fresh Tomatoes and Basil

*This is a delightful supper in late summer or fall when tomatoes are at their best. For the most fiber, try to buy whole-wheat noodles. Serve with extra Parmesan to sprinkle over top.*

| | | |
|---|---|---|
| 6 oz | fettuccine noodles (or 2 cups/500 mL dried medium egg noodles) | 175 g |
| 1 tbsp | olive oil | 15 mL |
| 3 | large cloves garlic, minced | 3 |
| 4 | tomatoes, diced | 4 |
| 1 tsp | crushed dried basil leaves (or 1/2 cup/125 mL chopped fresh) | 5 mL |
| Pinch | granulated sugar | Pinch |
| 1/4 cup | chopped fresh parsley leaves | 50 mL |
| | Salt and pepper | |
| 1/4 cup | grated Parmesan cheese | 50 mL |

In large pot of boiling water, cook noodles until al dente (tender but firm); drain well. Meanwhile, in heavy skillet, heat oil over medium heat. Add garlic, tomatoes, basil (if using dried) and sugar; cook for 5 minutes, stirring occasionally. Add parsley, fresh basil (if using), and salt and pepper to taste.

Add tomato mixture and Parmesan to noodles; toss well. (If sauce is too thick, add a few spoonfuls of pasta cooking liquid.)

*Makes 2 servings.*

**Nutrition Bonus**
One serving is a very high source of vitamins A and C and dietary fiber and a high source of calcium, iron and folacin.

**Easy Summer Supper**
Fettuccine with Fresh Tomatoes and Basil (this page)
Tossed green salad with Blue Cheese Dressing (page 80)
Sliced fresh peaches

**PER SERVING:**
490 calories
19 g protein
13 g total fat
  4 g saturated fat
  10 mg cholesterol
77 g carbohydrate
  7 g dietary fiber
479 mg sodium

# Pasta with Broccoli, Mushrooms and Cauliflower in Basil-Cream Sauce

*Your family will love this quick and easy pasta dish. The variety of vegetables you can use is limitless — try adding carrots, snow peas, celery or green beans. Evaporated milk gives a rich creamy sauce with a minimum of fat.*

**Nutrition Bonus**
One serving is a very high source of calcium, vitamin C, folacin and dietary fiber and a high source of iron and vitamin A.

**Pasta with Tomato Basil Sauce**
Cook 1 lb (500 g) of pasta (any kind) in a large pot of boiling water until tender yet firm; drain. Toss with 3 cups (750 mL) Tomato Basil Sauce (page 152). Top with freshly grated Parmesan. Makes 4 to 5 servings.

**Pasta with Shrimp and Tomato Basil Sauce**
Prepare as above and add 1 lb (500 g) cooked, peeled large shrimp. Makes 4 to 5 servings.

| | | |
|---|---|---|
| 4 cups | broccoli florets | 1 L |
| 4 cups | cauliflower florets | 1 L |
| 4 oz | whole-wheat noodles or spaghettini | 125 g |
| 1 tbsp | olive or vegetable oil | 15 mL |
| 3 | cloves garlic, minced | 3 |
| 2 1/2 cups | thickly sliced mushrooms | 625 mL |
| 1/2 cup | chopped fresh basil leaves (or 4 tsp /20 mL crushed dried) | 125 mL |
| 4 tsp | all-purpose flour | 20 mL |
| 1/2 tsp | each salt and pepper | 2 mL |
| 1 | can (385 mL) 2% evaporated milk (or 1 1/2 cups/375 mL 2% milk) | 1 |
| 1/4 cup | grated Parmesan cheese | 50 mL |

In large pot of boiling water, cook broccoli and cauliflower until tender-crisp, about 5 minutes. With slotted spoon, remove vegetables and set aside. Add pasta to boiling cooking water; cook until al dente (tender but firm), about 10 minutes. Drain well.

Meanwhile, in nonstick skillet, heat oil over medium heat. Add garlic; cook, stirring, for 30 seconds. Increase heat to medium-high. Add mushrooms and dried basil if using; cook for 3 to 5 minutes until mushrooms are browned and tender, stirring often. Sprinkle evenly with flour, salt and pepper; cook, stirring, for 1 minute.

Stir in milk; boil for 1 minute. Stir in broccoli, cauliflower and Parmesan; cook for 1 minute. Stir in fresh basil (if using). Add noodles and toss to combine well.

*Makes 4 servings.*

**PER SERVING:**
315 calories
19 g protein
8 g total fat
  3 g saturated fat
  13 mg cholesterol
45 g carbohydrate
  7 g dietary fiber
541 mg sodium

## MAKE AHEAD

Baked lasagne can be covered and refrigerated for up to three days or frozen for up to one month. Thaw at room temperature for at least three hours. Reheat, partially covered, in microwave, or tent with foil and cook in 350°F (180°C) oven for 30 minutes. Remove foil and cook another 10 to 15 minutes until hot and bubbling.

*Nutrition Bonus*
One serving is a very high source of calcium and a high source of vitamin A.

# Triple-Cheese Lasagne

*If making this for a special occasion, add sliced mushrooms and chopped sweet green or red pepper to the tomato sauce.*

| | | |
|---|---|---|
| 1 | can (19 oz/540 mL) tomatoes | 1 |
| 1 | can (14 oz/398 mL) tomato sauce | 1 |
| 2 | onions, chopped | 2 |
| 2 | cloves garlic, minced | 2 |
| 1/4 cup | chopped fresh parsley leaves | 50 mL |
| 2 tsp | granulated sugar | 10 mL |
| 1 tsp | each crushed dried basil, thyme and oregano leaves | 5 mL |
| | Pepper | |
| 8 oz | lasagne noodles (9 to 11) | 250 g |
| 2/3 cup | grated Parmesan cheese | 150 mL |
| 2 cups | cottage cheese | 500 mL |
| 1 | egg, lightly beaten | 1 |
| 1 tsp | crushed dried oregano leaves | 5 mL |
| | Pepper | |
| 2 cups | shredded part-skim mozzarella cheese (1/2 lb/250 g) | 500 mL |

**Sauce:** In saucepan, combine tomatoes, tomato sauce, onions, garlic, parsley, sugar, basil, thyme, oregano and pepper to taste; bring to boil. Reduce heat and simmer, uncovered and stirring occasionally, for 30 minutes or until spaghetti-sauce consistency.

In large pot of boiling water, cook lasagne noodles until al dente (tender but firm). Drain and rinse under cold running water; drain well.

Reserve 3 tbsp (50 mL) of the Parmesan cheese for topping. In bowl, combine remaining Parmesan cheese, cottage cheese, egg, oregano and pepper to taste. Set aside.

**PER SERVING:**
323 calories
25 g protein
9 g total fat
  5 g saturated fat
  51 mg cholesterol
35 g carbohydrate
  3 g dietary fiber
991 mg sodium

Reserve 1/2 cup (125 mL) of the tomato sauce for topping. In 13- x 9-inch (3.5 L) baking dish, spread just enough of the tomato sauce to cover bottom sparingly; top with layer of lasagne noodles. Cover with one-third of the cottage cheese mixture, then one-third of the mozzarella cheese. Repeat with remaining sauce, noodles and cheeses to make 3 layers of each. Top with reserved tomato sauce; sprinkle with reserved Parmesan cheese. Bake, uncovered, in 350°F (180°C) oven for 45 minutes or until hot and bubbly. Let cool slightly before serving.

*Makes 8 servings.*

---

Dishes that use prepared foods such as canned tomatoes (like lasagne) are usually high in sodium. Even though there is no added salt in this dish, there is still a considerable amount of sodium. Here is where most of it comes from:

|  | *mg sodium/ 1 serving* |
|---|---|
| Canned tomatoes | 111 |
| Tomato sauce | 310 |
| Parmesan cheese | 155 |
| Cottage cheese | 255 |
| Mozzarella cheese | 149 |

To reduce sodium, substitute 1 can (5.5 oz/156 mL) tomato paste plus 1 cup (250 mL) water for the tomato sauce; sodium will then be 695 mg/serving.

# Creamy Penne with Tomatoes

*Creamy and delicious pasta dishes can also be low in fat. Using ricotta cheese and lower fat milk keeps the fat down in this easy-to-make dish.*

**Nutrition Bonus**
One serving is a high source of calcium, iron, folacin and dietary fiber.

| | | |
|---|---|---|
| 1 tbsp | olive oil | 15 mL |
| 1 | onion, chopped | 1 |
| 2 | cloves garlic, minced | 2 |
| 1 | can (28 oz/796 mL) tomatoes | 1 |
| 1/4 tsp | hot red pepper flakes or chili paste | 1 mL |
| 1/2 cup | chopped fresh parsley leaves | 125 mL |
| 2 tbsp | chopped fresh oregano leaves (or 2 tsp/10 mL crushed dried) | 25 mL |
| 1 cup | ricotta cheese | 250 mL |
| 1/4 cup | 2% milk | 50 mL |
| 1 lb | penne pasta (about 5 cups/1.25 L) | 500 g |
| | Salt and pepper | |
| 1/4 cup | grated Parmesan cheese | 50 mL |

In heavy saucepan, heat oil over medium heat. Add onion and garlic; cook for 3 minutes. Purée tomatoes and add to saucepan along with hot red pepper flakes; bring to boil. Reduce heat and simmer, uncovered, for 20 minutes or until thickened. Add parsley and oregano; remove from heat. In food processor or blender, purée ricotta and milk until smooth; stir into tomato mixture.

Meanwhile, in large pot of boiling water, cook penne for 8 to 10 minutes or until tender but firm. Drain well and toss with sauce. Season with salt and pepper to taste. Sprinkle with Parmesan cheese.

*Makes 6 servings.*

**PER SERVING:**
395 calories
15 g protein
8 g total fat
 3 g saturated fat
 14 mg cholesterol
66 g carbohydrate
 5 g dietary fiber
518 mg sodium

# Thai Noodles with Broccoli

*Here's a quick and easy stir-fry with Thai flavors.*

| | | |
|---|---|---|
| 4 oz | rice vermicelli noodles | 125 g |
| 5 cups | small broccoli florets | 1.25 L |
| 1 tbsp | vegetable oil | 15 mL |
| 2 | cloves garlic, minced | 2 |
| 1 | fresh red chili pepper, seeded and chopped (or 1/4 tsp/1 mL dried hot red pepper flakes) | 1 |
| 3 tbsp | oyster or hoisin sauce | 50 mL |
| 2 tbsp | fresh lime juice | 25 mL |
| 1 tbsp | fish sauce | 15 mL |
| 1 tbsp | minced fresh gingerroot | 15 mL |
| 1 tbsp | granulated sugar | 15 mL |
| 3 | green onions, chopped | 3 |
| 1 tbsp | toasted sesame seeds (optional) | 15 mL |

Soak rice noodles in warm water for 15 minutes; drain. In large pot of boiling water, cook broccoli for 2 minutes; add noodles and cook for 1 minute or until tender. Drain.

Meanwhile, in wok or large nonstick skillet, heat oil over medium heat. Add garlic; cook, stirring constantly, for 1 minute. Stir in chili pepper, oyster sauce, lime juice, fish sauce, gingerroot and sugar; cook, stirring, for 1 minute. Add noodle mixture; cook, stirring, for 1 minute. Sprinkle with green onions and sesame seeds.

*Makes 4 servings.*

**Nutrition Bonus**
One serving is an excellent source of vitamin C.

Fish sauce is available at Oriental grocery stores, some specialty stores and supermarkets. It smells terrible but adds a delicious flavor and is often used in Thai cooking. It will keep on your shelf for a few years. If unavailable, use soy sauce.

Rice vermicelli noodles are available in many supermarkets. If unavailable use any thin noodle. Cook regular noodles in boiling water until nearly tender. Add broccoli and cook until the broccoli is tender-crisp and the noodles are al dente.

**PER SERVING:**
180 calories
3 g protein
4 g total fat
  trace saturated fat
  0 mg cholesterol
34 g carbohydrate
  3 g dietary fiber
713 mg sodium

# Deep-Dish Vegetable Pizza

*This scrumptious pizza is very filling. Two slices are plenty for dinner along with a salad.*

| | Whole-Wheat Pizza Dough (page 180) | |
|---|---|---|
| 1 cup | tomato sauce | 250 mL |
| 1 tbsp | finely chopped fresh garlic | 15 mL |
| 1 tsp | each crushed dried oregano and basil leaves | 5 mL |
| 1 tsp | vegetable oil | 5 mL |
| 2 cups | thinly sliced onions | 500 mL |
| 2 cups | sliced mushrooms | 500 mL |
| | Salt and pepper | |
| 4 cups | broccoli pieces (3/4-inch/2 cm) | 1 L |
| 3 cups | shredded part-skim mozzarella cheese | 750 mL |

***Nutrition Bonus***
One serving is a very high source of calcium, vitamin C, folacin and dietary fiber and a high source of iron and vitamin A.

***Larger Regular Pizza***
This recipe also makes two 16- x 12-inch (40 x 30 cm) pizzas. Bake in 475°F (240°C) oven for 13 to 15 minutes or until crust is crisp and top is bubbling.

***Children's Party***
Deep-Dish Vegetable Pizza (this page)
Crudités with Creamy Fresh Dill Dip (page 31)
Best-Ever Date Squares (page 182)
Oatmeal Raisin Cookies (page 186)
Chocolate Milk (page 219)

Divide dough into 2 pieces.* Roll out each piece to fit 10-inch (25 cm) round quiche or cake pan that's at least 1 inch (2.5 cm) deep.

In small bowl, combine tomato sauce, garlic, oregano and basil; set aside.

In nonstick skillet, heat oil over medium heat. Add onions; cook, stirring, over medium-low heat for 5 to 10 minutes or until tender. Add mushrooms; cook over medium heat, stirring occasionally, until lightly browned and liquid has evaporated. Season with salt and pepper to taste; set aside.

In large pot of boiling water, cook broccoli for 2 minutes or until bright green; drain and cool under cold running water to prevent any further cooking. Drain well and set aside.

Spread tomato mixture over dough. Cover with broccoli, then with mushroom mixture. Sprinkle with cheese. Bake in 450°F (230°C) oven for 25 to 35 minutes or until crust is browned and top is bubbly.

*Makes 2 pizzas.*

**PER 1/4 PIZZA:**
362 calories
20 g protein
12 g total fat
  5 g saturated fat
  23 mg cholesterol
45 g carbohydrate
  6 g dietary fiber
711 mg sodium

*This method makes a thick crust. If you want a thin crust, divide dough into three portions and freeze the extra dough to make another pizza later.

138

# Spinach and Zucchini Pie

*Similar to a crustless quiche or frittata, this is ideal with toast and salad or sliced tomatoes for brunch, lunch or dinner. Or, cut into small squares and serve warm or cold as an hors d'oeuvre, or cut into wedges and serve as a first course.*

| | | |
|---|---|---|
| 1 tsp | olive oil | 5 mL |
| 1 | medium onion, chopped | 1 |
| 1 | clove garlic, minced | 1 |
| 2 cups | thinly sliced unpeeled zucchini | 500 mL |
| 1/2 cup | grated part-skim mozzarella cheese | 125 mL |
| 1/4 cup | chopped fresh parsley leaves | 50 mL |
| 4 | eggs, lightly beaten | 4 |
| 1 | pkg (10 oz/300 g) frozen chopped spinach, thawed and drained | 1 |
| 3/4 tsp | salt | 4 mL |
| 1/4 tsp | pepper | 1 mL |
| Pinch | ground nutmeg | Pinch |

*Nutrition Bonus*
One serving is a very high source of vitamin A and folacin and a high source of calcium.

In nonstick skillet, heat oil over medium heat. Add onion and garlic; cook until onion is tender. Add zucchini; cook, stirring, for 5 minutes.

In bowl, combine cheese, parsley, eggs, spinach, salt, pepper and nutmeg; stir in zucchini mixture. Spoon into lightly greased 9-inch (23 cm) pie plate. Bake in 325°F (160°C) oven for 35 to 45 minutes or until set but still moist in center. Serve hot or cold.

*Makes 4 main-course servings.*

**PER MAIN-COURSE SERVING:**
159 calories
12 g protein
9 g total fat
  3 g saturated fat
  222 mg cholesterol
9 g carbohydrate
  3 g dietary fiber
612 mg sodium

**MAKE AHEAD**

Stew can be covered and refrigerated for up to two days.

*Nutrition Bonus*

For an average adult, one serving is a very high source of vitamin A (contributing 152% of the daily requirement), a very high source of vitamin C and folacin and a high source of calcium, iron and dietary fiber.

When making any kind of stew, try to make it a day in advance and refrigerate. Any fat will solidify on the surface and then can easily be removed. As well, stews always taste better the next day because the flavors blend and develop.

# Winter Vegetable Stew

*Serve this satisfying yet light stew in large shallow soup or pasta bowls. Other vegetables can be added to or substituted for the vegetables suggested. Broccoli, green beans, cooked kidney beans or chick-peas, asparagus in season, snow peas or other quick-cooking vegetables can be added to the stew when you add the zucchini.*

| | | |
|---|---|---|
| 1 tbsp | vegetable oil | 15 mL |
| 2 | onions, coarsely chopped | 2 |
| 4 | large cloves garlic, minced | 4 |
| 2 | leeks | 2 |
| 2 | each potatoes and carrots | 2 |
| 1 | sweet potato | 1 |
| Quarter | small rutabaga | Quarter |
| 3 cups | water (preferably vegetable cooking water) or chicken stock | 750 mL |
| 1 1/2 tsp | each crushed dried oregano and thyme leaves | 7 mL |
| 1 | small zucchini (unpeeled), cut in chunks | 1 |
| | Salt and pepper | |
| 1/3 cup | chopped fresh parsley leaves | 75 mL |
| 1/3 cup | grated Parmesan cheese | 75 mL |

In large nonstick saucepan, heat oil over medium heat. Add onions and garlic; cook, stirring occasionally, until tender.

Discard tough green parts of leeks; cut leeks in half lengthwise and wash under cold running water. Cut into 3/4-inch (2 cm) pieces; add to saucepan. Peel potatoes, carrots, sweet potato and rutabaga; cut into 1-inch (2.5 cm) cubes and add to pan.

Stir in water, oregano and thyme; bring to boil. Cover and simmer until vegetables are tender, about 30 minutes. Stir in zucchini, and salt and pepper to taste; simmer for 5 minutes or until all vegetables are tender, adding more water if desired. Ladle into bowls; sprinkle with parsley and Parmesan cheese.

*Makes 4 servings.*

**PER MAIN-COURSE SERVING:**
239 calories
8 g protein
6 g total fat
  2 g saturated fat
  7 mg cholesterol
40 g carbohydrate
  6 g dietary fiber
208 mg sodium

**MAKE AHEAD**

Can be covered and refrigerated for up to one day. Add fresh herbs just before serving.

# Tuscan White Kidney Beans and Tomato

*You'll want to have a little of this left over — it's delicious cold. Good as a main course with a green salad and whole-wheat pita bread, it's a high-fiber dinner that's easy to make.*

*Nutrition Bonus*
One serving has a whopping 20 grams of fiber. Health professionals recommend we get about 25 to 35 grams of fiber daily. One serving is also a very high source of iron, folacin and vitamin C (providing 95% of an adult's daily requirement) and a high source of vitamin A.

| | | |
|---|---|---|
| 1 tbsp | olive oil | 15 mL |
| 1 | onion, thinly sliced | 1 |
| 1 | clove garlic, minced | 1 |
| 1 | large tomato, coarsely chopped | 1 |
| 1 | small sweet green pepper, diced | 1 |
| 1/2 tsp | crushed dried basil leaves (or 3 tbsp/50 mL chopped fresh) | 2 mL |
| 1/2 tsp | crushed dried oregano leaves | 2 mL |
| 1 | can (19 oz/540 mL) white kidney beans, drained and rinsed | 1 |
| | Salt and pepper | |
| 1/2 cup | chopped fresh parsley leaves | 125 mL |

In small heavy saucepan, heat oil over medium heat. Add onion; cook until tender. Stir in garlic, tomato and green pepper; cook for 1 minute. Stir in basil (if using dried), oregano, kidney beans, and salt and pepper to taste; simmer over low heat for 5 minutes or until heated through and flavors are blended. Stir in parsley and basil (if using fresh).

*Makes 2 servings.*

**PER MAIN-COURSE SERVING:**
339 calories
18 g protein
8 g total fat
  1 g saturated fat
  0 mg cholesterol
52 g carbohydrate
  20 g dietary fiber
633 mg sodium

### MAKE AHEAD

Cover and refrigerate up to one day. Add water if necessary when reheating.

# Moroccan Vegetable Cous Cous

*Here's a great example of how tasty and nutritious vegetarian cooking can be. Instead of cous cous, you can use rice, orzo (the rice-shaped pasta) or bulgur. Season to taste with more coriander and lemon juice if desired.*

| | | |
|---|---|---|
| 2 tbsp | olive oil | 25 mL |
| 3 | onions, chopped | 3 |
| 2 tbsp | minced fresh gingerroot | 25 mL |
| 1 tsp | each turmeric, cinnamon and granulated sugar | 5 mL |
| 1/2 tsp | each ground coriander and cumin | 2 mL |
| 2 1/2 cups | cubed peeled sweet potato | 625 mL |
| 2 cups | water or vegetable stock | 500 mL |
| 1 cup | sliced carrots | 250 mL |
| 1/4 tsp | crushed dried hot red pepper flakes | 1 mL |
| 1 | sweet green or red pepper, chopped | 1 |
| 1 1/2 cups | cubed firm-style tofu (or 2 cups/ 500 mL cooked chick-peas)* | 375 mL |
| 1 | pkg (10 oz/284 g) fresh spinach, stems removed and coarsely chopped | 1 |
| 1/4 cup | chopped fresh coriander (cilantro) leaves | 50 mL |
| 1 tbsp | fresh lemon juice | 15 mL |
| 1/2 tsp | each salt and pepper | 2 mL |
| 1 1/2 cups | cous cous | 375 mL |

In large nonstick skillet heat oil over medium heat. Stir in onions, ginger, turmeric, cinnamon, sugar, coriander and cumin; cook, stirring often, for 5 minutes or until onions are softened. Add sweet potato, water, carrots and hot pepper flakes; cook, covered and stirring occasionally, for 15 minutes or until sweet potatoes are almost tender.

Add green pepper, tofu and spinach; cook, stirring frequently, for 5 minutes or until potatoes are fork-tender and spinach is wilted. Stir in coriander and lemon juice. Season with salt and pepper.

### Nutrition Bonus

One serving is a very high source of vitamin A (providing 201% of an adult's daily requirement), a very high source of iron, vitamin C and folacin and a high source of calcium. It also contains a very high amount of dietary fiber.

### Vegetarian Dinner Menu

Stuffed Mushroom Croustades (page 27)
Moroccan Vegetable Cous Cous (this page)
Arugula and Radicchio Salad with Balsamic Vinaigrette (page 62)
Plum Tart (page 215) with Honey Lime Sauce (page 35)

### PER SERVING:

382 calories
15 g protein
9 g total fat
  1 g saturated fat
  0 mg cholesterol
63 g carbohydrate
  8 g dietary fiber
256 mg sodium

Meanwhile, in saucepan, bring 2 1/2 cups (625 mL) water to boil; add cous cous, cover and remove from heat. Let stand for 5 minutes; fluff with fork and spoon into individual bowls or plates. Top with vegetable mixture.

*Makes 6 servings.*

\* If using canned chick-peas, use one 19-oz (540 mL) can, drained and rinsed.

---

### How much pasta to cook?

Appetites for pasta vary widely, depending on what else you are eating with the meal, your age, your size, the type of meal and other factors. Catelli recommends 85 grams of dry pasta as a standard serving size and provides this guide to estimate the measure.

| | *85 g Dry (approximate)* |
|---|---|
| **Long Pasta:** | |
| • spaghetti, vermicelli, fettuccine, linguine | bunch - 3/4 inch (2 cm) in diameter |
| **Shaped Pasta:** | |
| • alphabet, soup noodles, stars, rings | 1/2 cup (125 mL) |
| • macaroni, small shells | 3/4 cup (175 mL) |
| • penne, radiatore, fusilli, wagon wheels, small bows | 1 cup (250 mL) |
| • large shells, rigatoni | 1 1/3 cups (325 mL) |
| • rotini, medium bows; fine, medium and broad noodles | 1 2/3 cups (400 mL) |

## Nutrition Bonus

One serving is a very high source of vitamin C (providing 117% of an adult's daily requirement), a very high source of iron, vitamin A and folacin and a high source of calcium. It also contains a very high amount of dietary fiber.

## Tofu

Tofu has a mild taste and can be used in everything from appetizers to desserts. It's cheap, nutritious and relatively low in calories and fat. Tofu or soybean curd is one of the best sources of nonanimal protein you can find, as well as being rich in phosphorus and iron. The amount of calcium in tofu varies depending on how it was made. Check the label and buy the kind that has calcium sulphate or other calcium compound in the list of ingredients. Also compare labels for fat content; some kinds have much more than others.

Tofu is usually sold in a custardlike cake form, covered in water, packed either in 1-lb (500 g) plastic tubs or vacuum-packs. Check the "best before" date to make sure it is fresh. Cut the firm tofu into cubes and add it to soups or salads. Mash the soft tofu and season with fresh herbs or spices, mustard, Parmesan or garlic; add a little yogurt or sour cream and serve as a dip or sauce or salad dressing.

Store tofu in the refrigerator and change the water it is packaged in every day. It will stay fresh for up to 7 days.

**PER SERVING:**
217 calories
14 g protein
9 g total fat
  1 g saturated fat
  0 mg cholesterol
26 g carbohydrate
  8 g dietary fiber
428 mg sodium

# Bulgur Wheat, Tofu and Sweet Peppers

*This tasty main-course vegetarian dish is a good source of protein and fiber.*

| | | |
|---|---|---|
| 1/2 cup | coarse or medium bulgur* | 125 mL |
| 2 tsp | olive oil | 10 mL |
| 2 | cloves garlic, minced | 2 |
| 1 tsp | each ground cumin and coriander | 5 mL |
| 1 | sweet red pepper, cut in strips | 1 |
| 6 oz | firm-style tofu, cut in cubes (1 cup/250 mL) | 175 g |
| 1/3 cup | water | 75 mL |
| 2 tbsp | wine or cider vinegar | 25 mL |
| 1/8 tsp | hot pepper sauce | 0.5 mL |
| Half | pkg (10 oz/284 g) fresh spinach, washed, stemmed and cut in strips (4 cups/1 L) | Half |
| 1/2 tsp | salt | 2 mL |
| | Pepper | |

Place bulgur in bowl and add enough boiling water to cover by 2 inches (5 cm); soak for 20 minutes. Drain thoroughly in sieve.

In large nonstick skillet, heat oil over medium heat. Add garlic; cook for a few seconds. Stir in cumin and coriander; stir in red pepper. Cover and cook for 5 minutes.

Stir in tofu, then add bulgur, water, vinegar and hot pepper sauce; cook, uncovered, for 2 minutes or until bulgur is nearly tender, stirring often. Add spinach; cook, stirring, for 2 to 3 minutes or until slightly wilted. Add salt, and pepper to taste.

*Makes 3 servings.*

*See page 60 for information on bulgur wheat.

# Bulgur Pilaf with Fresh Basil, Mushrooms and Tomatoes

*Dotted with vegetables and sprinkled with nuts, this makes a tasty side dish for meat or poultry, or to serve as part of a vegetarian dinner.*

**Nutrition Bonus**

One serving is a high source of dietary fiber.

| | | |
|---|---|---|
| 3/4 cup | bulgur | 175 mL |
| 1 tbsp | olive oil | 15 mL |
| 1 | onion, finely chopped | 1 |
| 2 | cloves garlic, minced | 2 |
| 1 1/2 cups | sliced mushrooms | 375 mL |
| 1 | large tomato, diced | 1 |
| 1/2 cup | chopped fresh basil leaves* | 125 mL |
| 1/2 tsp | salt | 2 mL |
| | Pepper | |
| 1/4 cup | toasted slivered almonds (see note on page 147) | 50 mL |

**Vegetarian dinner**

Bulgur Pilaf with Fresh Basil, Mushrooms and Tomatoes (this page)
Baked Leeks au Gratin (page 164) OR
Orange Sherried Sweet Potatoes (page 171)
Herbed Green Beans with Garlic (page 164)
Olive and Rosemary Soda Bread (page 181)
Frozen Lemon Cream (page 201) with Raspberry Coulis (page 199)
Applesauce Raisin Spice Cake (page 191)

Place bulgur in bowl and add enough boiling water to cover by 2 inches (5 cm). Soak for 20 minutes or until tender. Drain thoroughly.

In nonstick skillet, heat oil. Add onion; cook, stirring, over medium heat until softened. Stir in garlic and mushrooms; cook until mushrooms are tender, about 3 minutes.

Stir in bulgur, tomato, basil, salt, and pepper to taste; cook, stirring, for 2 to 3 minutes or until heated through. Sprinkle with almonds.

*Makes 6 side-dish servings.*

*If fresh basil is not available, use 1/2 cup (125 mL) chopped fresh parsley and 1 tbsp (15 mL) crushed dried basil leaves.

**PER SERVING:**

128 calories
4 g protein
5 g total fat
  1 g saturated fat
  0 mg cholesterol
18 g carbohydrate
  4 g dietary fiber
198 mg sodium

## MAKE AHEAD

Before baking, cover and refrigerate for up to one day. Add another 1/2 cup (125 mL) stock. Bake as directed.

*Nutrition Bonus*
One serving is a high source of dietary fiber.

Barley has a slightly nutty flavor and soft texture. Use it as you would rice or other grains: add to soups, use as a side dish or as a main dish combined with vegetables, herbs and spices.

# Barley and Parsley Pilaf

*Red onion adds crunch and flavor to this intriguing rice dish. It goes very nicely with most meat or poultry or as part of a vegetarian meal.*

| | | |
|---|---|---|
| 3/4 cup | pearl barley | 175 mL |
| 3/4 cup | brown rice | 175 mL |
| 1/2 cup | hot vegetable or chicken stock | 125 mL |
| 1/2 cup | chopped red or green onion | 125 mL |
| 1 cup | chopped fresh parsley leaves | 250 mL |
| 1 tsp | salt | 5 mL |
| 1/4 tsp | pepper | 1 mL |

In saucepan, cook barley in 3 cups (750 mL) boiling water for 30 minutes or until tender; drain.

In another saucepan, bring 2 cups (500 mL) water to boil; add rice, cover, reduce heat and simmer for 30 minutes or until rice is tender and water is absorbed.

In 6-cup (1.5 L) casserole, combine barley, rice, stock, onion, parsley, salt and pepper. Bake, covered, in 350°F (180°C) oven for 20 minutes or until heated through.

*Makes 8 servings.*

**PER SERVING:**
138 calories
3 g protein
1 g total fat
  trace saturated fat
  0 mg cholesterol
30 g carbohydrate
  5 g dietary fiber
341 mg sodium

# Curried Fruit with Rice

**MAKE AHEAD**

Fruits and sauce can be prepared and set aside for up to six hours.

*Light and juicy fruits plus curry make a fresh, pleasing flavor-and-texture combination. Along with rice, they go well with roast or grilled lamb or baked ham. Perfect for entertaining, the curry looks terrific on a platter surrounded with the rice.*

*Nutrition Bonus*

One serving is a very high source of vitamin C and a high source of vitamin A.

| | | |
|---|---|---|
| 2 cups | cantaloupe or honeydew melon balls | 500 mL |
| 1 cup | diced fresh pineapple | 250 mL |
| 1 cup | sliced peeled peaches, strawberries, grapes or mandarin oranges (or combination) | 250 mL |
| 1 | banana, sliced | 1 |
| 1 cup | vegetable or chicken stock | 250 mL |
| 2 tsp | curry powder or paste | 10 mL |
| 1 1/2 tsp | cornstarch | 7 mL |
| 1/2 cup | finely chopped chutney | 125 mL |
| 1/4 cup | raisins | 50 mL |
| 2 tbsp | butter | 25 mL |
| 5 cups | hot cooked rice | 1.25 L |
| 1/4 cup | toasted slivered almonds* | 50 mL |

In bowl, combine melon, pineapple, peaches (or combination) and banana; set aside.

In saucepan, combine stock, curry powder and cornstarch, mixing well; bring to boil over medium heat, stirring constantly. Combine reserved fruits, chutney and raisins; add to hot curry sauce. Add butter; stir until melted.

Spoon hot rice around edge of shallow serving dish; spoon curry mixture into center and garnish with almonds.

*Makes 8 servings.*

*To toast almonds, spread on baking sheet and roast in 350°F (180°C) oven for 5 to 8 minutes or until lightly golden.

**PER SERVING:**
319 calories
6 g protein
6 g total fat
  2 g saturated fat
  8 mg cholesterol
62 g carbohydrate
  3 g dietary fiber
168 mg sodium

# Beet Risotto

*Dana McCauley, Toronto food writer and chef, helped test some of the recipes in this book and contributed this colorful rice dish. Best served immediately as a first course or as a main course with a green salad and grilled meats, fish or vegetables, it's a dish to make when you have company in the kitchen.*

**Nutrition Bonus**
One serving is a high source of folacin.

Arborio is an Italian rice used mainly in risotto. Try to buy the top quality labeled Superfino or carnarboli. If Arborio rice isn't available, use a long-grain parboiled white rice.

| | | |
|---|---|---|
| 5 cups | chicken or vegetable stock | 1.25 L |
| 2 tsp | vegetable or olive oil | 10 mL |
| 1/2 cup | finely chopped onion | 125 mL |
| 2 | cloves garlic, minced | 2 |
| 1 | small bay leaf | 1 |
| 1 1/2 cups | Arborio rice | 375 mL |
| 1 1/2 cups | chopped cooked beets (or one 14-oz/398 mL can, drained and chopped) | 375 mL |
| 1 tsp | finely grated lemon rind | 5 mL |
| 1 tbsp | fresh lemon juice | 15 mL |
| 1/4 cup | grated Parmesan cheese | 50 mL |
| 1/4 to 1/2 tsp | pepper | 1 to 2 mL |
| | Salt | |
| 2 tbsp | chopped fresh parsley leaves | 25 mL |

In saucepan, bring stock to low simmer.

Meanwhile, in shallow wide nonstick saucepan or large skillet, heat oil over medium heat. Add onion, garlic and bay leaf; cook, covered and stirring often, for 5 minutes or until onion is softened.

Add rice, stirring constantly for 2 minutes or until rice is evenly coated. Add 1 cup (250 mL) of the hot stock; cook, stirring constantly, until liquid is absorbed. Add remaining hot stock 1/2 cup (125 mL) at a time, cooking and stirring until each addition is absorbed before adding next. This should take 20 to 30 minutes total cooking time.

Stir in beets, lemon rind and lemon juice; cook for 1 minute longer or until rice is soft and creamy but still slightly crunchy and beets are heated through. Stir in cheese, pepper, and salt to taste. Discard bay leaf. Place in large shallow bowl; sprinkle with parsley.

*Makes 6 servings.*

**PER SERVING:**
265 calories
10 g protein
4 g total fat
 1 g saturated fat
 3 mg cholesterol
45 g carbohydrate
 2 g dietary fiber
747 mg sodium

# Brown Rice with Currants

**MAKE AHEAD**

Can be prepared and refrigerated for up to two hours. Reheat gently and add fresh basil just before serving.

*This flavorful rice dish goes well with Tomatoes Florentine (page 157), Baked Leeks au Gratin (page 164) or fish or meat, and makes enough for a company meal.*

| | | |
|---|---|---|
| 1/2 cup | currants | 125 mL |
| 2 tbsp | sherry | 25 mL |
| 1 tsp | butter | 5 mL |
| 1 | onion, chopped | 1 |
| 2 cups | brown rice | 500 mL |
| 4 cups | vegetable or chicken broth | 1 L |
| 1 tsp | crushed dried basil leaves (or 1/3 cup/75 mL chopped fresh) | 5 mL |
| | Salt and pepper | |

When using dried herbs, use the leaf form, not ground; add to the liquid early in the recipe. If using fresh herbs, I usually add them at the end of the cooking period for maximum flavor.

To reduce sodium use a low-sodium stock or water.

When shopping for lower sodium stocks or broth, read nutrition labels carefully. Some healthy or light claims may not be for sodium but for fat or cholesterol.

In bowl, soak currants in sherry, and set aside.

In heavy saucepan, melt butter over medium heat. Add onion; cook, stirring, until tender. Add rice and stir to mix well.

Bring stock to boil; pour over rice. Stir in basil (if using dried), and salt and pepper to taste. Simmer, covered, until water has been absorbed, about 40 minutes. Stir in currants and sherry and basil (if using fresh).

*Makes 8 servings.*

**PER SERVING:**
219 calories
6 g protein
2 g total fat
  1 g saturated fat
  1 mg cholesterol
43 g carbohydrate
  3 g dietary fiber
210 mg sodium

**COMPARE:**

| | mg sodium/serving |
|---|---|
| Recipe made with: | |
| • stock from 4 Oxo cubes and 4 cups (1 L) water | 606 |
| • canned chicken broth and water (2 cups/500 mL of each) | 403 |
| • canned chicken broth (1 cup/250 mL) and water (3 cups/750 mL) | 210 |
| • homemade stock without added salt | 30 |
| • water | 17 |

# Sauces

FOR TWO YEARS I WAS A NATIONAL JUDGE for Wiser's Deluxe Culinary Competition in Montreal. Most of the other judges were very experienced, award-winning chefs. It was here that I learned that the real test of a chef is his or her sauces. The judges would quickly decide how well meat was cooked, arranged and garnished, but the sauce for the meat would be tasted and discussed at great length. It had to be silky smooth, full of flavor but not overpowering, not too thick but not watery either. The sauces we tasted were exquisite, made from long-simmering stocks and enriched with butter and cream.

Now we want more variety in tastes and ingredients, and as a result, a whole new collection of sauces is in vogue. Red peppers are slowly roasted, then puréed, to blanket a plate for tender, juicy chicken breasts. Sun-ripened mangoes, puréed with lemon or lime juice, complement perfectly cooked fish.

Most home cooks don't have wonderful homemade stock bases on hand. We want tasty sauces we can make in five to ten minutes. We want light sauces that are not loaded with calories, cholesterol and fat. Here is a selection of sauces that will fool even the most serious diners. They're full of flavor, yet low in fat, especially when compared to traditional sauces. And most are very quick to prepare.

---

*Reducing fat content in sauces*
- To remove fat from pan juices, skim fat off surface. Or throw in ice cubes; the fat will adhere to the ice and can be easily removed. Or pour juices into a container and put in freezer; remove solid fat from surface.
- To thicken cold juices, add 2 tbsp (25 mL) flour per cup (250 mL) of juice and heat, stirring, until thickened and smooth.
- Boil down pan juices if they're too thin.
- If using canned beef or chicken stock, refrigerate.

The fat will solidify on top and lift off easily.
- Use yogurt or no-fat sour cream or milk as a base for cold, cream-type sauces, instead of cream or mayonnaise. To heat yogurt or sour cream, mix in 2 tsp (10 mL) flour per cup (250 mL) to prevent separating.
- Instead of whipped cream, use fruits such as strawberries or raspberries puréed in a food processor or blender. They are low in fat and calories and make delicious sauces to serve with other fruits, ice creams, sherbets or cakes.

Or use the Honey Lime Sauce on page 35. It's delicious.
- Many desserts are too sweet and need whipped cream or crème fraîche to tone them down. You won't need the whipped cream if you reduce the amount of sugar in puddings, pies and fruit desserts instead.

MAKE AHEAD

Sauce can be covered and refrigerated for up to one week.

*Holiday Turkey Dinner*
Roast turkey with Blackberry Sauce (this page)
Glazed Brussels Sprouts with Pecans (page 158)
Baked Squash with Ginger (page 173) or Turnips Paysanne (page 175)
Orange Sponge Cake (page 190) with Sherry Orange Sauce (page 204) and Fruit sorbets (pages 198 to 203)

PER TBSP:
35 calories
trace protein
0 g total fat
  0 g saturated fat
  0 mg cholesterol
8 g carbohydrate
  trace dietary fiber
2 mg sodium

# Blackberry Sauce

*This sauce is delicious with turkey, chicken and ham. Conventional gravy is much higher in fat than this sweet yet tart sauce. Currant jelly can be used instead of blackberry.*

| | | |
|---|---|---|
| 1 cup | blackberry jelly | 250 mL |
| 1/3 cup | frozen orange juice concentrate | 75 mL |
| 1/3 cup | brandy | 75 mL |
| 1/4 cup | red wine vinegar or balsamic vinegar | 50 mL |

In small saucepan, combine jelly, orange juice concentrate, brandy and vinegar. Heat over low heat until jelly is melted; stir well.

*Makes about 2 cups (500 mL).*

MAKE AHEAD

Sauce can be covered and refrigerated for up to two days

PER TBSP:
12 calories
1 g protein
trace total fat
  trace saturated fat
  1 mg cholesterol
1 g carbohydrate
  0 g dietary fiber
43 mg sodium

# Dill Mustard Sauce

*Serve with hot or cold fish dishes and seafood, as a dressing for salads, or with chicken or turkey, or toss with cold cooked pasta.*

| | | |
|---|---|---|
| 1/3 cup | plain low-fat yogurt | 75 mL |
| 1/3 cup | cottage cheese or no-fat sour cream | 75 mL |
| 1/4 cup | chopped fresh dill* leaves | 50 mL |
| 1 1/2 tsp | Dijon mustard | 7 mL |
| | Salt and pepper | |

In blender or bowl, combine yogurt, cottage cheese, dill and mustard; blend or whisk until smooth. Season with salt and pepper to taste.

*Makes 2/3 cup (150 mL).*

*Fresh dill gives this sauce excellent flavor; if not available, substitute 2 tbsp (25 mL) chopped fresh parsley leaves and 1 tsp (5 mL) dried dillweed.

If using cottage cheese, a blender (not a food processor) is needed to get a smooth sauce.

**MAKE AHEAD**

Sauce can be covered and refrigerated for up to three days.

# Tomato Basil Sauce

*I use this sauce often, either over spaghetti, macaroni or other pasta, or as a base for pizza. Use the dried leaf form of basil and oregano, not ground; crush the herbs by rubbing them between the palms of your hands before adding to the sauce. If I have fresh basil on hand, I add at least 1/2 cup (125 mL) coarsely chopped basil just before tossing sauce with pasta. Top pasta with freshly grated Parmesan cheese.*

**Nutrition Bonus**
One serving is a high source of vitamin C.

| 1 tbsp | extra virgin olive oil | 15 mL |
|---|---|---|
| 2 | onions, finely chopped | 2 |
| 2 | cans (each 28 oz/796 mL) plum tomatoes | 2 |
| 1 | can (5 1/2 oz/156 mL) tomato paste | 1 |
| 2 | cloves garlic, minced | 2 |
| 1 | large bay leaf | 1 |
| 2 tbsp | crushed dried basil leaves | 25 mL |
| 2 tsp | crushed dried oregano leaves | 10 mL |
| 1 cup | coarsely chopped fresh basil or parsley leaves (optional) | 250 mL |
| | Salt, pepper and granulated sugar | |

**PER 1/2 CUP:**
58 calories
2 g protein
2 g total fat
　trace saturated fat
　0 mg cholesterol
10 g carbohydrate
　2 g dietary fiber
228 mg sodium

　　In large nonstick saucepan, heat oil over medium-low heat. Add onions; cook, stirring often, until tender.
　　In food processor, purée tomatoes; add to pan along with tomato paste, garlic, bay leaf, basil and dried oregano. Simmer, uncovered, for 20 to 30 minutes or until thickened slightly. (If sauce thickens too quickly, cover for remaining cooking time.) Add fresh basil (if using); season with salt, pepper and sugar to taste.
*Makes about 6 cups (1.5 L).*

**MAKE AHEAD**

Sauce can be covered and refrigerated for up to two days; reheat gently.

# Tarragon and Mushroom Sauce

*This is really a great-tasting sauce that's similar in taste to a Béarnaise sauce but with much less butter. It is delicious served warm with lentil burgers, steak, meatballs and other meats or poultry.*

Photo:
*Scallops and Shrimp in Thai Lemon Cream with Julienne Vegetables (page 120)*

| 1 tbsp | butter | 15 mL |
|---|---|---|
| 1 cup | chopped fresh mushrooms (about 4 oz/125 g) | 250 mL |
| 2 tbsp | chopped green onion | 25 mL |
| 2 tbsp | all-purpose flour | 25 mL |
| 1/2 tsp | crushed dried tarragon leaves | 2 mL |
| 2 cups | hot beef, chicken or vegetable stock | 500 mL |

PER TBSP:
9 calories
trace protein
1 g total fat
  trace saturated fat
  1 mg cholesterol
1 g carbohydrate
  trace dietary fiber
70 mg sodium

In saucepan, melt butter over medium heat. Add mushrooms and onion; cook, stirring occasionally, until tender and most of the liquid is evaporated. Sprinkle with flour and tarragon; cook, stirring, for 2 minutes.

Bring stock to boil; gradually pour into mushroom mixture, whisking constantly. Cook, stirring constantly, until boiling and thickened slightly. Simmer, uncovered, for 10 minutes or until reduced to about 1 1/2 cups (375 mL). Serve warm.

*Makes 1 1/2 cups (375 mL).*

## MAKE AHEAD

Sauce can be covered and refrigerated for up to three days. Reheat over hot, not boiling, water.

# Yogurt Hollandaise

*Use this sauce with vegetables, eggs or fish. It is like a Hollandaise in taste but is made with yogurt instead of butter.*

| 1 cup | plain (1 to 2%) yogurt | 250 mL |
|-------|------------------------|--------|
| 2 tsp | fresh lemon juice | 10 mL |
| 3 | egg yolks | 3 |
| 1/2 tsp | salt | 2 mL |
| 1/2 tsp | Dijon mustard | 2 mL |
| Pinch | pepper | Pinch |
| 1 tbsp | chopped fresh dill or parsley leaves (optional) | 15 mL |

PER TBSP:
17 calories
1 g protein
1 g total fat
  trace saturated fat
  34 mg cholesterol
1 g carbohydrate
  0 g dietary fiber
69 mg sodium

In top of nonaluminum double boiler or saucepan,* whisk together yogurt, lemon juice, egg yolks, salt, mustard and pepper. Heat over simmering water, stirring constantly, for 10 to 15 minutes or until thickened and sauce coats back of wooden spoon. (Sauce could become thinner after about 10 minutes of cooking, then will thicken again.) Stir in dill (if using). Serve warm.

*Makes about 1 1/4 cups (300 mL).*

*Egg-yolk mixtures cooked in an aluminum pan will discolor.

Photo:
*Plum Tart (page 215)*

**MAKE AHEAD**

Salsa can be covered and refrigerated for up to two days.

# Tomato Salsa

*Serve this Mexican staple as a topping for tacos or tostadas, over cottage cheese, as a low-fat dip with Belgian endive wedges or low-fat chips, as a filling for pita bread or as an accompaniment to meats. You might like to add more coriander to taste.*

| | | |
|---|---|---|
| 4 | large tomatoes, diced | 4 |
| 1 | large sweet green pepper, diced | 1 |
| 1 | fresh hot chili pepper, or 1 pickled jalapeño pepper, or 2 canned green chili peppers, seeded and diced | 1 |
| 1/4 cup | chopped fresh coriander (cilantro) leaves | 50 mL |
| 1 tbsp | grated onion | 15 mL |
| 1 | clove garlic, minced | 1 |
| 1 tsp | crushed dried oregano leaves | 5 mL |
| | Salt and pepper | |

In bowl, combine tomatoes, green pepper, chili pepper, coriander, onion, garlic and oregano, mixing well. Season with salt and pepper to taste.

*Makes 4 cups (1 L).*

*Nutrition Bonus*
One serving is a very high source of vitamin C.

For other sauce recipes, see:
Red Pepper Purée (page 158)
Curry Sauce (page 94)
Pesto (page 46)
For dessert sauces, see pages 195 to 219
Honey Lime Sauce (page 35)
Creamy Herb Sauce (page 31)

**PER 1/2 CUP**:
23 calories
1 g protein
trace total fat
   0 g saturated fat
   0 mg cholesterol
5 g carbohydrate
   1 g dietary fiber
8 mg sodium

## Lower-Fat Choices For Sauces

| Sauce for | Instead of | g fat per 2 tbsp (25 mL) | Choose | g fat per 2 tbsp (25 mL) |
|---|---|---|---|---|
| Asparagus, broccoli, fish and eggs benedict | Conventional Hollandaise | 8+ | Yogurt Hollandaise (page 153) | 2 |
| Pork | Homemade gravy | 6+ | Cinnamon Applesauce (page 206) | trace |
| | | | Red Pepper Purée (page 158) | 1 |
| Beef | Homemade gravy | 6+ | Pan juices (fat removed) | 0 to 2 (approx) |
| Steak | Béarnaise Sauce | 7+ | Tarragon and Mushroom Sauce (page 152) | 1 |
| Chicken and turkey | Homemade gravy | 6+ | Pan juices (fat removed) | 0 to 2 (approx) |
| | | | Cranberry sauce | trace |
| | | | Blackberry Sauce (page 151) | 0 |
| Hot or cold poached salmon and other fish | Cream sauces | 3+ | Creamy Herb Sauce (page 31) | trace |
| | Mayonnaise | 22 | Dill Mustard Sauce (page 151) | 1 |
| Pasta | Butter- and cream-based sauces | 10+ | Tomato Basil Sauce (page 152) | trace |
| | Conventional pesto | 7+ | Pesto (page 46) | 1 |

# Vegetables

I ALWAYS LOOK FORWARD TO THE CHANGE in seasons because of the new vegetables it brings to the table. What could possibly taste better than the first bite of June's tender asparagus, July's juicy tomatoes full of sun-sweetened flavor or August's first feed of locally grown, sweet and juicy corn-on-the-cob? I enjoy the vegetables as much as, if not more than, the meat portion of a meal.

Not only are vegetables delicious, they also play an important role in a healthy diet and have anti-cancer effects (see page 4). Many vegetables are good sources of fiber, vitamins (especially A and C), phytochemicals and minerals, as well as being low in fat and calories. It's the butter, oil and cream you serve with vegetables that add the fat and calories, not the vegetables themselves.

As long as you don't add extra butter or other fats, vegetables will help you maintain your ideal weight and lower your total fat intake to no more than 30 percent of your daily calorie intake.

When planning meals, include both fresh and raw vegetables. Make sure you have a pleasing combination of colors, flavors and textures. For instance, don't serve turnip, cauliflower and parsnip at the same meal. They're all strongly flavored, similar in texture and lacking in color contrast. Include bright green, deep-yellow and orange vegetables as much as possible, not only for their visual appeal but for their nutrients.

For the most fiber and vitamins:

- Don't peel vegetables if the skins are edible (potatoes, zucchini, cucumber). They contain fiber as well as nutrients.
- Don't discard the seeds if they're edible (e.g., those in tomatoes and cucumbers). They are excellent sources of fiber.
- Eat a variety of vegetables both raw and cooked.
- Don't overcook vegetables. See page 5 for information on retaining vitamins when cooking vegetables.
- Refer to the table on page 161 to see which vegetables have the most fiber.

**MAKE AHEAD**

Tomatoes can be assembled, covered and set aside at room temperature for up to four hours before heating.

# Tomatoes Florentine

*These are an attractive make-ahead addition to a buffet table or dinner. Garlic enthusiasts could add another clove.*

| 6 | tomatoes | 6 |
|---|---|---|
| 2 tsp | olive oil | 10 mL |
| 1 | small onion, finely chopped | 1 |
| 1 | clove garlic, minced | 1 |
| 1 | pkg (12 oz/340 g) frozen chopped spinach, thawed and drained | 1 |
| 1/4 tsp | each salt and pepper | 1 mL |

| | *Topping:* | |
|---|---|---|
| 2 tbsp | fine fresh bread crumbs | 25 mL |
| 2 tbsp | chopped fresh parsley leaves | 25 mL |
| 2 tbsp | grated Parmesan cheese | 25 mL |

**Nutrition Bonus**
One serving is a very high source of vitamin A and a high source of vitamin C and folacin.

Cut a slice from top of each tomato. Scoop out pulp to halfway down tomato and save for sauce or soup.

In skillet, heat oil. Add onion and garlic; cook over medium heat for 3 minutes or until tender. Stir in spinach, salt and pepper. Spoon into tomatoes. Arrange in ovenproof serving dish or on baking sheet.

**Topping:** Combine bread crumbs, parsley and cheese; sprinkle over tomatoes. Bake in 400°F (200°C) oven for 20 minutes or until heated through.

*Makes 6 servings.*

**Tomatoes Provençal**
Cut 6 tomatoes in half crosswise. Combine 1/2 cup (125 mL) fine fresh bread crumbs, 1 large clove garlic, minced, 1/4 cup (50 mL) chopped fresh parsley leaves and 1 tbsp (15 mL) olive oil; sprinkle over tomato halves. Bake on baking sheet in 400°F (200°C) oven for 15 minutes or until heated through. Makes 6 servings.

**PER SERVING:**
63 calories
3 g protein
3 g total fat
  1 g saturated fat
  2 mg cholesterol
9 g carbohydrate
  3 g dietary fiber
178 mg sodium

*Nutrition Bonus*
One serving is a very high source of vitamin C.

# Glazed Brussels Sprouts with Pecans

*Traditional with a turkey dinner, this dish can be easily doubled or tripled. Walnuts can be used instead of pecans. Just make sure they are fresh.*

| | | |
|---|---|---|
| 2 cups | small Brussels sprouts | 500 mL |
| 1 tbsp | butter | 15 mL |
| 2 tsp | granulated sugar | 10 mL |
| 2 tbsp | coarsely chopped pecans | 25 mL |
| | Salt and pepper | |

Trim base of sprouts and outside leaves. Steam sprouts over boiling water for 8 to 10 minutes or until tender.

In skillet, melt butter over medium heat; add sugar and stir until melted. Add Brussels sprouts and pecans, stirring to coat well; cook for 1 to 2 minutes. Season with salt and pepper to taste.

*Makes 4 servings.*

**PER SERVING:**
76 calories
2 g protein
6 g total fat
  2 g saturated fat
  8 mg cholesterol
7 g carbohydrate
  2 g dietary fiber
39 mg sodium

**MAKE AHEAD**

Red pepper purée can be covered and refrigerated for up to five days. Reheat gently over low heat or in microwave.

*Nutrition Bonus*
One serving is a very high source of vitamin C (providing 168% of an adult's daily requirement), and also a very high source of vitamin A and folacin.

Roasted red peppers have a wonderful rich flavor. They're usually quickly roasted under a broiler or on the barbecue until they char and blacken. I recommend roasting them slowly just until they blister, not until they char.

# Asparagus with Red Pepper Purée

*Serve this colorful dish as a first course in asparagus season.*

| | | |
|---|---|---|
| 2 | large sweet red peppers | 2 |
| 2 tsp | extra-virgin olive oil | 10 mL |
| 1/4 tsp | crushed dried thyme leaves | 1 mL |
| | Pepper | |
| 2 lb | asparagus | 1 kg |

Roast peppers on baking sheet in 375°F (190°C) oven for 18 minutes. Turn and roast on other side for 18 to 20 minutes longer or until peppers are blistered and soft. Let cool. Using fingers and small knife, peel skin from peppers (it should come off easily); discard seeds and liquid. In food processor or blender, purée together red peppers, oil, thyme, and pepper to taste. Set aside.

Wash and break tough ends off asparagus; cook in large pot of boiling water for 5 to 8 minutes or until tender-crisp; drain thoroughly.

Spoon hot pepper purée onto individual plates. Arrange hot asparagus on top.

*Makes 6 servings.*

**PER SERVING:**
54 calories
3 g protein
2 g total fat
  trace saturated fat
  0 mg cholesterol
8 g carbohydrate
  3 g dietary fiber
13 mg sodium

**MAKE AHEAD**

Vegetables can be prepared a few hours in advance; cook just before serving.

*Nutrition Bonus*
One serving is a very high source of vitamin A (providing 140% of an adult's daily requirement).

*Lemon-Ginger Carrots*
In a small saucepan, combine 1 tbsp (15 mL) each butter, granulated sugar and lemon juice and 1 tsp (5 mL) each grated lemon rind and grated fresh gingerroot; cook until sugar dissolves. Toss with 2 to 3 cups (500 to 750 mL) hot cooked carrots.

Add butter at the end of the cooking of vegetables to get maximum flavor with minimum fat.

*Spring Dinner Party Menu*
Asparagus with Red Pepper Purée (page 158)
Marinated Leg of Lamb with Coriander (page 110)
Bulgur Pilaf with Fresh Basil, Mushrooms and Tomatoes (page 145)
Steamed cherry tomatoes and snow peas or Sautéed Zucchini with Yogurt and Herbs (page 168) or Stir-Fried Vegetables with Ginger and Garlic (page 170)
Fresh Strawberry Sorbet (page 199)

**PER SERVING:**
56 calories
1 g protein
2 g total fat
  1 g saturated fat
  5 mg cholesterol
9 g carbohydrate
  2 g dietary fiber
58 mg sodium

# Tarragon Carrots

*Onion and tarragon add extra flavor and color to carrots. Cook them in the oven or microwave to retain the vitamins, and save time by slicing the carrots and onions in the food processor.*

| 2 cups | thinly sliced carrots | 500 mL |
|---|---|---|
| 2 | small onions, thinly sliced | 2 |
| 2 tbsp | water | 25 mL |
| 1 tsp | crushed dried tarragon leaves (or 1 tbsp/15 mL chopped fresh tarragon) | 5 mL |
| | Salt and pepper | |
| 2 tsp | butter | 10 mL |

Lightly oil large sheet of foil or 6-cup (1.5 L) microwaveable dish. Arrange carrots and onion in center; sprinkle with water, tarragon, and salt and pepper to taste. Wrap tightly or cover. Bake in 350°F (180°C) oven for 30 minutes, or microwave on High for 10 to 12 minutes, or until tender. Stir in butter.

*Makes 4 servings.*

MAKE AHEAD

Vegetables (including blanching of broccoli) can be prepared, covered and refrigerated for up to one day. Stir-fry just before serving.

*Nutrition Bonus*
One serving is a very high source of vitamin C (providing 148% of an adult's daily requirement) and a high source of vitamin A and folacin.

PER SERVING:
47 calories
2 g protein
2 g total fat
  trace saturated fat
  0 mg cholesterol
6 g carbohydrate
  2 g dietary fiber
144 mg sodium

# Broccoli and Sweet Pepper Stir-Fry

*This bright red, yellow and green vegetable dish tastes as good as it looks.*

| | | |
|---|---|---|
| 1 | bunch broccoli (about 1 lb/500 g) | 1 |
| 1 | each sweet red and yellow pepper | 1 |
| 1 tbsp | canola or sesame oil | 15 mL |
| 1 | onion, chopped | 1 |
| 1 to 2 tbsp | grated fresh gingerroot | 15 to 25 mL |
| 1/4 cup | chicken stock | 50 mL |
| 1 tbsp | soy sauce | 15 mL |
| 1 tbsp | toasted sesame seeds (optional) | 15 mL |

Peel tough broccoli stems. Cut stems and florets into pieces about 1 1/2 inches (4 cm) long. Blanch in large pot of boiling water for 2 to 3 minutes or until bright green and tender-crisp; drain and cool under cold running water. Drain again and dry on paper towels. Core and seed peppers; cut into thin strips.

In large nonstick skillet or wok, heat oil over medium heat. Add onion and gingerroot; stir-fry for 1 minute. Add peppers and stir-fry for 2 to 3 minutes, adding chicken stock when necessary to prevent sticking or scorching. Add broccoli; stir-fry until heated through. Sprinkle with soy sauce, and sesame seeds (if using).

*Makes 8 servings.*

MAKE AHEAD

Cabbage can be covered and refrigerated for up to two days. Reheat to serve.

# Braised Red Cabbage

*Here's a colorful and flavorful vegetable that's especially good with pork or poultry. To retain a bright red color when cooking red cabbage, include an acid such as vinegar or lemon juice in the cooking liquid.*

| | | |
|---|---|---|
| Half | medium red cabbage | Half |
| 1 | cooking apple | 1 |
| 1/3 cup | water | 75 mL |
| 1/4 cup | white wine vinegar | 50 mL |
| | Salt and pepper | |
| 2 tbsp | (approx) liquid honey or granulated sugar | 25 mL |

PER SERVING:
75 calories
1 g protein
trace total fat
　0 g saturated fat
　0 mg cholesterol
19 g carbohydrate
　3 g dietary fiber
10 mg sodium

Remove outer leaves and center core of cabbage. Slice thinly to make about 5 cups/1.25 L. Peel, core and slice apple. In large skillet or heavy saucepan, combine cabbage, apple, water and vinegar; bring to boil. Reduce heat and simmer, covered and stirring occasionally, for 50 to 60 minutes or until cabbage is very tender.

Season with salt, pepper and honey to taste to make dish sweet and sour. Adjust seasonings if necessary.

*Makes 4 servings.*

---

## *Best Vegetable Sources of Fiber*

**VERY HIGH SOURCE OF FIBER** - more than 6 grams of fiber serving

| | g of fiber |
|---|---|
| Kidney Beans | 8.3 g |
| Corn, sweet on/off cob (12 inch/30 cm ear) | 6.7 g |
| Navy Beans | 6.9 g |

**HIGH SOURCE OF FIBER** - 4 to 6 grams of fiber per serving

| | g of fiber |
|---|---|
| Green Peas | 5.4 g |
| Baked Potato, flesh and skin - 1 potato (200 g) | 4.6 g |
| Lentils | 4.4 g |
| Sweet Potato, boiled without skin, mashed | 4.1 g |
| Baby Lima Beans | 4.1 g |

**SOURCE OF FIBER** - 2 to 4 grams of fiber per serving

| | g of fiber |
|---|---|
| Squash, Hubbard, boiled mashed | 3.4 g |
| Brussels Sprouts | 3.4 g |
| Chick-Peas | 3.3 g |
| Parsnips | 3.1 g |
| Vegetables, mixed | 3.1 g |
| Spinach | 3.0 g |
| Broccoli | 3.0 g |

(Measurements are for 1/2 cup (125 mL) cooked vegetables unless otherwise noted.)

**MAKE AHEAD**

Casserole can be assembled (except for bread crumbs), covered and refrigerated for up to 24 hours. Sprinkle with bread crumbs and bake as directed.

*Nutrition Bonus*
One serving is a very high source of vitamin C.

# Scalloped Cabbage au Gratin

*This makes a delicious dish that adds some protein to a meatless meal. It also goes well with hot or cold beef, pork and lamb.*

| | | |
|---|---|---:|
| 4 cups | coarsely shredded cabbage | 1 L |
| 1 | can (28 oz/796 mL) tomatoes, drained and chopped | 1 |
| 2 tsp | granulated sugar | 10 mL |
| 1 tsp | crumbled dried oregano leaves | 5 mL |
| 1/4 tsp | each paprika, salt and pepper | 1 mL |
| 1/2 cup | shredded light Cheddar-style cheese | 125 mL |
| 1 cup | fresh whole-wheat bread crumbs | 250 mL |

In saucepan of boiling water, cook cabbage for about 6 minutes or until fork-tender; drain well. Spoon into lightly greased 6-cup (1.5 L) baking dish.

In bowl, combine tomatoes, sugar, oregano, paprika, salt and pepper; spoon evenly over cabbage. Sprinkle with cheese, then bread crumbs. Bake, uncovered, in 350°F (180°C) oven for 30 minutes or until heated through.

*Makes 6 servings.*

**PER SERVING:**
80 calories
5 g protein
2 g total fat
  1 g saturated fat
  6 mg cholesterol
11 g carbohydrate
  2 g dietary fiber
360 mg sodium

# Two-Cabbage Stir-Fry

MAKE AHEAD

Vinegar mixture and vegetables can be set aside for up to four hours before cooking.

*Red and green cabbage stir-fried with ginger and onion is a delicious, colorful vegetable dish that's especially good with pork and turkey. It's quick to make and can easily be doubled.*

| | | |
|---|---|---|
| 1 tbsp | rice vinegar | 15 mL |
| 1 tbsp | water | 15 mL |
| 1 tsp | soy sauce | 5 mL |
| 1 tsp | cornstarch | 5 mL |
| 1 tbsp | canola oil | 15 mL |
| 1 tsp | chopped fresh gingerroot | 5 mL |
| 1 | small onion, chopped | 1 |
| 1 cup | thinly sliced red cabbage | 250 mL |
| 1 cup | thinly sliced green cabbage | 250 mL |

Rice vinegar is a mild, sweet vinegar, available in the Chinese food section of many supermarkets. If not available, substitute cider vinegar and a pinch of sugar.

In small dish, mix together vinegar, water, soy sauce and cornstarch; set aside.

In nonstick skillet or wok, heat oil over medium heat. Add ginger and onion; stir for 1 minute. Add red and green cabbage and stir-fry until tender, 3 to 5 minutes.

Pour in vinegar mixture and stir-fry until liquid comes to a boil, about 1 minute.

*Makes 3 servings.*

*Fall Dinner Menu*
Pork Tenderloin with Rosemary and Thyme (page 107)
Two-Cabbage Stir-Fry (this page)
Mashed Potatoes with Garlic and Onions (page 169)
Peach Blueberry Crisp (page 207)

PER SERVING:
64 calories
1 g protein
5 g total fat
  trace saturated fat
  0 mg cholesterol
6 g carbohydrate
  1 g dietary fiber
102 mg sodium

MAKE AHEAD

Trimmed and cooked beans can be rinsed under cold water, drained and set aside for up to six hours before continuing with recipe.

Leave beans whole or cut into lengths: 1 lb (500 g) green beans cut into 1-inch (2.5 cm) lengths = 4 cups (1 L); cut into 1 1/2-inch (4 cm) lengths = 6 cups (1.5 L)

PER SERVING:
59 calories
2 g protein
2 g total fat
  1 g saturated fat
  5 mg cholesterol
10 g carbohydrate
  3 g dietary fiber
23 mg sodium

# Herbed Green Beans with Garlic

*Herbs, onion and garlic enhance the flavor of beans without adding calories or fat.*

| 1 lb | green beans | 500 g |
|---|---|---|
| 2 tsp | butter or olive oil | 10 mL |
| 1 | small onion, thinly sliced | 1 |
| 1 | clove garlic, minced | 1 |
| 1 tbsp | chopped fresh thyme or oregano leaves (or 1/2 tsp/2 mL crushed dried leaf) | 15 mL |
| | Salt and pepper | |

Trim beans. In saucepan of rapidly boiling water, cook beans for 4 to 5 minutes or until tender-crisp; drain.

In nonstick skillet or saucepan, melt butter over medium heat. Add onion and garlic; cook, stirring occasionally, until onion is tender. Stir in beans, thyme, and salt and pepper to taste; cook until heated through.

*Makes 4 servings.*

MAKE AHEAD

Leeks can be assembled and set aside for up to six hours.

Be sure to cook leeks until they are fork-tender. Undercooked leeks are tough and seem to have less flavor. Cooked and cooled leeks drizzled with Orange Vinaigrette (page 80) or Tarragon Vinaigrette (page 79) are a delicious first course.

PER SERVING:
83 calories
3 g protein
4 g total fat
  1 g saturated fat
  2 mg cholesterol
12 g carbohydrate
  2 g dietary fiber
75 mg sodium

# Baked Leeks au Gratin

*Though leeks are available nearly all year round, they're in season and most reasonably priced during the fall. They're delicious with any cut of meat or poultry, or as part of an all-vegetable dinner.*

| 4 | large leeks | 4 |
|---|---|---|
| 2 tsp | olive oil | 10 mL |
| | Salt and pepper | |
| 2 tbsp | grated Parmesan cheese | 25 mL |
| 1 tsp | water | 5 mL |

Trim base and tough green leaves from leeks, leaving tender green and white parts. Cut leeks in half lengthwise; wash under cold running water and drain. Place leeks, cut side up, in single layer in microwaveable dish or on lightly oiled foil. Sprinkle with oil; season with salt and pepper to taste. Sprinkle with cheese. Add 1 tsp (5 mL) water to dish. Cover dish or wrap in foil. Microwave on High for 10 minutes, or bake in 350°F (180°C) oven for 25 minutes, or until very tender.

*Makes 4 servings.*

**MAKE AHEAD**

Dish can be covered and refrigerated for up to two days; reheat gently in oven or microwave or on stove top.

**Nutrition Bonus**
One serving is a very high source of vitamin C (providing 125% of an adult's daily requirement) and a high source of iron, vitamin A and folacin.

**October-November Friday Night Dinner Menu**
Lemon Chicken Schnitzel (page 86)
Baked Leeks au Gratin (page 164)
Baked Squash with Ginger (page 173)
Tossed green salad with Creamy Caesar Dressing (page 81)
Plum Tart (page 215)

**Microwave Method**
In 10-inch (25 cm) round microwaveable dish, place leeks, cut side up, in single layer.
Add 1 tbsp (15 mL) water to dish. Dot with butter and season with salt and pepper to taste. Cover dish and slightly vent; microwave on High for 5 minutes or until leeks are nearly tender. Add red peppers and cover and slightly vent; microwave on High for 2 minutes or until vegetables are tender.

**PER SERVING:**
94 calories
2 g protein
3 g total fat
　2 g saturated fat
　8 mg cholesterol
17 g carbohydrate
　3 g dietary fiber
49 mg sodium

# Braised Red Peppers and Leeks

*This dish goes well with lamb, pork or beef, but don't use more red pepper than called for — it could overpower the subtle flavor of the leeks.*

| | | |
|---|---|---|
| 6 | medium leeks | 6 |
| 1 | large sweet red pepper | 1 |
| 1/2 cup | chicken stock or water | 125 mL |
| 1 tbsp | butter | 15 mL |
| | Salt and pepper | |

Trim base and tough green leaves from leeks, leaving tender green and white parts. Cut leeks in half lengthwise; wash under cold running water and drain. Cut into 1/2-inch (1 cm) thick slices to make about 4 cups (1 L). Core and seed red pepper; cut into thin 1-inch (2.5 cm) long strips.

In saucepan, combine chicken stock and leeks; cover and simmer for 5 to 10 minutes or until almost tender. Add red pepper; cover and simmer for 5 to 10 minutes or until tender. If too much liquid, uncover and cook for 1 to 2 minutes. Add butter, and salt and pepper to taste.

*Makes 4 servings.*

**MAKE AHEAD**

Vegetables can be prepared up to point of baking and set aside for up to four hours.

*Nutrition Bonus*
One serving is a very high source of vitamin A (providing 131% of an adult's daily requirement) and a high source of folacin.

# Foil-Steamed Spring Vegetables

*These vegetables are delicious with fish or chicken. In winter, use parsnips, snow peas or beans instead of asparagus and cut the parsnips and carrots into 1/2-inch (1 cm) pieces. White pearl onions, which are the size of small grapes, are sold in 2-cup (500 mL) boxes. They keep for a month or two in a cool, dry place. If not available, use the white and tender green part of 2 to 3 bunches of green onions.*

| | | |
|---|---|---|
| 8 oz | pearl onions | 250 g |
| 12 oz | young carrots | 375 g |
| 8 oz | asparagus | 250 g |
| 2 tbsp | water | 25 mL |
| 1 tbsp | butter | 15 mL |
| 1 | bay leaf | 1 |
| 1/2 tsp | salt | 2 mL |
| Pinch | white pepper | Pinch |

In large pot of boiling water, blanch pearl onions for 2 minutes; remove with slotted spoon. Cut off root end and gently squeeze to remove skin. In same pot of boiling water, blanch carrots for 2 minutes; drain and rinse under cold running water. Drain again. Snap tough ends from asparagus.

On large piece of heavy-duty foil, arrange vegetables in single layer. Sprinkle with water and dot with butter; add bay leaf, salt and pepper. Fold foil over vegetables and seal. Bake in 375°F (190°C) oven for 20 to 30 minutes or until vegetables are tender.

*Makes 6 servings.*

**PER SERVING:**
59 calories
2 g protein
2 g total fat
  1 g saturated fat
  5 mg cholesterol
10 g carbohydrate
  2 g dietary fiber
249 mg sodium

## Steam Cooking

To steam food means to cook over, not in, boiling water or other liquid. Foods wrapped in foil, then baked or barbecued, steam in their own liquids.

Herbs, salt, sugar or spices can be added to the foods or to the liquid before steaming. The advantage of steaming is that vegetables retain their flavor, color and vitamins, and fish is moist and flavorful. Food can be steamed in the oven, on top of the stove or on the barbecue.

## Equipment for Steaming

There are a number of steamers on the market, but you don't have to have special equipment.

- Wrap foods in foil, then cook in the oven or on the barbecue.
- For stove-top cooking, you can use a deep pot with a tight-fitting lid and something to keep the food above the liquid. This could be a steamer with perforated petals and short legs, a flat-bottomed metal colander or one with feet, or a metal strainer. Large foods such as chicken or pudding can be placed on an inverted heat-proof plate or bowl, or on custard cups or a wire rack. A wok with a rack inside, and covered with a lid (or foil if the lid isn't tight-fitting), can also be used.
- To oven-steam, use a roasting pan with a trivet, wire rack or anything that is heat-proof to keep the food above the liquid.
- Steam-cook in a deep-fryer with basket set over water instead of oil.
- Use a clay baker.

# Sautéed Zucchini with Yogurt and Herbs

*Sautéed zucchini dressed with yogurt or sour cream is one of my favorite quick-vegetable recipes.*

| | | |
|---|---|---|
| 1 lb | zucchini (about 3 small) | 500 g |
| 2 tsp | butter or soft margarine | 10 mL |
| 1 | small onion, sliced and separated into rings | 1 |
| 1 tsp | all-purpose flour | 5 mL |
| 1/3 cup | 1% plain yogurt or 1% sour cream | 75 mL |
| 2 tbsp | chopped fresh parsley leaves | 25 mL |
| 1/2 tsp | crushed dried oregano and/or basil leaves (or 2 tbsp/25 mL chopped fresh) | 2 mL |
| | Salt and pepper | |

Trim ends from zucchini. In food processor or by hand, slice zucchini thinly.

In nonstick skillet, melt butter over medium heat. Add onion; cook, stirring, until tender. Add zucchini and oregano and/or basil (if using dried) and cook, stirring often, just until barely tender, about 5 minutes.

Mix flour into yogurt; stir into zucchini. Add parsley, oregano and/or basil (if using fresh), and salt and pepper to taste. Stir to coat well.

*Makes 6 servings.*

***30-Minute Summer Dinner***
Sole Fillets with Lemon and Parsley (page 115)
Sautéed Zucchini with Yogurt and Herbs (this page)
Tomatoes Provençal (page 157)
Tiny boiled potatoes in skins
Fresh strawberries or cantaloupe

**PER SERVING:**
34 calories
1 g protein
2 g total fat
  1 g saturated fat
  4 mg cholesterol
4 g carbohydrate
  1 g dietary fiber
25 mg sodium

**MAKE AHEAD**

Potatoes can be covered and refrigerated for up to one day. Reheat in microwave at High for 5 minutes or in 325 to 350°F (160 to 180°C) oven for 20 to 30 minutes.

# Mashed Potatoes with Garlic and Onions

*These everyday vegetables are delicious when mixed. The onions and garlic add wonderful flavor to the potatoes. The potatoes can also be cooked with only the onion or only the garlic.*

| | | |
|---|---|---|
| 6 | potatoes (about 2 lb/1 kg) | 6 |
| 4 | large cloves garlic | 4 |
| 2 tsp | butter | 10 mL |
| 2 | onions, finely chopped | 2 |
| 1 tbsp | water | 15 mL |
| 1/2 cup | (approx) milk, buttermilk or potato cooking water | 125 mL |
| | Salt and pepper | |
| | Chopped fresh dill, chives or green onions (optional) | |

Peel potatoes and cut into quarters. In saucepan of boiling water, cook potatoes and garlic until tender, about 20 minutes.

Meanwhile, in nonstick skillet, melt butter over medium-low heat. Add onions and water; cook, stirring occasionally, for 10 to 15 minutes or until onions are tender, reducing heat if necessary to prevent onions from browning.

Drain potatoes and return to pan (including garlic); heat over low heat for 1 to 2 minutes, shaking pan to dry potatoes. With potato masher, mash potatoes with half of the milk, adding remaining milk to taste (amount of milk will vary depending on kind of potatoes and may be as much as 1 cup/250 mL). Stir in onions; add salt and pepper to taste. Sprinkle with dill (if using).

*Makes 6 servings.*

**PER SERVING:**
142 calories
3 g protein
2 g total fat
  1 g saturated fat
  4 mg cholesterol
30 g carbohydrate
  2 g dietary fiber
26 mg sodium

**COMPARE:**

| | g dietary fiber per 4 1/2-inch (12 cm) long potatoes |
|---|---|
| 1 large baked potato with skin | 4.6 |
| 1 large baked potato, flesh only | 3.4 |
| 1 boiled peeled potato | 2.1 |

**MAKE AHEAD**

Prepare vegetables and blanch beans, broccoli, carrots and cauliflower up to six hours in advance.

# Stir-Fried Vegetables with Ginger and Garlic

*The wonderful colors and flavor combination in this dish complement any meat from chicken and lamb to beef. You need only add rice to complete the main course. For a one-dish meal, add chicken, turkey, shellfish, ham or tofu to the stir-fry and serve over hot pasta.*

| | | |
|---|---|---|
| 1 1/3 cups | green beans (4 oz/125 g) | 325 mL |
| 1 | large stalk broccoli | 1 |
| 2 | medium carrots, diagonally sliced | 2 |
| Half | small cauliflower, cut in florets | Half |
| 1 | sweet red or yellow pepper, cut in 1-inch (2.5 cm) pieces | 1 |
| 2 tbsp | vegetable oil | 25 mL |
| 1 | medium red onion, thinly sliced | 1 |
| 3 | cloves garlic, minced | 3 |
| 1 | small zucchini, diagonally sliced | 1 |
| 2 tbsp | minced fresh gingerroot | 25 mL |
| 1 1/2 cups | snow peas, trimmed (4 oz/125 g) | 375 mL |
| 2 tbsp | soy sauce | 25 mL |
| | Salt and pepper | |

*Nutrition Bonus*

One serving is a very high source of vitamin C (providing 112% of an adult's daily requirement), a very high source of vitamin A and a high source of folacin.

Because of its high sodium content, use soy sauce sparingly. Naturally brewed and sodium-reduced soy sauces are lower in sodium than chemically brewed ones.

Cut beans on the diagonal into 1 1/2-inch (4 cm) lengths. Cut broccoli into florets; peel stem; slice on the diagonal.

In large pot of boiling water, blanch beans, broccoli, carrots and cauliflower separately just until tender-crisp. Remove and immediately rinse under cold running water to prevent further cooking; drain thoroughly.

Twenty minutes before serving, heat about 2 tsp (10 mL) of the oil in large nonstick skillet over medium-high heat. Add onion and 1 clove of garlic; stir-fry for 3 to 4 minutes. Add zucchini and some of the ginger and more garlic; stir-fry for 3 minutes, adding more oil if necessary. If pan is full, transfer vegetables to baking dish and keep warm in 250°F (120°C) oven. Add as many of the blanched vegetables as you can stir-fry at one time, plus some of the garlic and ginger; stir-fry for 2 to 3 minutes or until hot. Add to baking dish; keep warm. Stir-fry remaining vegetables, adding a small amount of oil as necessary. Stir-fry red pepper and snow peas until tender-crisp. Combine all vegetables; toss with soy sauce, and salt and pepper to taste.

*Makes 8 servings.*

**PER SERVING:**
92 calories
3 g protein
4 g total fat
  trace saturated fat
  0 mg cholesterol
13 g carbohydrate
  4 g dietary fiber
231 mg sodium

MAKE AHEAD

Potatoes can be covered and refrigerated in casserole dish for up to two days; reheat in microwave or in 350°F (180°C) oven for about 25 minutes or until hot.

# Orange Sherried Sweet Potatoes

*Sweet potatoes go well with turkey, goose or ham. Instead of sherry, you can substitute ginger, maple syrup or crushed pineapple (adjust amount to taste).*

| | | |
|---|---|---|
| 4 | sweet potatoes (unpeeled), about 2 1/2 lb (1.25 kg) | 4 |
| 1 tbsp | butter | 15 mL |
| | Grated rind of half an orange | |
| 1/4 cup | fresh orange juice | 50 mL |
| 2 tbsp | (approx) sherry | 25 mL |
| 2 tbsp | packed brown sugar | 25 mL |
| Pinch | freshly grated nutmeg | Pinch |
| | Salt and pepper | |

*Nutrition Bonus*
Sweet potatoes are extremely high in beta carotene, which the body converts into vitamin A. For an adult's daily requirements one serving of Orange Sherried Sweet Potatoes provides 359% of vitamin A and 80% of vitamin C, and is a high source of folacin and dietary fiber.

In pot of boiling water, cook potatoes until tender, 30 to 40 minutes. Drain and let cool slightly; peel. While still warm, mash potatoes with butter, orange rind and juice, sherry, sugar, nutmeg, and salt and pepper to taste. Return to saucepan and heat over medium heat until hot.

*Makes 5 servings.*

PER SERVING:
221 calories
3 g protein
2 g total fat
  1 g saturated fat
  6 mg cholesterol
47 g carbohydrate
  5 g dietary fiber
42 mg sodium

**MAKE AHEAD**

Parsnips can be covered and refrigerated for up to two days; reheat gently.

# Parsnip Purée

*Parsnips were one of the few vegetables I really disliked as a child. Now I absolutely love them, especially this way or cooked around a roast chicken. You can use carrots, turnips or squash instead of parsnips in this recipe. When buying parsnips, remember that the small ones are more tender and sweet than the older fat ones.*

| 5 | medium parsnips (1 lb/500g) | 5 |
|---|---|---|
| 2 tbsp | 1% milk | 25 mL |
| 1 1/2 tsp | butter | 7 mL |
| 1 1/2 tsp | sherry (optional) | 7 mL |
| Pinch | freshly ground nutmeg | Pinch |
| | Salt and pepper | |

*Nutrition Bonus*

One serving is a very high source of folacin and dietary fiber and a high source of vitamin C.

Puréed vegetables, because of their creamy texture, can be served instead of a vegetable with a cream sauce. Puréed parsnips team well with green beans, broccoli or other green vegetables that have been steamed or boiled. Serve with any meats or poultry. For a slightly milder flavor, combine puréed parsnips or turnips with mashed potatoes.

Peel parsnips and cut into chunks to make about 2 1/2 cups (625 mL). In saucepan of boiling water, cook parsnips for 12 to 15 minutes or until tender; drain well. Transfer to food processor, blender or food mill; purée until smooth. Add milk, butter, sherry (if using), nutmeg, and salt and pepper to taste; process or stir until smooth. Return to saucepan to reheat or spoon into serving dish; cover and keep warm.

*Makes 4 servings.*

**PER SERVING:**
155 calories
3 g protein
2 g total fat
   1 g saturated fat
   4 mg cholesterol
34 g carbohydrate
   7 g dietary fiber
36 mg sodium

MAKE AHEAD

Squash can be covered and refrigerated for up to two days.

# Baked Squash with Ginger

*Ginger is a particularly nice accent for squash. Grated orange rind also heightens the flavor and can be used instead of ginger. Serve with roast pork, chicken, turkey or fish.*

| 2 1/4 lb | hubbard or butternut squash (or 2 acorn squash) | 1 kg |
|---|---|---|
| 2 tbsp | packed brown sugar | 25 mL |
| 1 tbsp | butter | 15 mL |
| 1 tsp | grated fresh gingerroot (or 1 tsp/5 mL ground ginger) | 5 mL |
| | Salt, pepper and freshly grated nutmeg | |

Cut squash in half; scoop out seeds. Cover squash with foil and place on baking sheet. Bake in 400°F (200°C) oven for 40 to 60 minutes or until tender. (Or place in microwaveable dish, partially cover and microwave on High for 10 to 15 minutes.)

Scoop out pulp; mash or purée with 2 or 3 on-off turns in food processor. Stir in sugar, butter, ginger, and salt, pepper and nutmeg to taste. Transfer to baking dish and reheat, covered, in microwave or 350°F (180°C) oven until hot.

*Makes 6 servings.*

An average-size acorn squash weighs about 1 1/2 lb (750 g) and yields about 1 1/2 cups (375 mL) cooked, mashed squash.

- 1 1/2 lb (750 g) chunk of hubbard squash, covered and microwaved at High for 10 minutes, yields 2 3/4 cups (675 mL) purée.
- 3 lb whole butternut squash, peeled and cubed (about 11 cups/3 L) and steamed for 10 to 12 minutes or microwaved on High for 10 minutes, yields 4 cups (1 L) purée.

**PER SERVING:**
85 calories
1 g protein
2 g total fat
  1 g saturated fat
  5 mg cholesterol
18 g carbohydrate
  3 g dietary fiber
24 mg sodium

**MAKE AHEAD**

Dish can be covered and refrigerated for up to two days. Reheat in microwave or oven. Sprinkle with parsley just before serving.

# Mashed Rutabaga with Carrots and Orange

*Adding mashed carrots to rutabaga (yellow turnip), along with a pinch of brown sugar and a dollop of butter, mellows the rutabaga.*

| | | |
|---|---|---|
| 1 | small rutabaga (yellow turnip) | 1 |
| 4 | carrots | 4 |
| 2 tbsp | packed brown sugar | 25 mL |
| 2 tbsp | frozen orange juice concentrate, thawed | 25 mL |
| 1 tbsp | butter | 15 mL |
| 1/2 tsp | grated orange rind (optional) | 2 mL |
| Pinch | freshly grated nutmeg | Pinch |
| | Salt and pepper | |
| | Chopped fresh parsley leaves | |

*Nutrition Bonus*
One serving is a very high source of vitamin A (providing 92% of an adult's daily requirement) and a high source of vitamin C.

Peel turnip and carrots; cut into 3/4-inch (2 cm) chunks. In separate pots of boiling water, cook turnips and carrots until very tender. Drain well and mash with potato masher or in food processor.

In baking dish, combine turnip, carrots, sugar, orange juice concentrate, butter, orange rind (if using), nutmeg, and salt and pepper to taste. Sprinkle with parsley.

*Makes 8 servings.*

**PER SERVING:**
72 calories
1 g protein
2 g total fat
  1 g saturated fat
  4 mg cholesterol
14 g carbohydrate
  2 g dietary fiber
52 mg sodium

**MAKE AHEAD**

Vegetables can be cooked and set aside for up to four hours; reheat and add parsley just before serving.

# Turnips Paysanne

*Either white turnips or a yellow rutabaga can be used in this recipe but the rutabaga will take longer to cook. To save time, use the food processor to slice the vegetables.*

| 1 | small rutabaga or 4 to 6 white turnips (about 2 lb/1 kg) | 1 |
|---|---|---|
| 1 cup | sliced celery | 250 mL |
| 1 cup | sliced carrots | 250 mL |
| 1 | large clove garlic, minced | 1 |
| 1 | onion, chopped | 1 |
| 1 cup | chicken or vegetable stock | 250 mL |
| 1/4 cup | chopped fresh parsley leaves | 50 mL |
| 1 tbsp | butter | 15 mL |
|  | Salt and pepper |  |

*Nutrition Bonus*
One serving is a very high source of vitamin A and a high source of vitamin C.

Peel and dice turnips. In heavy saucepan, combine turnip, celery, carrots, garlic, onion and stock; bring to boil. Cover, reduce heat and simmer until tender, about 20 minutes.

Uncover and cook until liquid is reduced to a glaze. Sprinkle with parsley, butter, and salt and pepper to taste.

*Makes 6 servings.*

**PER SERVING:**
74 calories
2 g protein
2 g total fat
  1 g saturated fat
  5 mg cholesterol
12 g carbohydrate
  3 g dietary fiber
196 mg sodium

# Muffins, Breads, Cakes and Cookies

NOTHING SMELLS BETTER than freshly baked breads, muffins, cookies and cakes. And nothing tastes better either. Low in fat (if you don't spread extra butter on the breads or muffins) and a good source of fiber and carbohydrates, the following treats make excellent snacks and are an important part of every balanced meal.

Moderation is the key to all good eating habits, and this applies to sweets as well. Enjoy them, but eat them in reasonable amounts.

### MAKE AHEAD

Muffins can be stored in airtight container for up to two days or frozen for up to one month.

**Nutrition Bonus**
One serving is a high source of dietary fiber.

Plump raisins, apricots and other dried fruits by steeping them in hot water before using them in recipes. Plumping adds moisture while preventing the fruit from drawing moisture from the batter during baking.

**PER MUFFIN:**
188 calories
4 g protein
6 g total fat
  1 g saturated fat
  19 mg cholesterol
34 g carbohydrate
  5 g dietary fiber
276 mg sodium

## Banana Apricot Bran Muffins

*Start your day with one of these fruity muffins, a glass of milk and some fresh fruit.*

| | | |
|---|---|---:|
| 1 1/2 cups | whole-wheat flour | 375 mL |
| 1 tbsp | baking powder | 15 mL |
| 1/2 tsp | baking soda | 2 mL |
| 1/2 tsp | salt | 2 mL |
| 1/2 cup | chopped dried apricots | 125 mL |
| 1 1/2 cups | well-mashed ripe bananas (about 4) | 375 mL |
| 2/3 cup | 1% plain yogurt | 150 mL |
| 1/3 cup | liquid honey | 75 mL |
| 1/4 cup | vegetable oil | 50 mL |
| 1 | egg, lightly beaten | 1 |
| 1 cup | bran cereal (All-Bran, 100% Bran) | 250 mL |

In large bowl, combine flour, baking powder, baking soda and salt. Stir in apricots.

In separate bowl, whisk together bananas, yogurt, honey, oil and egg. Stir in cereal. Pour over flour mixture and stir just enough to moisten, being careful not to overmix.

Spoon into lightly greased nonstick muffin tins. Bake in 400°F (200°C) oven for 20 minutes or until tops are firm to the touch.

*Makes 12 muffins.*

MAKE AHEAD

Muffins can be stored in airtight container for up to two days or frozen for up to one month.

**Nutrition Bonus**
One serving is a very high source of vitamin A.

Wheat bran and wheat germ are sold in the grain sections of supermarkets. Because they have some fat, store them in the refrigerator or freezer to prevent them from becoming rancid. Use in muffins, biscuits, bread and cookies. They are an excellent source of fiber.

**PER MUFFIN:**
191 calories
4 g protein
6 g total fat
  1 g saturated fat
  18 mg cholesterol
35 g carbohydrate
  4 g dietary fiber
207 mg sodium

# Pumpkin Raisin Muffins

*These are my daughter Susie's favorite muffins to bake. They are so moist you don't need to add any butter.*

| | | |
|---|---|---|
| 1 cup | whole-wheat flour | 250 mL |
| 3/4 cup | wheat bran | 175 mL |
| 2/3 cup | packed brown sugar | 150 mL |
| 2 tsp | cinnamon | 10 mL |
| 2 tsp | baking powder | 10 mL |
| 1/2 tsp | each baking soda, nutmeg and salt | 2 mL |
| 1 cup | raisins | 250 mL |
| 1 cup | mashed or canned cooked pumpkin | 250 mL |
| 1/2 cup | 1% plain yogurt | 125 mL |
| 1/4 cup | vegetable oil | 50 mL |
| 1 | egg, lightly beaten | 1 |

In large bowl, combine flour, bran, sugar, cinnamon, baking powder, baking soda, nutmeg and salt. Stir in raisins.

In separate bowl, whisk together pumpkin, yogurt, oil and egg. Pour over flour mixture and stir just enough to moisten, being careful not to overmix.

Spoon into lightly greased nonstick muffin tins. Bake in 400°F (200°C) oven for 25 minutes or until tops are firm to the touch.

*Makes 12 muffins.*

---

*Successful Muffins:*
• Mix liquid and dry ingredients only until all of the flour is moistened, about 15 to 20 strokes. Batter will be lumpy.
• Once muffin batter has been mixed, it should go into the oven right away. Therefore, be sure to grease or spray muffin pans and have all ingredients ready (including grated vegetables etc.) before combining. Bake muffins in the top third of the oven for best results.
• Muffins are done when they are firm to the touch. For moist muffins, don't overbake. Cool muffins in pans about 5 minutes before removing to rack.
Freezing muffins: Muffins keep well in the freezer for up to 2 months. Reheat frozen muffins at 400°F (200°C) for about 25 minutes. To reheat one frozen muffin in the microwave, wrap in paper towel and cook on High for 30 to 40 seconds.
Storing muffins: Muffins are best eaten fresh but may be stored in an airtight container for 2 to 4 days at room temperature or refrigerated for 4 to 7 days.

MAKE AHEAD

Batter can be covered and refrigerated for up to two weeks. Baked muffins can be frozen for up to one month.

*Nutrition Bonus*
One serving is a high source of dietary fiber.

**SUBSTITUTING WHOLE-WHEAT FLOUR FOR ALL-PURPOSE FLOUR IN BAKING**

As a general rule, you can substitute whole-wheat flour for half of the all-purpose flour called for in a recipe. For example, if a recipe calls for 1 cup (250 mL) of all-purpose flour, you can use 1/2 cup (125 mL) all-purpose flour and 1/2 cup (125 mL) whole-wheat flour.

Using all whole-wheat flour results in a heavier product. In some cases, such as oatmeal cookies, this is fine; in others such as cakes, it may be undesirable. Experiment with your favorite recipes to see how much whole-wheat flour you can substitute.

**PER MUFFIN:**
206 calories
5 g protein
6 g total fat
  1 g saturated fat
  28 mg cholesterol
37 g carbohydrate
  5 g dietary fiber
208 mg sodium

# Refrigerator Applesauce-Spice Bran Muffins

*I like to make these when I have overnight guests because you can mix up the batter in advance, refrigerate it and make delicious, hot muffins in only the time it takes to bake them. If you wish, use reconstituted skim milk powder in place of milk. These moist and flavorful muffins are very high in fiber.*

| | | |
|---|---|---|
| 3 cups | wheat bran | 750 mL |
| 2 cups | whole-wheat flour | 500 mL |
| 1 cup | all-purpose flour | 250 mL |
| 1 1/2 cups | raisins or chopped dates | 375 mL |
| 1 tbsp | cinnamon | 15 mL |
| 1 1/2 tsp | each baking powder and baking soda | 7 mL |
| 1 tsp | each salt, ground ginger and nutmeg | 5 mL |
| | Grated rind of 1 lemon or orange | |
| 1 cup | applesauce | 250 mL |
| 3/4 cup | granulated sugar | 175 mL |
| 1/2 cup | vegetable oil | 125 mL |
| 3 | eggs | 3 |
| 2 1/4 cups | low-fat milk | 550 mL |
| 1/2 cup | fancy molasses | 125 mL |

In large bowl, combine bran, whole-wheat and all-purpose flours, raisins, cinnamon, baking powder, baking soda, salt, ginger, nutmeg and rind.

In separate bowl, beat together applesauce, sugar, oil and eggs until well mixed. Stir in milk and molasses. Add to dry ingredients. Stir just enough to moisten, being careful not to overmix. (Batter can be covered and refrigerated up to 2 weeks.)

Spoon into lightly greased nonstick muffin tins. Bake in 400°F (200°C) oven for 20 minutes or until tops are firm to the touch.

*Makes 24 muffins.*

# Oatmeal Carrot Muffins

*Grated carrot adds flavor and helps keep the muffins moist.*
*They are delicious in a packed lunch or for breakfast.*

**MAKE AHEAD**

Muffins can be stored in airtight container for up to two days or frozen for up to one month.

| 1 1/4 cups | buttermilk* | 300 mL |
|---|---|---|
| 1 1/2 cups | quick-cooking rolled oats | 375 mL |
| 1 cup | grated carrots | 250 mL |
| 1/4 cup | packed brown sugar | 50 mL |
| 1/4 cup | canola oil | 50 mL |
| 2 | eggs, lightly beaten | 2 |
| 1 1/2 tsp | grated orange rind | 7 mL |
| 1 1/2 cups | all-purpose flour | 375 mL |
| 3/4 cup | raisins | 175 mL |
| 1/4 cup | granulated sugar | 50 mL |
| 1 tbsp | baking powder | 15 mL |
| 1/2 tsp | salt | 2 mL |

*Nutrition Bonus*
One serving is a high source of vitamin A.

**PREPARING MUFFIN PANS**
For best results, use nonstick pans and spray with a vegetable coating spray or lightly oil. Paper liners are not recommended for lower fat muffins because the paper tends to stick to the muffins.

In bowl, pour buttermilk over oats; stir to mix. Let stand for 5 minutes. Stir in carrots, sugar, oil, eggs and orange rind.

In large bowl, combine flour, raisins, sugar, baking powder and salt. Pour buttermilk mixture over top and stir just enough to moisten, being careful not to overmix.

Spoon into lightly greased nonstick muffin tins. Bake in 400°F (200°C) oven for 20 minutes or until tops are firm to the touch.

*Makes 12 muffins.*

*Instead of buttermilk, you can use soured milk. To sour 1 1/4 cups (300 mL) milk, measure 4 tsp (20 mL) vinegar or lemon juice into measuring cup and fill to 1 1/4 cups (300 mL) with milk.

---

*Whole-wheat Flour*
- Whole-wheat flour contains 11 grams fiber per 1 cup (250 mL), while the same amount of all-purpose contains 4 grams.
- Whole-wheat flour is made from the whole grain of wheat. Along with fiber, it also contains a small amount of fat. All-purpose flour has had the bran and germ removed from the wheat. It is enriched with B vitamins, thiamine, riboflavin, niacin and iron, but it doesn't have the fiber, other vitamins or trace minerals that whole-wheat flour does.
- Because of the fat content, whole-wheat flour doesn't have the same shelf life as all-purpose flour, which will keep for up to two years. Whole-wheat flour will keep 6 weeks to 6 months, depending on the milling method, before it turns rancid. For this reason, buy whole-wheat flour in small amounts unless you use it regularly.

**PER MUFFIN:**
228 calories
6 g protein
6 g total fat
  1 g saturated fat
  37 mg cholesterol
38 g carbohydrate
  2 g dietary fiber
206 mg sodium

**MAKE AHEAD**

Dough can be frozen for up to three weeks.

*Nutrition Bonus*
One serving is a very high source of iron, folacin and dietary fiber.

You can use this dough in our Deep-Dish Vegetable Pizza (page 138).

*All-Dressed Pizza*
Spread pizza dough with tomato sauce seasoned with oregano and basil. Then finish with your favorite toppings. Try:
• chopped red, yellow, green or purple peppers
• blanched broccoli florets
• sliced mushrooms
• sliced regular, cherry or sun-dried tomatoes
• artichoke hearts, halved
• grated partly skimmed mozzarella cheese
Bake in lower half of 475°F (240°C) oven for 13 to 16 minutes or until crust is golden brown and cheese is bubbly.

# Whole-Wheat Pizza Dough

*Use this basic dough for any type of pizza. It's very quick and easy to make in a food processor. Whole-wheat flour adds color, flavor, fiber and vitamins.*

| | | |
|---|---|---|
| 1 tsp | granulated sugar | 5 mL |
| 1 cup | warm water | 250 mL |
| 1 | pkg active dry yeast (or 1 tbsp/15 mL) | 1 |
| 1 1/2 cups | all-purpose flour | 375 mL |
| 1 1/2 cups | whole-wheat flour | 375 mL |
| 1 tsp | salt | 5 mL |
| 2 tbsp | vegetable oil | 25 mL |

In large mixing bowl, dissolve sugar in warm water. Sprinkle yeast over water and let stand for 10 minutes or until foamy. Meanwhile, in separate bowl, combine all-purpose and whole-wheat flours and salt.

Stir oil into foamy yeast mixture. Stir in about half of the flour mixture. Add more flour, mixing until dough can be gathered into a slightly sticky ball (you may need a little more or less than 3 cups/750 mL of flour).

On lightly floured surface, knead dough for about 5 minutes or until smooth and elastic, adding flour as necessary to prevent dough from sticking to counter. Cut dough in half; cover with waxed paper and let stand for 10 minutes.

On lightly floured surface, use a rolling pin to roll each piece of dough into a 12-inch (30 cm) circle, about 1/4-inch (5 mm) thick.

Transfer rounds to 2 lightly oiled pizza pans or baking sheets. Carefully, using fingers, stretch dough into large circles.

Let dough rise for about 15 minutes before adding toppings. For a thicker crust, let dough rise for 30 minutes. Add toppings just before baking.

*Makes two 12-inch (30 cm) pizza rounds.*

**PER PIZZA:**
786 calories
24 g protein
16 g total fat
  1 g saturated fat
  0 mg cholesterol
140 g carbohydrate
  15 g dietary fiber
1159 mg sodium

*Food Processor Variation*
In measuring cup, combine sugar and warm water; add yeast and let stand until foamy. In food processor bowl, combine whole-wheat flour and 1 cup (250 mL) of all-purpose flour and salt. Add oil to yeast mixture. While processing, pour yeast mixture into feed tube. Process 30 seconds. Turn onto floured board and knead in enough of the remaining flour to prevent dough from sticking to board. Roll out as in Whole-Wheat Pizza Dough.

**MAKE AHEAD**

Bread can be wrapped in plastic bag or foil and stored for up to two days at room temperature or frozen for up to five weeks.

*Whole-Wheat*
*Irish Soda Bread*
Prepare Olive and Rosemary Soda Bread but omit the olives and rosemary and add 1 cup (250 mL) raisins along with the flour.

*After-Theatre Supper*
Nova Scotia Seafood Chowder (page 48)
Arugula and Radicchio Salad with Balsamic Vinaigrette (page 62)
Olive and Rosemary Soda Bread (this page)
Lemon Sorbet (page 203)
Oatmeal Raisin Cookies (page 186)

# Olive and Rosemary Soda Bread

*Quick and easy to prepare, this bread dough can be mixed in a few minutes, then popped into the oven. From breakfast to dinner, this suits any meal deliciously.*

| | | |
|---|---|---|
| 3 cups | whole-wheat flour | 750 mL |
| 1 cup | all-purpose flour | 250 mL |
| 2 tbsp | granulated sugar | 25 mL |
| 2 tsp | baking powder | 10 mL |
| 1 1/2 tsp | baking soda | 7 mL |
| 1 tsp | salt | 5 mL |
| 1/4 cup | finely chopped pitted black olives | 50 mL |
| 1 1/2 tsp | dried whole-leaf rosemary (or 4 tsp/20 mL fresh) | 7 mL |
| 1 3/4 cups | buttermilk (or 1 2/3 cups/400 mL milk, plus 2 tbsp/25 mL vinegar) | 425 mL |
| 2 tbsp | vegetable oil | 25 mL |
| 1/2 tsp | coarse salt (optional) | 2 mL |

In large bowl, combine whole-wheat and all-purpose flours, sugar, baking powder, baking soda and salt. Stir in olives and half of the dried or fresh rosemary. Add buttermilk and oil; stir to make soft dough. Turn out onto lightly floured surface; knead about 10 times until smooth.

Place dough on lightly greased baking sheet; flatten into circle about 2 1/2 inches (6 cm) thick. Cut large "X" about 1/4 inch (5 mm) deep on top. Brush top with water. Sprinkle with remaining rosemary, and coarse salt (if using). Bake in 350°F (180°C) oven for 40 to 50 minutes or until toothpick inserted in center comes out clean.

*Makes 1 large loaf, about 16 slices.*

**PER SLICE:**
140 calories
5 g protein
3 g total fat
  trace saturated fat
  1 mg cholesterol
25 g carbohydrate
  3 g dietary fiber
331 mg sodium

**MAKE AHEAD**

Squares can be covered and refrigerated for up to five days.

# Best-Ever Date Squares

*Sometimes called matrimonial cake, these are my husband's favorite squares.*

| | | |
|---|---|---|
| 2 cups | packed chopped pitted dates (10 oz/350 g) | 500 mL |
| 1 cup | cold coffee | 250 mL |
| 2 tbsp | packed brown sugar | 25 mL |
| | Grated rind and juice of half an orange | |
| 1 tbsp | fresh lemon juice | 15 mL |

| | *Crumb Mixture:* | |
|---|---|---|
| 1 1/4 cups | all-purpose flour | 300 mL |
| 1 tsp | baking powder | 5 mL |
| 1/2 tsp | baking soda | 2 mL |
| 1/2 tsp | salt | 2 mL |
| 2/3 cup | butter | 150 mL |
| 1 1/4 cups | rolled oats | 300 mL |
| 3/4 cup | lightly packed brown sugar | 175 mL |

In small saucepan, combine dates, coffee, brown sugar and orange rind; bring to boil. Reduce heat and simmer, uncovered, until soft enough to mash and consistency of jam (runny but easy to spread), about 10 minutes. Remove from heat; stir in orange and lemon juices. Let cool.

**Crumb Mixture:** In bowl, stir together flour, baking powder, baking soda and salt. With pastry blender or 2 knives, cut in butter until size of small peas. Stir in rolled oats and sugar. Press half of mixture firmly into lightly greased 9-inch (2.5 L) square cake pan. Spread date mixture evenly over crumb mixture. Top with remaining crumbs, pressing lightly. Bake in 325°F (160°C) oven for 25 minutes or until lightly browned. Let cool in pan. Cut into squares.

*Makes 25 squares.*

**PER SQUARE:**
149 calories
2 g protein
5 g total fat
  3 g saturated fat
  13 mg cholesterol
25 g carbohydrate
  2 g dietary fiber
133 mg sodium

MAKE AHEAD

Squares can be refrigerated in airtight container for up to five days or frozen for up to three weeks.

# Almond Apricot Squares

*Apricots add extra flavor to these tasty and attractive-looking squares.*

| | | |
|---|---|---|
| 3/4 cup | packed dried apricots | 175 mL |

| ***Base:*** | | |
|---|---|---|
| 1/4 cup | cold butter | 50 mL |
| 1 cup | all-purpose flour | 250 mL |
| 1/4 cup | granulated sugar | 50 mL |
| 2 tbsp | 1% plain yogurt | 25 mL |

| ***Top:*** | | |
|---|---|---|
| 2 | eggs | 2 |
| 1/2 cup | granulated sugar | 125 mL |
| Pinch | salt | Pinch |
| 1/2 cup | slivered almonds | 125 mL |

In small saucepan, combine apricots with enough water to cover. Cover and bring to boil; remove from heat. (Alternatively, place apricots in microwaveable dish, add just enough water to cover. Cover and microwave on High for 1 minute.) Let stand for 1 minute. Drain, let cool and chop apricots finely; set aside.

**Base:** In bowl and using pastry blender or 2 knives, cut butter into flour until it resembles fine crumbs. Stir in sugar and yogurt, combining well. Press evenly into lightly greased 8-inch (2 L) square cake pan. Bake in 350°F (180°C) oven for 20 minutes.

**Top:** Meanwhile, in bowl, beat eggs with sugar and salt until light; stir in apricots. Pour over base. Sprinkle almonds evenly over top. Bake in 350°F (180°C) oven for 30 minutes or until set and golden brown. Let cool slightly in pan. Cut into squares.

*Makes 18 squares.*

**PER SQUARE:**
123 calories
2 g protein
5 g total fat
  2 g saturated fat
  31 mg cholesterol
18 g carbohydrate
  1 g dietary fiber
35 mg sodium

MAKE AHEAD

Squares are best the same day but can be stored in airtight container for up to five days or frozen for up to three weeks.

# Date and Almond Meringue Bars

*One of my mother's recipes, these go well with frozen desserts such as Grapefruit Ice (page 202) or other fruit sorbets.*

| | | |
|---|---|---:|
| 1 3/4 cups | chopped dates | 425 mL |
| 3/4 cup | water | 175 mL |
| 1/3 cup | butter or soft margarine | 75 mL |
| 1/3 cup | granulated sugar | 75 mL |
| 2 | eggs, separated | 2 |
| 1 tsp | vanilla | 5 mL |
| 3/4 cup | all-purpose flour | 175 mL |
| 3/4 cup | whole-wheat flour | 175 mL |
| 1 tsp | baking powder | 5 mL |
| 1/2 cup | packed brown sugar | 125 mL |
| 1/4 cup | slivered almonds (optional) | 50 mL |

In saucepan, simmer dates and water until mixture is thick and soft, about 4 minutes.

In mixing bowl, cream butter; beat in granulated sugar, mixing well. Beat in egg yolks and vanilla until well mixed. Beat in all-purpose and whole-wheat flours and baking powder until mixed. Pat into lightly greased 9-inch (2.5 L) square cake pan. Spread date paste on top.

In bowl, beat egg whites until soft peaks form; gradually beat in brown sugar until stiff peaks form. Spread over date mixture. Sprinkle with almonds (if using). Bake in 350°F (180°C) oven for 30 to 35 minutes or until golden.

*Makes about 25 squares.*

**PER SQUARE:**
123 calories
2 g protein
4 g total fat
    2 g saturated fat
    24 mg cholesterol
22 g carbohydrate
    2 g dietary fiber
43 mg sodium

Photo:
***Lemon and Fresh Blueberry Tart (page 208)***

MAKE AHEAD

Cookies can be stored in airtight container for up to one month.

# Almond Meringues

*It's hard to find good-tasting cookies that are low in fat. These are both.*

| | | |
|---|---|---:|
| 1/4 cup | slivered almonds | 50 mL |
| 3 | egg whites | 3 |
| 1/2 cup | granulated sugar | 125 mL |
| 1 tbsp | cornstarch | 15 mL |
| 1/4 tsp | almond extract | 1 mL |

For a crisper cookie, leave baked cookies in turned-off oven overnight.

Toast almonds on baking sheet in 325°F (160°C) oven for 6 minutes or until golden. Let cool. Reduce oven temperature to 225°F (110°C).

In large bowl and using electric mixer, beat egg whites until soft peaks form; gradually beat in sugar, then cornstarch and almond extract until stiff peaks form. Fold in almonds.

Line baking sheets with foil, shiny side down. Drop batter by small spoonfuls onto prepared pan. Bake in 225°F (110°C) oven for 2 hours or until cookies can be easily removed from foil. Let cool.

*Makes 30 cookies.*

PER COOKIE:
22 calories
1 g protein
1 g total fat
    trace saturated fat
    0 mg cholesterol
4 g carbohydrate
    trace dietary fiber
6 mg sodium

Photo:
***Pumpkin Raisin Muffins***
*(page 177)*
***Oatmeal Raisin Cookies***
*(page 186)*
***Breakfast Bran-and-Fruit Mix** (page 221)*

**MAKE AHEAD**

Cookies can be stored in airtight container for up to two weeks or wrapped well and frozen for up to one month.

# Oatmeal Raisin Cookies

*These cookies are a family favorite, especially of my son Jeff.*

| | | |
|---|---|---|
| 1/2 cup | butter or margarine | 125 mL |
| 3/4 cup | granulated sugar | 175 mL |
| 1/2 cup | lightly packed brown sugar | 125 mL |
| 1 | egg | 1 |
| 1 cup | whole-wheat flour | 250 mL |
| 1 cup | rolled oats | 250 mL |
| 1/4 cup | wheat germ | 50 mL |
| 1 tsp | baking powder | 5 mL |
| 1 tsp | baking soda | 5 mL |
| 1 1/2 cups | raisins | 375 mL |

In mixing bowl, cream butter; beat in granulated and brown sugars and egg, creaming together thoroughly. Add flour, oats, wheat germ, baking powder and baking soda; mix well. Stir in raisins.

Drop by spoonfuls onto lightly greased baking sheets. Flatten slightly with floured fork. Bake in 350°F (180°C) oven for 12 to 15 minutes or until light golden.

*Makes about 40 cookies.*

**PER COOKIE:**
95 calories
1 g protein
3 g total fat
  2 g saturated fat
  13 mg cholesterol
17 g carbohydrate
  1 g dietary fiber
70 mg sodium

MAKE AHEAD

Cookies can be stored in airtight container for up to 10 days.

# Daphna's Meringue Kisses

*Daphna Rabinovitch is the test kitchen manager at* Canadian Living *magazine and is a terrific cook. When Daphna made these light cookies, they disappeared before they hardly had time to cool. If miniature chocolate chips are unavailable, use any small chocolate chips.*

Daphna's cookies are softer and chewier than the Almond Meringues because they bake for a shorter time at a higher temperature.

| 3 | egg whites | 3 |
|---|---|---|
| Pinch | salt | Pinch |
| 3/4 cup | granulated sugar | 175 mL |
| 3/4 cups | miniature semisweet chocolate chips | 175 mL |
| 1 tsp | cornstarch or potato starch | 5 mL |
| 1/2 tsp | vanilla | 2 mL |

In bowl and using electric mixer, beat egg whites with salt until soft peaks form. Beat in sugar, 2 tbsp (25 mL) at a time, until stiff shiny peaks form. Sprinkle with chocolate chips, cornstarch and vanilla; gently fold into whites.

Using pastry bag fitted with 1-inch (2.5 cm) tip, or two spoons, pipe into 1-inch (2.5 cm) kisses on foil-lined baking sheets. Bake in 300°F (150°C) oven, rotating pans halfway through, for 25 to 30 minutes or until just starting to turn golden and tops are firm to the touch. Let cool on foil for 10 minutes, then on racks.

*Makes about 40 cookies.*

PER COOKIE:
32 calories
trace protein
1 g total fat
  1 g saturated fat
  0 mg cholesterol
6 g carbohydrate
  trace dietary fiber
4 mg sodium

**MAKE AHEAD**

Bread can be wrapped well and stored for up to five days or frozen for up to five weeks.

# Apricot, Orange and Pecan Loaf

*A favorite with all my recipe tasters, this wonderful bread keeps very well. Serve for tea, snacks, brunch or lunch with salad, soup or dessert.*

| | | |
|---|---|---|
| 1 cup | all-purpose flour | 250 mL |
| 1 cup | whole-wheat flour | 250 mL |
| 1 cup | raisins | 250 mL |
| 2/3 cup | skim milk powder | 150 mL |
| 1/2 cup | packed brown sugar | 125 mL |
| 1/2 cup | finely chopped dried apricots | 125 mL |
| 1/3 cup | wheat germ | 75 mL |
| 1/4 cup | chopped almonds or pecans | 50 mL |
| 2 tsp | baking powder | 10 mL |
| 1/2 tsp | each baking soda and salt | 2 mL |
| 3 | eggs | 3 |
| 3/4 cup | fresh orange juice | 175 mL |
| 1/2 cup | vegetable oil | 125 mL |
| 1/2 cup | fancy molasses | 125 mL |
| 2 | bananas | 2 |

In large bowl, combine all-purpose and whole-wheat flours, raisins, skim milk powder, sugar, apricots, wheat germ, almonds, baking powder, baking soda and salt.

In separate bowl or food processor, beat eggs until foamy; beat in orange juice, oil, molasses and bananas until well mixed. Pour over dry ingredients and stir just until moistened.

Pour into 2 lightly greased 8- x 4-inch (1.5 L) loaf pans. Bake in 325°F (160°C) oven for 1 hour or until toothpick inserted in center comes out clean. Let cool in pan on wire rack for 15 minutes. Turn out onto rack and let cool completely.

*Makes 2 loaves, 18 slices each.*

**PER SLICE:**
120 calories
3 g protein
4 g total fat
  trace saturated fat
  18 mg cholesterol
19 g carbohydrate
  1 g dietary fiber
78 mg sodium

MAKE AHEAD

Cake can be wrapped in foil or plastic wrap and stored at room temperature for up to four days or frozen for up to one month.

# Cinnamon Coffee Cake

*Serve this easy-to-make extra-moist cake with fresh fruit or sorbet for any meal at any time of day.*

| | | |
|---|---|---|
| 1 cup | plain yogurt | 250 mL |
| 1 tsp | baking soda | 5 mL |
| 1/4 cup | butter or soft margarine | 50 mL |
| 1 cup | lightly packed brown sugar | 250 mL |
| 1 | egg | 1 |
| 1 tsp | vanilla | 5 mL |
| 1 1/2 cups | all-purpose flour | 375 mL |
| 2 tsp | baking powder | 10 mL |

| | *Topping:* | |
|---|---|---|
| 1/2 cup | lightly packed brown sugar | 125 mL |
| 1 tbsp | cinnamon | 15 mL |

In small bowl, combine yogurt and baking soda, mixing well; set aside. (Mixture will increase in volume.)

In large mixing bowl, beat butter with sugar until well mixed. Add egg and vanilla; beat well, about 2 minutes. Mix flour and baking powder; add to butter mixture alternately with yogurt mixture, making 3 additions of dry and 2 of wet. Spread half the batter in greased and floured 9-inch (2.5 L) square cake pan.

**Topping:** Combine sugar and cinnamon, mixing well. Sprinkle half over batter in pan.

Cover with remaining batter. Sprinkle with remaining topping. Bake in 350°F (180°C) oven for 35 minutes or until toothpick inserted in center comes out clean. Let cool for 10 to 15 minutes in pan. Cut into squares.

*Makes 12 servings.*

**PER SERVING:**
206 calories
3 g protein
5 g total fat
   3 g saturated fat
   29 mg cholesterol
38 g carbohydrate
   1 g dietary fiber
207 mg sodium

# Orange Sponge Cake

*This cake is delicious on its own or with fresh fruit or dessert sauces. Or you can ice it with Orange Icing (page 191), or serve with sherbet or Raspberry Coulis (page 199). Make sure you use large eggs at room temperature.*

To make a larger cake, recipe can be doubled. Baking time will then be 55 minutes.

| 4 | eggs, separated | 4 |
|---|---|---|
| 3/4 cup | granulated sugar | 175 mL |
| 1 tbsp | grated orange rind | 15 mL |
| 1/2 cup | fresh orange juice | 125 mL |
| 1 cup | all-purpose flour | 250 mL |
| 1 tsp | baking powder | 5 mL |
| Pinch | salt | Pinch |
| 2 tsp | icing sugar | 10 mL |

In mixing bowl, beat together egg yolks, sugar, orange rind and juice until very light in color. Add flour and baking powder; beat until combined.

In separate bowl, beat egg whites and salt until stiff peaks form. Mix a small amount of whites into yolk mixture, then fold yolk mixture into whites.

Pour batter into ungreased 10-inch (4 L) tube pan with removable bottom. Bake in 325°F (160°C) oven for 45 to 55 minutes or until golden brown and cake springs back when lightly touched. Invert and let hang to cool completely before removing from pan. Sift icing sugar over top.

*Makes 12 servings.*

**PER SERVING:**
118 calories
3 g protein
2 g total fat
　1 g saturated fat
　72 mg cholesterol
22 g carbohydrate
　trace dietary fiber
43 mg sodium

**MAKE AHEAD**

Cake can be wrapped well and refrigerated for up to four days or frozen for up to one month.

*Lemon Icing*
Using yogurt instead of butter makes a creamy low-fat icing. In mixing bowl, combine 1 1/2 cups (375 mL) icing sugar (sifted), 2 tbsp (25 mL) plain yogurt, 1 tsp (5 mL) each grated lemon rind and lemon juice until smooth.

Applesauce Raisin Spice Cake with Lemon Icing has 189 calories and 3 g fat per serving.

*Orange Icing*
Substitute orange rind and juice for lemon rind and juice.

**PER SLICE:**
162 calories
3 g protein
3 g total fat
  1 g saturated fat
  14 mg cholesterol
34 g carbohydrate
  2 g dietary fiber
125 mg sodium

# Applesauce Raisin Spice Cake

*Full of flavor, this delicious moist cake looks attractive when made in a bundt or tube pan. It's easy to make and keeps well. Serve it with fresh fruit desserts, poached pears or sorbets.*

| | | |
|---|---|---|
| 1 3/4 cups | granulated sugar | 425 mL |
| 1/4 cup | butter, at room temperature | 50 mL |
| 1 | egg | 1 |
| 1/2 cup | plain (1 to 2%) yogurt | 125 mL |
| 2 cups | applesauce | 500 mL |
| 1 tsp | vanilla | 5 mL |
| | Grated rind of 1 medium orange | |
| 1 1/2 cups | all-purpose flour | 375 mL |
| 1 1/4 cups | whole-wheat flour | 300 mL |
| 1 cup | raisins | 250 mL |
| 1/4 cup | wheat bran | 50 mL |
| 4 tsp | cinnamon | 20 mL |
| 2 tsp | baking soda | 10 mL |
| 1/2 tsp | ground nutmeg | 2 mL |

Butter and flour a 10-inch (25 cm) bundt pan.

In mixing bowl, beat sugar with butter until well mixed. Beat in egg until light in color. Beat in yogurt until mixed. Beat in applesauce, vanilla and orange rind.

In separate bowl, combine all-purpose and whole-wheat flours, raisins, bran, cinnamon, baking soda and nutmeg; stir to mix. Pour over applesauce mixture and stir just until combined.

Pour into prepared pan and bake in 325°F (160°C) oven for 60 to 70 minutes or until toothpick inserted in center comes out clean. Let cool in pan on rack for 20 minutes, then turn out onto rack and let cool completely.

*Makes 24 slices.*

MAKE AHEAD

Cake can be wrapped well and stored at room temperature for up to three days or frozen for up to one month. Defrost, wrapped, at room temperature.

# Prune Cake with Lemon Icing

*Orange rind and juicy cooked prunes are a winning combination in this easy-to-make cake. It's ideal for dessert, along with fresh fruit, for packed lunches or for feeding a crowd of kids. Sprinkle it with icing sugar or ice with Lemon Icing.*

| | | |
|---|---|---|
| 1 1/2 cups | prunes | 375 mL |
| 1/4 cup | butter or soft margarine | 50 mL |
| 1 cup | 1% plain yogurt | 250 mL |
| 3/4 cup | packed brown sugar | 175 mL |
| 1/3 cup | granulated sugar | 75 mL |
| 2 | eggs | 2 |
| 1 1/2 cups | all-purpose flour | 375 mL |
| 1 cup | whole-wheat flour | 250 mL |
| 2 tsp | baking powder | 10 mL |
| 1 tsp | cinnamon | 5 mL |
| 1/2 tsp | each baking soda and salt | 2 mL |
| | Grated rind of 1 orange | |
| | Lemon Icing (page 191), optional | |

Prune Cake with Lemon Icing has 240 calories and 4 grams fat per piece (1/16 of cake).

In saucepan or microwaveable dish, cover prunes with water and bring to boil. Let stand for 15 minutes or until cool; drain. Remove pits and chop prunes to make about 1 1/2 cups (375 mL); set aside.

In mixing bowl, cream butter; beat in yogurt and brown and granulated sugars until smooth. Beat in eggs until well mixed. Add all-purpose and whole-wheat flours, baking powder, cinnamon, baking soda, salt and orange rind; beat well. Stir in prunes.

Pour into lightly greased and floured 10-inch (3 L) springform pan. Bake in 350°F (180°C) oven for 40 minutes or until toothpick inserted in center comes out clean.

When cool, ice with Lemon Icing if desired.

*Makes 16 servings.*

**PER SERVING WITHOUT ICING:**
201 calories
4 g protein
4 g total fat
  2 g saturated fat
  36 mg cholesterol
39 g carbohydrate
  4 g dietary fiber
194 mg sodium

## *Best Fruit Sources of Fiber*

**VERY HIGH SOURCE OF FIBER** - more than 6 grams of fiber serving

| | *g of fiber* |
|---|---|
| Figs, dried uncooked | 20 g |
| Dates, pitted, chopped | 13 g |
| Apricots, dried, uncooked | 11 g |
| Blackberries, raw | 8 g |
| Raisins, seedless | 7 g |
| Prunes, dried, uncooked | 6 g |
| Raspberries, raw | 6 g |

**HIGH SOURCE OF FIBER** - 4 to 6 grams of fiber per serving

| | *g of fiber* |
|---|---|
| Kiwifruit (medium) (2) | 6 g |
| Papaya, raw, 1 | 5 g |
| Pears (medium) (1) | 5 g |
| Blueberries, raw | 4 g |
| Mango, raw, 1 | 4g |

**SOURCE OF FIBER** - 2 to 4 grams of fiber per serving

| | *g of fiber* |
|---|---|
| Apple, medium (150 g), raw with skin | 3 g |
| Strawberries, whole | 3 g |
| Cantaloupe (1/2) | 2 g |
| Orange, medium, peeled (1) | 2 g |
| Peach (medium) (1) | 2 g |
| Bananas (1) | 2 g |
| Cherries, raw | 2 g |
| Grapes, raw | 2 g |
| Plums (2) | 2 g |

Source: Health Canada
(Measurements are for 1 cup (250 mL) unless otherwise noted.)

# Desserts

D ESSERTS ARE DEFINITELY PART of a healthy diet. This section of the cookbook offers many delicious desserts that are not high in fat or calories. Remember that fresh strawberries, juicy peaches and sweet cherries are among the delights of summer. And what tastes better after a two- or three-course dinner than a homemade fruit sorbet? The Plum Tart (page 215) or the Raspberry Meringue Torte (page 210) will take top billing on any dessert table.

We do have to be careful, however, with more conventional desserts. They can easily lead us astray when it comes to reducing the fat content in our diet. Most cookies are deadly, and mousses, chocolate desserts and whipped-cream confections are usually filled with fat. But don't despair: you don't have to deprive yourself forever of these dessert choices. Just be aware of their high fat content and savor them in moderation. Save them for special occasions, enjoy small servings and select lower-fat dishes for the rest of the meal.

To help you find a balance, many of the recipes in this section are for fruit desserts. They are low in fat yet full of flavor. They are also high in vitamins, minerals and fiber. You will find them a delight to both the eye and the palate! Enjoy!

---

### MAKE AHEAD
Sauce can be refrigerated in airtight container for up to one week.

**Nutrition Bonus**
One serving is a very high source of vitamin C and a high source of folacin and dietary fiber.

**PER SERVING:**
136 calories
3 g protein
1 g total fat
  trace saturated fat
  3 mg cholesterol
30 g carbohydrate
  5 g dietary fiber
32 mg sodium

## Blackberries with Orange Cream Sauce

*In Vancouver, where I grew up, blackberries grow wild, and it wasn't until I moved to Toronto that I realized what a high-priced treat they were. One of my favorite traditions was the annual Elliott family's blackberry expedition to Lulu Island (where the majority of Richmond is now). In just a few hours, we would fill large baskets with huge, juicy Himalayan blackberries — lots to eat raw, some for pies and the rest to make into jelly.*

| | | |
|---|---|---|
| 2 1/2 cups | fresh blackberries | 625 mL |
| 1 cup | Orange Cream Sauce (page 219) | 250 mL |

Wash blackberries. Remove any stems. Spoon sauce onto individual dessert plates and top with blackberries. Alternatively, spoon blackberries into stemmed glasses and pour sauce over top.

*Makes 4 servings.*

MAKE AHEAD

Sauce can be refrigerated in airtight container for up to three days.

*Nutrition Bonus*
One serving is a very high source of vitamin C (providing 103% of an adult's daily requirement).

PER SERVING:
77 calories
1 g protein
1 g total fat
  0 g saturated fat
  0 mg cholesterol
19 g carbohydrate
  4 g dietary fiber
3 mg sodium

# Strawberries with Raspberry Rhubarb Sauce

*For a truly low-fat dessert, dress up strawberries, cherries, plums, blackberries or other fresh seasonal fruit with a delicious fruit sauce.*

| | | |
|---|---|---|
| 4 cups | strawberries | 1 L |
| 1 1/2 cups | Raspberry Rhubarb Sauce (page 218) | 375 mL |

Wash, then hull strawberries. Divide among stemmed glasses. Pour Raspberry Rhubarb Sauce over top.

*Makes 6 servings.*

---

*Dessert Toppings*
Apple pie with Cheddar cheese, blueberry pie with vanilla ice cream, pumpkin pie with whipped cream — these innocent toppings can add large amounts of fats and calories.

Ice cream varies considerably in the amount of fat it contains; do read labels and choose ones with lower-fat content. Or eat smaller amounts of the higher-fat ice creams less frequently.

*Compare:*
Strawberries served with 1/4 cup (50 mL) whipped cream instead of with Raspberry Rhubarb Sauce have 10 g fat and 143 calories per serving.

**Fat Content of Commercial Dessert Toppings**

| | Grams fat per 1/4 cup (50 mL) |
|---|---|
| Whipping cream (unwhipped) | 21 |
| Whipped cream | 11 |
| Sour cream 14% fat | 8 |
| Whipped cream (pressurized) | 4 |
| Dream Whip with 2% milk | 2 |
| | Grams fat per 1/2 cup (125 mL) |
| Ice cream (vanilla, 16% fat) | 12 |
| Ice cream (vanilla, 10% fat) | 7 |
| Frozen yogurt (avg.) | 3 |
| Ice cream (vanilla, 1% fat) | 1 |
| | Grams fat per 1 oz/28 g (2 tbsp/25 mL) |
| Mascarpone cheese | 13 |
| Cheddar cheese | 10 |
| Cream cheese (35% b.f.) | 10 |
| Quark (7% b.f.) | 2 |

**Fat Content of Dessert Sauces from this book**

| | Grams fat per 1/4 cup (50 mL) |
|---|---|
| Custard Sauce (page 210) | 2.2 |
| Raspberry Rhubarb Sauce (page 218) | 1.0 |
| Easy Chocolate Sauce (page 219) | 0.5 |
| Orange Cream Sauce (page 219) | 0.2 |
| Raspberry or Strawberry Coulis (page 199) | 0.1 |
| Sherry Orange Sauce (page 204) | 0.1 |

**MAKE AHEAD**

Sauce can be refrigerated in airtight container for up to two days.

# Peaches with Raspberry Yogurt Sauce

*You can use fresh or frozen raspberries or strawberries in this sauce. In fact, it's truly delicious over any fresh fruit.*

| 4 | fresh ripe peaches | 4 |
|---|---|---|
|  | Fresh raspberries or mint leaves |  |

| | *Raspberry Yogurt Sauce:* | |
|---|---|---|
| 1 cup | frozen unsweetened raspberries | 250 mL |
| 1/2 cup | plain yogurt | 125 mL |
| 2 tbsp | (approx) granulated sugar or liquid honey | 25 mL |

Raspberries are high in dietary fiber.

**Raspberry Yogurt Sauce:** In food processor or blender, process raspberries, yogurt and sugar until smooth. Add extra sugar to taste. Refrigerate.

Peel peaches (blanch in boiling water to make peeling easier). Slice and spoon into individual dishes. Spoon sauce over top. (Or spoon sauce onto plates; arrange peaches on top.) Garnish with fresh raspberries or mint.

*Makes 4 servings.*

**PER SERVING:**
96 calories
2 g protein
1 g total fat
  trace saturated fat
  2 mg cholesterol
22 g carbohydrate
  3 g dietary fiber
21 mg sodium

**MAKE AHEAD**

Pears can be poached, cooled in liquid, covered and refrigerated for up to two days. Sauce can be refrigerated in airtight container for up to two weeks.

Poached fruit can be served in the poaching liquid. Remove cooled fruit from liquid and strain liquid. Boil poaching liquid until reduced to 1 cup (250 mL); let cool, then serve over poached fruit.

# Poached Pears with Chocolate Sauce

*Many other fruits, such as peaches, plums, apricots and apples, can also be poached. Serve them with Easy Chocolate Sauce or one of the other fruit dessert sauces in this book, such as Raspberry Coulis (page 199).*

| | | |
|---|---|---|
| 3 cups | water | 750 mL |
| 1/2 cup | granulated sugar | 125 mL |
| | Grated rind and juice of 1 lemon | |
| 1 | vanilla bean and/or cinnamon stick | 1 |
| 4 | pears | 4 |
| 1/2 cup | Easy Chocolate Sauce (page 219) | 125 mL |

In large saucepan, combine water, sugar, lemon rind and juice, vanilla bean and/or cinnamon stick; bring to boil, stirring until sugar is dissolved.

Peel, halve and core pears; add to boiling syrup. (Pears should be covered in liquid; if not, double the amount of poaching liquid or poach in batches.) Reduce heat to medium-low and simmer gently for 15 to 20 minutes or until pears are almost tender (time will vary depending on type and ripeness; remember, pears will continue to cook while cooling). Remove from heat and let cool in liquid.

Drain pears thoroughly and pat dry on paper towels. Arrange on individual plates. Drizzle with Easy Chocolate Sauce. Serve at room temperature.

*Makes 8 small servings.*

**PER SMALL SERVING:**
134 calories
1 g protein
1 g total fat
  trace saturated fat
  0 mg cholesterol
34 g carbohydrate
  3 g dietary fiber
27 mg sodium

**MAKE AHEAD**

Sorbet can frozen for up to one month.

# Raspberry Sorbet with Strawberry Coulis

*Coulis is a purée of fruits or vegetables used as a sauce and makes the base for a pretty dessert for summer. Don't strain the raspberry mixture; the seeds are an excellent source of fiber. This looks very attractive when different kinds of sorbets are served on each plate and garnished with fresh raspberries or other fresh fruits.*

| | | |
|---|---|---|
| 1 | pkg (300 g) frozen unsweetened raspberries | 1 |
| 3/4 cup | hot water | 175 mL |
| 1/2 cup | granulated sugar | 125 mL |
| 1 cup | Strawberry Coulis (page 199) | 250 mL |

*Nutrition Bonus*

One serving is a very high source of vitamin C.

If unsweetened raspberries are unavailable, use one package (425 g) frozen raspberries in light syrup mixed with 1 tbsp (15 mL) lemon juice and 3/4 cup (175 mL) water.

In food processor, purée raspberries. Stir hot water and sugar until sugar dissolves; add to raspberries and process to mix.

*Freezing Instructions:*

**Method 1** - Ice-Cream Machine: Follow manufacturer's instructions.
**Method 2** - Food Processor: Freeze in shallow metal pan or bowl until almost firm. Break up mixture and process in food processor until hard, smooth slush. Pour into airtight container and freeze until firm, about 1 hour.
**Method 3** - Hand Method: Freeze in shallow metal pan or covered bowl until almost firm, about 3 hours. Beat by hand or electric mixer just until smooth and slushy. Pour into airtight container and freeze until firm, about 1 hour.
**To Serve:** Sorbet should not be rock-hard. Transfer to refrigerator 15 to 30 minutes before serving or process in food processor. Spoon into individual dishes or stemmed glasses. Pour Strawberry Coulis over top. (Or spoon sauce onto dessert plates; top with a scoop of sorbet.)

*Makes 6 servings.*

**PER SERVING:**
129 calories
1 g protein
trace total fat
   0 g saturated fat
   0 mg cholesterol
33 g carbohydrate
   3 g dietary fiber
2 mg sodium

**MAKE AHEAD**

Sorbet can be frozen for up to one month.

*Nutrition Bonus*
One serving is a very high source of vitamin C (providing 93% of an adult's daily requirement).

**PER SERVING:**
129 calories
1 g protein
trace total fat
  0 g saturated fat
  0 mg cholesterol
33 g carbohydrate
  2 g dietary fiber
2 mg sodium

# Fresh Strawberry Sorbet

*Fresh ripe strawberries make a delicious easy-to-make sorbet. Serve with other fruit ices or sorbets and fresh fruit, or with Orange Cream Sauce (page 219).*

| | | |
|---|---|---|
| 1 cup | granulated sugar | 250 mL |
| 1 cup | water | 250 mL |
| 4 cups | strawberries, washed and hulled | 1 L |
| | Juice of 2 oranges | |
| | Juice of 1 lemon | |
| | Unhulled strawberries | |

In saucepan, bring sugar and water to boil, stirring to dissolve sugar; boil for 2 minutes. Let cool. In food processor or blender, purée strawberries. Add sugar, syrup, orange juice and lemon juice; mix to combine.

Freeze and serve according to instructions in Raspberry Sorbet (page 198). Garnish each serving with strawberries.

*Makes 8 servings.*

**MAKE AHEAD**

Coulis can be refrigerated in airtight container for up to three days.

**PER 1/4 CUP:**
66 calories
trace protein
trace total fat
  0 g saturated fat
  0 mg cholesterol
17 g carbohydrate
  3 g dietary fiber
1 mg sodium

# Raspberry or Strawberry Coulis

In blender or food processor, purée 1 package (300 g) frozen raspberries or strawberries. If using unsweetened berries, add icing sugar to taste.

*Makes about 1 cup (250 mL) sauce.*

MAKE AHEAD

Sorbet can be frozen for up to one month.

# Apple Cinnamon Sorbet with Raspberry Coulis

*The sorbet for this light, colorful year-round dessert is full of flavor and is very good by itself or with Applesauce Raisin Spice Cake (page 191) or Pumpkin Raisin Muffins (page 177). Serve with fresh fruit such as grapes, sliced kiwifruit or strawberries, plus a fresh mint leaf.*

***Nutrition Bonus***
One serving is a very high source of vitamin C.

| | | |
|---|---|---|
| 1 cup | finely grated cored peeled apple | 250 mL |
| 2 tbsp | fresh lemon juice | 25 mL |
| 2 tbsp | Calvados or apple brandy (optional) | 25 mL |
| 1/2 tsp | cinnamon | 2 mL |
| 2 1/2 cups | water | 625 mL |
| 1 cup | granulated sugar | 250 mL |
| 2 1/2 cups | apple juice | 625 mL |
| 1 cup | Raspberry Coulis (page 199) | 250 mL |

In skillet, combine apple, lemon juice, Calvados (if using) and cinnamon; cook over medium heat, stirring, until apple is tender, about 3 minutes. In saucepan, bring water and sugar to boil; cook until sugar is dissolved. Remove from heat; stir in apple mixture and apple juice.

Freeze and serve according to instructions in Raspberry Sorbet (page 198). Serve drizzled with Raspberry Coulis.

*Makes 8 servings.*

PER SERVING:
176 calories
trace protein
trace total fat
  0 g saturated fat
  0 mg cholesterol
45 g carbohydrate
  2 g dietary fiber
6 mg sodium

MAKE AHEAD

Lemon Cream can be frozen for up to two weeks.

# Frozen Lemon Cream

*It's hard to tell that the base of this creamy dessert is yogurt. It's delicious on its own, but try it with a topping of fresh fruit such as strawberries, blueberries, peaches, bananas, papaya or kiwifruit.*

| | | |
|---|---|---:|
| 3 cups | low-fat yogurt | 750 mL |
| 3/4 cup | (approx) granulated sugar | 175 mL |
| 4 tsp | grated lemon rind (from 2 lemons) | 20 mL |
| 1/4 cup | fresh lemon juice | 50 mL |
| 2 tsp | vanilla | 10 mL |

In bowl, combine yogurt, sugar, lemon rind and juice and vanilla, mixing well. Add more sugar to taste. Freeze and serve according to instructions in Raspberry Sorbet (page 198).

*Makes 8 servings, about 1/2 cup (125 mL) each.*

*Nutrition Bonus*
One serving is a high source of calcium.

For a festive frozen dessert, use Frozen Lemon Cream as a filling between layers of Orange Sponge Cake (page 190) or sandwiched between Meringues (page 210), then freeze.

PER SERVING:
136 calories
5 g protein
1 g total fat
   1 g saturated fat
   6 mg cholesterol
26 g carbohydrate
   trace dietary fiber
64 mg sodium

**MAKE AHEAD**

Ice can be frozen for up to one month.

# Grapefruit Ice

*Fresh-squeezed grapefruit juice made into an ice is a delicious, refreshing dessert at any time of year. Arrange scoops of ice on individual plates with fresh grapefruit sections or other fresh fruit, or serve with cookies or squares.*

| 2 cups | granulated sugar | 500 mL |
|--------|------------------|--------|
| 2 cups | water | 500 mL |
| 6 | grapefruit | 6 |
| 1/4 cup | fresh lemon juice | 50 mL |

*Nutrition Bonus*
One serving is a very high source of vitamin C.

In saucepan, combine sugar and water, stirring to dissolve sugar. Bring to boil; boil for 5 minutes. Remove from heat. Grate rind from 1 of the grapefruits (grate only yellow part — white part is too bitter); stir into syrup. Let cool.

Squeeze juice from all grapefruit to measure 4 cups (1 L). Stir grapefruit juice and lemon juice into cool syrup.

Freeze and serve according to instructions in Raspberry Sorbet (page 198).

*Makes 12 servings.*

**PER SERVING:**
165 calories
trace protein
trace total fat
  0 g saturated fat
  0 mg cholesterol
42 g carbohydrate
  1 g dietary fiber
4 mg sodium

MAKE AHEAD

Sorbet can be frozen for up to two weeks.

# Lemon Sorbet

*This makes a light, refreshing no-fat dessert.*

| 2 cups | water | 500 mL |
|---|---|---|
| 1 cup | granulated sugar | 250 mL |
| | Grated rind and juice of 3 medium lemons | |

In saucepan, combine water, sugar, lemon rind and juice; bring to boil. Reduce heat and simmer for 5 minutes; let cool. Pour into metal pan and freeze until firm, at least 4 hours. Break frozen mixture into chunks; place in food processor and process until smooth. Or freeze according to page 198.

Spoon into airtight container; freeze until firm, 1 to 2 hours. To serve, place in refrigerator for 15 minutes or until slightly softened.

*Makes 5 servings.*

**PER SERVING:**
162 calories
trace protein
0 g total fat
 0 g saturated fat
 0 mg cholesterol
43 g carbohydrate
 trace dietary fiber
4 mg sodium

MAKE AHEAD

Yogurt Freeze can be frozen for up to two weeks.

# Yogurt Fruit Freeze

*This is a pleasure for dieters who are dessert lovers. It's also the perfect year-round treat for children. For kids, freeze in Popsicle containers after processing.*

| 2/3 cup | frozen orange juice concentrate (undiluted) | 150 mL |
|---|---|---|
| 2 | small bananas | 2 |
| 2 1/2 cups | plain yogurt | 625 mL |

In food processor or blender, process orange juice concentrate and bananas until smooth; stir in yogurt. (Or mash bananas and with electric mixer, beat in yogurt and orange juice concentrate until smooth.) Freeze and serve according to instructions in Raspberry Sorbet (page 198).

*Makes 8 servings.*

*Nutrition Bonus*
One serving is a very high source of vitamin C and a high source of folacin.

**PER SERVING:**
108 calories
5 g protein
1 g total fat
 1 g saturated fat
 5 mg cholesterol
20 g carbohydrate
 1 g dietary fiber
54 mg sodium

## MAKE AHEAD

Sauce can be covered and refrigerated for up to three days.

# Cantaloupe, Pear and Grapes with Sherry Orange Sauce

*This sauce is easy to make and keeps well in the refrigerator. Use any fresh fruit in season. Japanese pears, which look more like apples than pears, are available in the winter; they are very crisp and juicy and add a lot of crunch. Top this dessert with yogurt and brown sugar, or spoon over sherbet for another variation.*

| | | |
|---|---|---|
| 1 | cantaloupe | 1 |
| 1 | pear (Japanese or domestic), mango or papaya | 1 |
| 1 cup | red, green or black grapes | 250 mL |
| | *Sherry Orange Sauce:* | |
| 1/2 cup | granulated sugar | 125 mL |
| 1 tbsp | cornstarch | 15 mL |
| 1 tbsp | grated orange rind | 15 mL |
| 1/2 cup | orange juice | 125 mL |
| 1/2 cup | medium to dry sherry | 125 mL |
| 1 tbsp | fresh lemon juice | 15 mL |

**Nutrition Bonus**
One serving is a very high source of vitamin C (providing 85% of an adult's daily requirement) and a very high source of vitamin A.

Cut cantaloupe in half; discard seeds. Cut flesh into cubes or balls. Cut unpeeled pear into cubes (if using mango or papaya, peel and cut flesh into cubes). Cut grapes in half if large and remove any seeds. Combine fruit and spoon into stemmed wine or sherbet glasses.

**Sherry Orange Sauce:** In small saucepan, blend sugar with cornstarch; stir in orange rind and juice, sherry and lemon juice. Cook, stirring, over medium heat until sauce thickens, bubbles and becomes clear. Cook for 3 minutes, stirring constantly. Let cool. Spoon over fruit.

*Makes 6 servings.*

**PER SERVING:**
163 calories
1 g protein
1 g total fat
  trace saturated fat
  0 mg cholesterol
38 g carbohydrate
  2 g dietary fiber
11 mg sodium

# Melon with Blueberries

**MAKE AHEAD**

Fruit can be covered and refrigerated for up to four hours. Bring to room temperature before serving.

*This makes a quick refreshing dessert. Or try it as a first course or breakfast treat. Peaches, grapes, kiwifruit or other fresh fruit in season can be used instead of blueberries. If serving as a first course, omit the honey; arrange wedges of melon on individual salad plates, drizzle with lemon juice mixed with liqueur or lime juice, and garnish with blueberries.*

*Nutrition Bonus*
One serving is a very high source of vitamin C (providing 92% of an adult's daily requirement) and a high source of vitamin A and folacin.

| Half | cantaloupe | Half |
|---|---|---|
| Half | honeydew melon | Half |
| 2 cups | cubed seeded watermelon | 500 mL |
| 1 cup | blueberries | 250 mL |
| 2 tbsp | liquid honey | 25 mL |
| 2 tbsp | fresh lemon juice | 25 mL |
| 2 tbsp | melon or orange liqueur or sherry (optional) | 25 mL |
|  | Fresh mint leaves |  |

Cut flesh of cantaloupe and honeydew melon into cubes or balls. In glass serving bowl, combine cantaloupe, honeydew, watermelon and blueberries.

In small dish, combine honey and lemon juice; blend in liqueur (if using). Pour over melons; toss to mix. Serve in stemmed glasses and garnish with mint.

*Makes 6 servings.*

**PER SERVING:**
106 calories
1 g protein
1 g total fat
  0 g saturated fat
  0 mg cholesterol
27 g carbohydrate
  2 g dietary fiber
19 mg sodium

**MAKE AHEAD**

Applesauce can be refrigerated in airtight container for up to five days.

**Nutrition Bonus**
One serving is a high source of dietary fiber.

Serve this sauce with meats (especially pork) instead of gravy or other high-fat sauces, or as a dessert or breakfast fruit.

When making applesauce, add the sugar after the apples are cooked. If you add the sugar at the beginning, the apples will take longer to cook.

**Pear and Ginger Sauce**
Substitute pears for apples and ginger for cinnamon in Cinnamon Applesauce. Increase water to 1 cup (250 mL). Add sugar to taste. Serve over Apricot, Orange and Pecan Loaf (page 188).

# Cinnamon Applesauce

*Applesauce is so easy and quick to make, it isn't necessary to follow a recipe. Treat this one merely as a guide. The amount of sugar and cooking time will vary depending on the variety and ripeness of apples. To save time, don't peel or core apples; instead, pass cooked mixture through a food mill or sieve. If you want to keep the skin for more fiber and a chunky sauce or don't have a food mill, core the apples and chop coarsely; cook until apples are tender, then add sugar to taste. Grated lemon or orange rind or raisins can be added. Serve alone or with Applesauce Raisin Spice Cake (page 191).*

| 6 | apples (about 3 lb/1.5 kg) | 6 |
|---|---|---|
| 1/4 cup | water | 50 mL |
| 1 tbsp | fresh lemon juice | 15 mL |
| 3 tbsp | (approx) granulated sugar | 50 mL |
| 1 tsp | cinnamon | 5 mL |

Cut apples into quarters. In saucepan, combine apples, water and lemon juice; bring to boil. Reduce heat and simmer gently, uncovered and stirring often, until apples are tender, about 20 minutes.

Place food mill or sieve over mixing bowl. Pass apple mixture through food mill (skin and seeds will stay in top of mill). Add sugar and cinnamon to purée; stir to dissolve sugar. Taste and add more sugar if needed. (If sauce is too thin, return to saucepan and cook, stirring, over medium heat until thickened.)

*Makes 6 servings.*

**PER SERVING:**
126 calories
trace protein
1 g total fat
  trace saturated fat
  0 mg cholesterol
33 g carbohydrate
  4 g dietary fiber
1 mg sodium

MAKE AHEAD

Crisp can be covered and refrigerated for up to one day.

# Peach Blueberry Crisp

*It's hard to find a better-tasting fall dessert than this one. If you cook it in a microwave, it takes only 10 minutes.*

| | | |
|---|---|---|
| 6 cups | peeled, sliced fresh peaches | 1.5 L |
| 2 cups | blueberries | 500 mL |
| 1/3 cup | packed brown sugar | 75 mL |
| 2 tbsp | all-purpose flour | 25 mL |
| 2 tsp | cinnamon | 10 mL |

| | *Topping:* | |
|---|---|---|
| 1 cup | quick-cooking rolled oats | 250 mL |
| 1/3 cup | packed brown sugar | 75 mL |
| 1 tsp | cinnamon | 5 mL |
| 3 tbsp | butter, melted | 50 mL |

In 8-cup (2 L) baking dish, combine peaches and blueberries. Combine sugar, flour and cinnamon; add to fruit and toss to mix.

**Topping:** In small bowl, combine oats, sugar and cinnamon; drizzle with butter and toss to mix. Sprinkle over fruit mixture. Bake in 350°F (180°C) oven for 25 minutes, or microwave on High for 10 minutes, or until bubbling and fruit is barely tender. Serve warm or cold.

*Makes 8 servings.*

**PER SERVING:**
229 calories
3 g protein
5 g total fat
  3 g saturated fat
  12 mg cholesterol
46 g carbohydrate
  4 g dietary fiber
52 mg sodium

MAKE AHEAD

Meringue crust can be covered and stored in dry place at room temperature for up to six weeks. Assembled tart can be set aside for up to six hours.

# Lemon and Fresh Blueberry Tart

*Meringue on the bottom, lemon filling in the center and blueberries on the top make a luscious, amazingly low-fat dessert that's also lower in calories than a pie made with traditional pastry.*

### Meringue Crust:

| | | |
|---|---|---|
| 2 | egg whites | 2 |
| 1/2 cup | granulated sugar | 125 mL |
| 1/4 tsp | cornstarch | 1 mL |
| 1/2 tsp | vanilla | 2 mL |

### Lemon Filling:

| | | |
|---|---|---|
| 1/2 cup | granulated sugar | 125 mL |
| 5 tbsp | cornstarch | 75 mL |
| 1 1/2 cups | hot water | 375 mL |
| 2 | egg yolks | 2 |
| | Grated rind of 1 lemon and half a medium orange | |
| 1/3 cup | fresh lemon juice | 75 mL |

### Blueberry Topping:

| | | |
|---|---|---|
| 1/4 cup | granulated sugar | 50 mL |
| 2 tsp | cornstarch | 10 mL |
| 1/3 cup | water | 75 mL |
| 1 tsp | fresh lemon juice | 5 mL |
| 2 cups | fresh blueberries | 500 mL |

**Meringue Crust:** Line 8- or 9-inch (20 or 23 cm) pie plate with foil, dull side out. In medium bowl, beat egg whites until soft peaks form. Beat in sugar, 1 tbsp (15 mL) at a time, until stiff glossy peaks form. Beat in cornstarch, then vanilla. Spread into foil-lined pie plate, spreading meringue sides about 1/2 inch (1 cm) higher than pan. Bake in 275°F (140°C) oven for 1 hour. Reduce heat to 200°F (100°C); bake another 1 1/2 hours or until firm and dry. Let cool slightly on rack. While still warm, remove meringue from pie plate and peel off foil. Return meringue shell to pie plate.

PER SERVING:
186 calories
2 g protein
1 g total fat
  trace saturated fat
  55 mg cholesterol
43 g carbohydrate
  1 g dietary fiber
20 mg sodium

**Lemon Filling:** In small nonaluminum heavy saucepan, mix sugar with cornstarch. Stir in water and bring to boil over medium heat, stirring constantly. Reduce heat and boil gently for 3 minutes, stirring constantly.

In small bowl, beat egg yolks lightly; whisk in a little hot mixture, then slowly pour yolk mixture back into saucepan, stirring constantly. Cook over medium-low heat, stirring constantly, for 2 minutes. Remove from heat. Stir in lemon juice and grated lemon and orange rinds. Let cool slightly; pour into prepared pie shell.

**Blueberry Topping:** In heavy saucepan, combine sugar and cornstarch; stir in water and lemon juice. Cook, stirring, over medium heat until mixture thickens, comes to boil and becomes clear. Remove from heat. Add blueberries, stirring to coat well. Spoon over lemon filling. Refrigerate for 30 minutes before serving.

*Makes 8 servings.*

MAKE AHEAD

Meringues can be covered and stored in cool, dry place for up to six weeks. Custard can be covered and refrigerated for up to one day. Torte can be assembled and refrigerated for up to 1 1/2 hours before serving.

*Make-Ahead Summer Dinner*
Chilled Melon and Yogurt Soup (page 37)
Marinated Flank Steak (page 98)
Pasta Salad with Sweet Peppers and Dill (page 76)
Sliced tomatoes with basil
Whole-wheat buns
Raspberry Meringue Torte (this page)

*Strawberry Meringue Torte*
Prepare Raspberry Meringue Torte using strawberries. When berries are not in season, use 3 cups (750 mL) sliced peaches, bananas, kiwifruit, mangoes or other fresh fruit.

# Raspberry Meringue Torte

*Individually frozen raspberries are available in most supermarkets, making this torte a year-round treat. It's not as complicated as it looks. The meringues can be made well in advance, and the custard sauce early in the day, or even a day in advance; neither procedure takes very long. Use strawberries or other berries or fresh fruit when they are in season instead of raspberries.*

### Meringues:

| | | |
|---|---|---|
| 1 cup | granulated sugar | 250 mL |
| 1 tsp | cornstarch | 5 mL |
| 4 | egg whites | 4 |
| 1 tsp | vanilla | 5 mL |

### Custard Sauce:

| | | |
|---|---|---|
| 1/3 cup | granulated sugar | 75 mL |
| 3 tbsp | cornstarch | 50 mL |
| Pinch | salt | Pinch |
| 3 cups | milk | 750 mL |
| 4 | egg yolks | 4 |
| 3 tbsp | orange liqueur* | 50 mL |
| 2 tsp | vanilla | 10 mL |
| Pinch | grated nutmeg | Pinch |

### Fruit Layers:

| | | |
|---|---|---|
| 2 cups | blueberries | 500 mL |
| 2 cups | raspberries or strawberries | 500 mL |

**Meringues:** Line 2 baking sheets with foil, dull side up. Combine sugar and cornstarch; set aside. In large bowl, beat egg whites until soft peaks form; gradually beat in sugar mixture until stiff peaks form. Beat in vanilla. Spoon into two circles about 11 inches (28 cm) in diameter. Bake in upper third of 275°F (140°C) oven for 1 1/2 hours or until meringues are firm. While warm, carefully remove foil. (If foil is difficult to remove, meringues may not be cooked; return to 200°F (100°C) oven until foil can be removed.)

**PER SERVING:**
207 calories
5 g protein
3 g total fat
　1 g saturated fat
　91 mg cholesterol
40 g carbohydrate
　2 g dietary fiber
63 mg sodium


**CUSTARD SAUCE
PER 1/4 CUP:**
71 calories
3 g protein
2 g total fat
　1 g saturated fat
　70 mg cholesterol
10 g carbohydrate
　0 g dietary fiber
31 mg sodium

**Custard:** In nonaluminum saucepan or top of double boiler, combine sugar, cornstarch and salt; stir in milk. Cook, stirring constantly, over medium-low heat or simmering water until mixture thickens and comes to a simmer; cook for 5 minutes, stirring constantly.

In small bowl, beat egg yolks lightly; whisk in a little of hot mixture, then slowly pour yolk mixture back into saucepan, stirring constantly. Cook over low heat, stirring constantly, for about 2 minutes or until thickened slightly. Remove from heat. Stir in liqueur, vanilla and nutmeg; let cool.

**Fruit Layers:** Place one meringue on serving platter; spread with half of the custard. Arrange half of the blueberries and half of the raspberries over custard. Place second meringue on top; repeat with remaining custard and berries. Refrigerate until serving. To serve, cut into wedges.

*Makes 10 servings.*

*Instead of using an orange liqueur such as Grand Marnier, add 3 tbsp (50 mL) thawed orange juice concentrate plus 2 tbsp (25 mL) grated orange rind (rind from 2 medium oranges).

MAKE AHEAD

Crisp can be covered and refrigerated for up to one day.

# Pear Crisp with Ginger

*You'll enjoy the lemon and ginger flavors in this fall or winter dessert. The amount of juice will vary depending on the kind and size of pears used. Serve with Honey Lime Sauce (page 35).*

| | | |
|---|---|---|
| 8 | large pears, cored and sliced (about 12 cups/3 L) | 8 |
| 1 tsp | grated lemon rind | 5 mL |
| 2 tbsp | fresh lemon juice | 25 mL |
| 1 tbsp | grated fresh gingerroot (or 1 tsp/5 mL ground ginger) | 15 mL |
| 1/2 cup | granulated sugar | 125 mL |
| 1/4 cup | all-purpose flour | 50 mL |

| | *Topping:* | |
|---|---|---|
| 2/3 cup | rolled oats | 150 mL |
| 1/2 cup | packed brown sugar | 125 mL |
| 1/3 cup | whole-wheat flour | 75 mL |
| 1 tsp | cinnamon | 5 mL |
| 3 tbsp | butter, melted | 50 mL |

*Nutrition Bonus*
One serving is a high source of dietary fiber.

For extra calcium, add 1/4 cup (50 mL) powdered skim milk to the topping.

Recipe can be cut in half. Bake in 8-cup (2 L) dish.

In mixing bowl, toss pears with lemon rind and juice and ginger. Combine sugar and flour; sprinkle over pears and toss to mix. Spoon into lightly greased 12-cup (3 L) soufflé dish or baking dish.

**Topping:** Mix together oats, sugar, flour and cinnamon; drizzle with butter and toss to mix. Sprinkle over pear mixture.

Bake in 375°F (190°C) oven for 25 to 35 minutes or until bubbling and pears are tender. Serve hot or warm.

*Makes 10 servings.*

PER SERVING:
255 calories
2 g protein
5 g total fat
  2 g saturated fat
  9 mg cholesterol
55 g carbohydrate
  5 g dietary fiber
39 mg sodium

**MAKE AHEAD**

Clafouti can be set aside at room temperature for up to three hours. However, it's best served hot from the oven.

*Nutrition Bonus*
One serving is a high source of vitamin A.

*Apricot Raspberry Clafouti*
Arrange 1/2 cup (125 mL) fresh or frozen raspberries with apricots, sprinkle with sugar and continue as in recipe.

Instead of sprinkling top with icing sugar, sprinkle hot clafouti with 2 tbsp (25 mL) brown sugar and place under hot broiler for about 3 minutes or until dark golden.

# Apricot Clafouti

*Clafouti is a French baked-fruit custard dessert. It's easy to make with almost any kind of fruit besides apricots — cherries, plums, peaches, or whatever is available.*

| 4 cups | fresh apricots (or two 14 oz/398 mL cans, well drained) | 1 L |
|---|---|---|
| 1 tbsp | butter | 15 mL |
| 1/3 cup | granulated sugar | 75 mL |
| 3 | eggs | 3 |
| 1 1/3 cups | low-fat milk | 325 mL |
| 2/3 cup | all-purpose flour | 150 mL |
| 2 tsp | vanilla | 10 mL |
| 1 tsp | grated lemon rind | 5 mL |
| 1/2 tsp | cinnamon | 2 mL |
| | Icing sugar | |

Quarter and pit apricots. Grease 11-inch (27 cm) glass pie plate or large quiche dish with butter. Sprinkle with 1 tbsp (15 mL) of the granulated sugar. Arrange apricots, cut side down, in dish; sprinkle with 2 tbsp (25 mL) of the granulated sugar.

In mixing bowl, beat eggs with remaining sugar. Add milk, flour, vanilla, lemon rind and cinnamon; beat until smooth. (Or combine in food processor.) Pour over fruit.

Bake in 375°F (190°C) oven for 30 to 35 minutes or until top is browned and filling is set. Just before serving, sift icing sugar over top. Serve warm.

*Makes 8 servings.*

**PER SERVING:**
169 calories
6 g protein
4 g total fat
  2 g saturated fat
  86 mg cholesterol
27 g carbohydrate
  2 g dietary fiber
60 mg sodium

MAKE AHEAD

Cobbler can be set aside at room temperature for up to three hours.

# Old-Fashioned Peach Cobbler

*Make this delicious and comforting dessert in the summertime when peaches are juicy and plentiful.*

| | | |
|---|---|---|
| 1/2 cup | packed brown sugar | 125 mL |
| 2 tbsp | all-purpose flour | 25 mL |
| 1 tsp | grated lemon or orange rind (1 medium lemon) | 5 mL |
| 1/2 tsp | cinnamon | 2 mL |
| 4 cups | sliced peeled peaches* | 1 L |

| *Topping:* | | |
|---|---|---|
| 1 cup | all-purpose flour | 250 mL |
| 2 tbsp | granulated sugar | 25 mL |
| 1 tsp | baking powder | 5 mL |
| 1/4 tsp | baking soda | 1 mL |
| 1/4 tsp | salt | 1 mL |
| 2 tbsp | butter, chilled and cut in bits | 25 mL |
| 2/3 cup | buttermilk | 150 mL |

In bowl, combine sugar, flour, lemon rind and cinnamon. Add peaches; toss to mix. Spread in 8-cup (2 L) shallow glass baking dish; bake in 400°F (200°C) oven for 10 minutes.

**Topping:** In large bowl, combine flour, sugar, baking powder, baking soda and salt. Using fingers or 2 knives, cut in butter until size of small peas. With fork, stir in buttermilk until soft dough forms. Drop by spoonfuls in 8 evenly spaced mounds on hot fruit. Bake in 400°F (200°C) oven for 25 minutes or until top is golden.

*Makes 8 servings.*

*To make with canned peaches: use 3 cans (14 oz/398 mL each) peaches, thoroughly drained. If using frozen peaches, thaw completely and drain before using.

**PER SERVING:**
199 calories
3 g protein
3 g total fat
    2 g saturated fat
    9 mg cholesterol
41 g carbohydrate
    2 g dietary fiber
196 mg sodium

**MAKE AHEAD**

Tart can be set aside at room temperature for up to six hours.

# Plum Tart

*I love cooked plums in desserts and too often forget about how sweet, juicy and flavorful they are. Use any kind of plums; however, if they are quite ripe and sweet, reduce sugar to 3/4 cup (175 mL). This is the easiest and most fool-proof method possible of making pastry. Serve with Honey Lime Sauce (page 35).*

### Pastry:

| | | |
|---|---|---|
| 1 1/4 cups | all-purpose flour | 300 mL |
| 1/4 cup | butter | 50 mL |
| 2 tbsp | granulated sugar | 25 mL |
| 1 tsp | white vinegar | 5 mL |

### Filling:

| | | |
|---|---|---|
| 1 cup | granulated sugar | 250 mL |
| 1/4 cup | all-purpose flour | 50 mL |
| 1 tsp | cinnamon | 5 mL |
| | Grated rind and juice of 1 lemon | |
| 5 cups | quartered pitted fresh plums (about 2 lb/1 kg) | 1.25 L |

**Pastry:** In food processor, combine flour, butter, sugar and vinegar; process with on-off turns until mixture resembles oatmeal. Firmly and evenly pat mixture into bottom and slightly up sides of 9-inch (23 cm) flan pan or pie plate.

**Filling:** In bowl, combine sugar, flour, cinnamon and lemon rind. Add lemon juice and plums; toss to mix. Spoon evenly over pastry. Place flan pan on baking sheet; bake in 400°F (200°C) oven for 50 to 60 minutes or until filling is bubbling and plums are fork-tender. (It top browns too quickly, cover loosely with foil.) Let stand for at least 1 hour before serving.

*Makes 6 servings.*

**PER SERVING:**
405 calories
4 g protein
9 g total fat
 5 g saturated fat
 21 mg cholesterol
80 g carbohydrate
 3 g dietary fiber
79 mg sodium

**MAKE AHEAD**

Pie can be set aside for up to six hours.

# Rhubarb Crumb Pie

*My mom always made the best-tasting pies. This is one of her recipes that I love. A crumb topping reduces the amount of pastry needed. If you are using frozen rhubarb, be sure to thaw the rhubarb first so there won't be too much liquid.*

| | | |
|---|---|---|
| 1 1/4 cups | all-purpose flour | 300 mL |
| 1/2 tsp | salt | 2 mL |
| 1/4 cup | butter | 50 mL |
| 3 tbsp | ice water | 50 mL |

### Filling:

| | | |
|---|---|---|
| 1 cup | granulated sugar | 250 mL |
| 1/4 cup | all-purpose flour | 50 mL |
| | Grated rind of 1 medium orange or lemon | |
| 1 | egg, well beaten | 1 |
| 5 cups | sliced (fresh or thawed) rhubarb, cut in 1/2-inch (1 cm) pieces | 1.25 L |

### Topping:

| | | |
|---|---|---|
| 1/3 cup | packed brown sugar | 75 mL |
| 1/4 cup | quick-cooking rolled oats | 50 mL |
| 1/4 cup | whole-wheat flour | 50 mL |
| 1 tsp | cinnamon | 5 mL |
| 2 tbsp | butter, melted | 25 mL |

In mixing bowl, combine flour and salt. With pastry blender or 2 knives, cut in butter until consistency of oatmeal. Sprinkle with water; toss with fork to mix. Sprinkle evenly into 9-inch (23 cm) pie plate; press firmly over bottom and sides to create evenly thick pastry. Set aside.

**Filling:** Combine sugar, flour and orange rind; mix well. In another bowl, mix egg and rhubarb; add sugar mixture and stir to mix. Spoon into prepared pie shell.

**Topping:** In bowl, combine sugar, oats, flour and cinnamon; drizzle with butter, tossing to mix well. Sprinkle over filling. Bake in 400°F (200°C) oven for 45 to 60 minutes or until topping is golden brown and rhubarb is tender. (If top browns too quickly, cover loosely with foil after 30 minutes of baking.) Let stand for at least 1 hour before serving.

*Makes 8 servings.*

**Rhubarb Crisp with Oatmeal Topping**
Follow Rhubarb Crumb Pie but omit the pastry. Reduce flour in filling to 2 tbsp (25 mL) and omit egg; spoon into lightly greased 6-cup (1.5 L) baking dish. Sprinkle with topping. Bake in 375°F (190°C) oven for 40 to 50 minutes or until filling is bubbly and top is brown. Makes 6 servings.

**PER SERVING:**
343 calories
5 g protein
10 g total fat
 6 g saturated fat
 47 mg cholesterol
60 g carbohydrate
 3 g dietary fiber
246 mg sodium

MAKE AHEAD

Rhubarb can be covered and refrigerated for up to four days.

# Stewed Rhubarb

*Welcome spring with rhubarb. It's delicious cooked with sugar and orange and served for dessert with extra-thick sweetened yogurt or vanilla ice cream. Or enjoy it on its own for breakfast. Depending on whether you use frozen, hot house or home-grown rhubarb, the tartness will vary, so add more sugar if necessary.*

For a thicker sauce, stir 1 tbsp (15 mL) cornstarch into 2 tbsp (25 mL) orange juice; pour into hot sauce and cook, stirring, until mixture boils and thickens.

| | | |
|---|---|---|
| 1 lb | fresh or frozen rhubarb, cut in 3/4-inch (2 cm) pieces (3 cups/750 mL) | 500 g |
| 1/2 cup | (approx) granulated sugar | 125 mL |
| 1/2 cup | water | 125 mL |
| | Grated rind from half an orange | |

In nonaluminum saucepan, bring rhubarb, sugar and water to boil; reduce heat and simmer, uncovered, for about 10 minutes for fresh, 3 minutes for frozen, or until tender. Taste and add more sugar, if necessary.

*Makes 3 servings, about 1/2 cup (125 mL) each.*

**PER SERVING:**
157 calories
1 g protein
trace total fat
  0 g saturated fat
  0 mg cholesterol
39 g carbohydrate
  3 g dietary fiber
7 mg sodium

MAKE AHEAD

Sauce can be refrigerated in airtight container for up to three days.

# Raspberry Rhubarb Sauce

*This sauce has a delightful sweet-tart taste that's perfect over ice cream, fresh or frozen yogurt and sliced peaches or other fresh fruit.*

| | | |
|---|---|---|
| 2 1/2 cups | sliced (1/2 inch/1 cm thick) fresh or frozen rhubarb | 625 mL |
| 3/4 cup | water | 175 mL |
| 1/2 cup | granulated sugar | 125 mL |
| | Grated rind and juice of 1 lemon | |
| 2 cups | fresh raspberries (or 1 cup /250 mL thawed unsweetened raspberries*) | 500 mL |
| 1/4 tsp | cinnamon | 1 mL |

*Nutrition Bonus*
One serving is a high source of vitamin C.

*Frozen Lemon Cream with Raspberry Rhubarb Sauce*
Spoon alternate layers of Frozen Lemon Cream (page 201) and Raspberry Rhubarb Sauce into parfait glasses. Or pour sauce over Frozen Lemon Cream. Use about 1/4 cup (50 mL) sauce per person.

   In saucepan, combine rhubarb, water, sugar and lemon rind; bring to boil over medium heat. Reduce heat and simmer for 10 to 15 minutes or until tender. Remove from heat; stir in lemon juice, raspberries and cinnamon. Serve warm or cool.

*Makes about 3 cups (750 mL).*

*If measuring raspberries while frozen, use 2 cups (500 mL); if thawed, about 1 cup (250 mL).

| COMPARE: | |
|---|---|
| *2 tbsp (25 mL):* | **g fat** |
| • Orange Cream Sauce | 0.4 |
| • whipping cream | 10.0 |

PER 1/2 CUP:
97 calories
1 g protein
trace total fat
   0 g saturated fat
   0 mg cholesterol
24 g carbohydrate
   3 g dietary fiber
3 mg sodium

# Orange Cream Sauce

*Delicious over Lemon Sorbet (page 203) or with cake, this sauce also makes a creamy base for fresh fruit. For an attractive, light dessert, spread sauce over rimmed individual dessert plates and arrange three kinds of fresh fruit — strawberries, kiwifruit, sliced peaches, grapes or blackberries — artistically over the top.*

| | | |
|---|---|---|
| 1/4 cup | granulated sugar | 50 mL |
| 1 tbsp | frozen orange juice concentrate | 15 mL |
| | Grated rind of 1 orange | |
| 3/4 cup | plain or extra-thick yogurt | 175 mL |

In small mixing bowl, combine sugar, orange juice concentrate and rind; stir in yogurt, mixing well.
*Makes 1 cup (250 mL).*

**MAKE AHEAD**

Sauce can be refrigerated in airtight container for up to one week.

**Orange Cream Dressing**
Reduce sugar in Orange Cream Sauce to 2 tbsp (25 mL). Use with fruit salads.

**PER TBSP:**
22 calories
1 g protein
trace total fat
   trace saturated fat
   1 mg cholesterol
5 g carbohydrate
   trace dietary fiber
8 mg sodium

# Easy Chocolate Sauce

*Spoon this on ice cream, drizzle over bananas, pears or chocolate cake, or use as a dipping sauce for fresh fruit.*

| | | |
|---|---|---|
| 1 cup | unsweetened cocoa powder | 250 mL |
| 3/4 cup | granulated sugar | 175 mL |
| 3/4 cup | water | 175 mL |
| 1/2 cup | corn syrup | 125 mL |
| 1 tsp | vanilla | 5 mL |

In saucepan, combine cocoa and sugar; whisk in water and corn syrup. Bring to full boil over medium heat; boil for 2 minutes, stirring constantly. Remove from heat and stir in vanilla. Let cool (sauce will thicken upon cooling).
*Makes 2 cups (500 mL).*

**MAKE AHEAD**

Sauce can be refrigerated in airtight container for up to two weeks.

Cocoa powder is made from solid chocolate with the cocoa butter removed, therefore, it is much lower in fat than chocolate.
Choose chocolate recipes using cocoa powder instead of chocolate if other fat ingredients such as butter or oil are in comparatively similar amounts.

**Chocolate Milk**
Combine 2 tbsp (25 mL) Easy Chocolate Sauce with 3/4 cup (175 mL) milk. Serve hot or cold.

**PER TBSP:**
42 calories
trace protein
1 g total fat
   trace saturated fat
   0 mg cholesterol
10 g carbohydrate
   1 g dietary fiber
25 mg sodium

# Breakfasts

START YOUR DAY OFF RIGHT — WITH BREAKFAST! Here are some reasons why.
• Research has shown that the lack of morning fuel for children can affect their mental ability. Children who don't eat breakfast concentrate less than those who do. Children learn from example, so if you want them to eat breakfast, you should eat one yourself.
• If you eat breakfast, it is easier to maintain a healthy weight.
• Breakfast provides an easy way to satisfy some of the body's needs for fiber, vitamins and minerals in the form of cereal and fruits; if you don't eat breakfast, it is difficult to meet these daily requirements.

Breakfast-skippers can pick up nutrients at a morning coffee break if they choose the right foods — fresh fruit, bran muffins, whole-wheat bagels, yogurt, cottage cheese or light cream cheese. Avoid energy-only calories and high-fat items such as Danish pastries, doughnuts and too much butter. Spread cheese or peanut butter over a bagel rather than butter; these spreads have protein as well as fat.

Because we need fiber from grains as well as from fruits and vegetables, include both grains and fruit for breakfast. Try to also include a lower fat milk product. See page 225 for sample breakfast menus.

---

*Reducing Fat Content of Breakfasts*
- Instead of spreading butter or margarine over toast or pancakes, spread jam or maple syrup.
- Boil or poach eggs rather than fry them.
- Avoid bacon, Danish pastries and croissants.
- Consider nontraditional breakfast foods — leftover salad, rice, pasta or vegetable dishes. Soups and sandwiches can taste just as delicious in the morning as at noon or dinnertime.

---

## Make Ahead

Store in airtight container for up to two months.

**Nutrition Bonus**

One serving is a high source of iron and dietary fiber.

**Fall Brunch Menu**

Honeydew, cantaloupe and watermelon wedges with Honey-Lime Dip (page 35)
Eggs Florentine with Yogurt Hollandaise (pages 130 and 153)
Tomatoes Provençal (page 157)
Apricot, Orange and Pecan Loaf (page 188)
Fresh berries and sliced peaches with Raspberry Coulis (page 199)

**PER SERVING:**
139 calories
4 g protein
3 g total fat
  trace saturated fat
  0 mg cholesterol
29 g carbohydrate
  5 g dietary fiber
150 mg sodium

# Breakfast Bran-and-Fruit Mix

*With this mixture on your kitchen shelf, breakfast can be ready in a jiffy — just add sliced apples, peaches, blueberries, strawberries or banana, and top with yogurt or milk.*

| | | |
|---|---|---|
| 2 cups | bran flakes | 500 mL |
| 1 cup | All-Bran | 250 mL |
| 1/2 cup | sliced or chopped almonds, walnuts or pecans | 125 mL |
| 1/2 cup | chopped dried apricots | 125 mL |
| 1/2 cup | chopped prunes | 125 mL |
| 1/2 cup | raisins | 125 mL |

Combine bran flakes, All-Bran, almonds, apricots, prunes and raisins. Store in airtight container.

*Makes 10 servings, 1/2 cup (125 mL) each.*

**Nutrition Bonus**

One serving is a high source of calcium.

**PER SERVING:**
185 calories
6 g protein
2 g total fat
  1 g saturated fat
  5 mg cholesterol
41 g carbohydrate
  4 g dietary fiber
63 mg sodium

# Blender Breakfast

*Keep this in mind for days when you want breakfast on the run; it takes only a minute to make and is packed with nutrients.*

| | | |
|---|---|---|
| 1 | banana, peach or nectarine, peeled and cut in chunks | 1 |
| 1/2 cup | milk or plain yogurt | 125 mL |
| 1 tbsp | wheat bran | 15 mL |
| 1 tsp | liquid honey, granulated sugar or maple syrup (or more to taste) | 5 mL |

In blender or food processor, blend banana, milk, bran and honey until smooth. Pour into tall glass. Serve immediately.

*Makes 1 serving.*

MAKE AHEAD

Granola can be stored in airtight container for up to six weeks.

# Honey Raisin Granola

*This delicious, easy-to-make granola recipe is one of the few that doesn't use oil. It is much less expensive than store-bought and just as good. Serve with yogurt and fresh fruit.*

| 5 cups | quick-cooking rolled oats | 1.25 L |
|---|---|---|
| 1 cup | wheat bran | 250 mL |
| 1/2 cup | toasted wheat germ | 125 mL |
| 1/4 cup | chopped walnuts or almonds | 50 mL |
| 1/4 cup | each sesame seeds and sunflower seeds | 50 mL |
| 3/4 cup | liquid honey | 175 mL |
| 1 1/2 cups | raisins | 375 mL |

***Nutrition Bonus***
One serving is a high source of iron and dietary fiber.

In large bowl, combine oatmeal, bran, wheat germ, walnuts, sesame seeds and sunflower seeds; pour in honey, stirring to mix. Spread on 2 lightly greased baking sheets; squeeze together to form small clumps. Bake in 300°F (150°C) oven for 20 minutes or until golden brown, stirring often so granola will brown evenly. Stir in raisins. Let cool completely. Store in airtight containers.

*Makes 9 cups (2.25 L).*

**PER 1/2 CUP:**
226 calories
7 g protein
5 g total fat
   1 g saturated fat
   0 mg cholesterol
42 g carbohydrate
   6 g dietary fiber
5 mg sodium

## MAKE AHEAD

Best served immediately, but any leftover pancakes can be covered and refrigerated for up to two days or, layered between waxed paper, wrapped well and frozen up to two weeks. Reheat in toaster.

*Nutrition Bonus*
One serving is a high source of calcium.

For a restricted-fat diet, you can reduce the oil to 1 tbsp (15 mL), but pancakes will be slightly heavier in texture.

*Spring Brunch Menu*
Grapefruit Juice Spritzer (page 130)
Stewed Rhubarb (page 217)
Omelet à la Jardinière (page 131) or
Spinach and Zucchini Pie (page 139)
Asparagus with Orange Vinaigrette
(page 80)
Cinnamon Coffee Cake (page 189)
Fresh strawberries

*Summer Brunch Menu*
Broccoli Frittata (page 128)
Melon with Blueberries (page 205)
Olive and Rosemary Soda Bread
(page 181)
Refrigerator Applesauce-Spice Bran
Muffins (page 178)

**PER 2 PANCAKES:**
238 calories
7 g protein
7 g total fat
   1 g saturated fat
   39 mg cholesterol
39 g carbohydrate
   3 g dietary fiber
375 mg sodium

# Whole-Wheat Pancakes with Blueberries and Yogurt

*Use any fresh fruit in season as a topping for these feathery-light and tender pancakes. Peaches, strawberries and raspberries are delicious alternatives.*

| 3/4 cup | whole-wheat flour | 175 mL |
|---|---|---|
| 1/2 cup | all-purpose flour | 125 mL |
| 2 tbsp | granulated sugar | 25 mL |
| 1 tbsp | baking powder | 15 mL |
| 1/2 tsp | salt | 2 mL |
| 1 | egg, beaten | 1 |
| 1 1/4 cups | 1% milk | 300 mL |
| 2 tbsp | vegetable oil | 25 mL |

### Topping:

| 1/2 cup | low-fat yogurt | 125 mL |
|---|---|---|
| 2 tbsp | maple syrup | 25 mL |
| 2 cups | blueberries | 500 mL |

In mixing bowl, combine whole-wheat and all-purpose flours, sugar, baking powder and salt, stirring to mix. Pour in egg, milk and oil; stir just until dry ingredients are wet. (Don't worry about lumps.)

Heat nonstick skillet over medium heat until hot (a drop of water will sizzle or dance). Lightly grease pan if desired. Drop batter into skillet from large spoon to form rounds. Cook until bubbles start to pop on surface and underside is golden brown; turn and brown other side.

**Topping:** Combine yogurt and maple syrup, mixing well. Spoon over each pancake and top with blueberries.

*Makes about twelve 4-inch (10 cm) pancakes, or 6 servings.*

**MAKE AHEAD**

Muesli can be covered and refrigerated for up to three days.

**Nutrition Bonus**
One serving is a high source of calcium and dietary fiber.

For other breakfast and brunch dishes, see:
Eggs Florentine (page 130)
Omelet à la Jardiniere (page 131)
Spinach and Zucchini Pie (page 139)
Broccoli Frittata (page 128)
Breads and Muffins (pages 177 to 181)
Cinnamon Coffee Cake (page 189)
Applesauce Raisin Spice Cake (page 191)

**Winter Brunch Menu**
Grapefruit sections, pear wedges and grapes or kiwifruit halves
Broccoli Frittata (page 128)
Arugula and Radicchio Salad with Balsamic Vinaigrette (page 62)
Pumpkin Raisin Muffins (page 177)
Apple Cinnamon Sorbet (page 200) with Raspberry Coulis (page 199)

# Swiss Fruit Muesli

*Different from the packaged muesli in Canadian stores, especially in its creamy texture, this delicious Swiss breakfast is a make-ahead-meal-in-one-dish. If "no time" or "not hungry" first thing in the morning is your excuse for skipping breakfast, pack this in individual yogurt containers and eat on the way to school or at work. Add fresh berries, peaches or other fruits in season.*

| | | |
|---|---|---|
| 1/2 cup | rolled oats | 125 mL |
| 1/2 cup | hot water | 125 mL |
| 1 cup | plain yogurt | 250 mL |
| 1/4 cup | granulated sugar | 50 mL |
| 1/4 cup | raisins or chopped dried apricots | 50 mL |
| 2 tbsp | each wheat and oat bran | 25 mL |
| 1 | apple, cored and diced | 1 |

In bowl, combine oats and water; let stand for 10 minutes or until water is absorbed. Stir in yogurt, sugar, raisins, wheat bran, oat bran and apple.

*Makes 3 servings, about 3/4 cup (175 mL) each.*

**PER SERVING:**
251 calories
8 g protein
3 g total fat
  1 g saturated fat
  5 mg cholesterol
53 g carbohydrate
  5 g dietary fiber
61 mg sodium

## Breakfast Menus

Fresh fruit
Whole-grain cereal
Whole-wheat toast
Yogurt or thin slice of part-skim cheese
Milk

Cantaloupe wedges
Bran flakes
Whole-wheat toast
Yogurt

Fresh orange wedges
Whole-wheat English muffin
Poached egg
Milk
Coffee

Fresh fruit (melon, apple or berries) topped with yogurt, and sprinkled with cinnamon, sugar and wheat germ
Milk

Whole-wheat pita bread filled with cottage cheese and raisins
Orange juice
Milk

Hot oatmeal with milk
Half grapefruit
Whole-wheat toast
Milk

Whole-wheat toast spread with cottage cheese and topped with freshly grated nutmeg and fresh blueberries or other fruit
Milk

Swiss Fruit Muesli
(page 224)
Yogurt and sliced peaches or papaya

## Quick Breakfast Menus

Orange juice
Granola (page 222) (made with bran) topped with yogurt and fresh strawberries
Milk

Honeydew melon with blueberries
Whole-wheat English muffin with melted mozzarella cheese
Milk

Orange or apple juice
Breakfast Bran-and-Fruit Mix (page 221)
Milk

Refrigerator Bran Muffin (page 178)
Tomato juice
Blender Breakfast (page 221)
Milk

## Weekend Breakfast Menus

Whole-Wheat Pancakes with Blueberries and Yogurt (page 223)
Sliced mango with grapefruit sections

Fresh fruit or stewed figs
Poached eggs on whole-wheat toast
English muffins
Tomatoes Provençal (page 157)
Coffee

Melon with Blueberries (page 205)
Broccoli Frittata (page 128)
Pumpkin Raisin Muffins (page 177)
Milk

## APPENDIX A: What Is your BMI?
### To determine your BMI:

- Find your height in feet/inches or centimeters along the bottom or top of the chart. At this point, draw a line from the top to the bottom of the chart.
- Find your weight in pounds or kilograms along the sides of the chart. Draw a line across the chart.
- Mark an "X" where the two lines cross. Note the BMI range that the X is within.

### How does your weight rate?

#### BMI less than 20 (lines cross below the dotted area)

You are thin! If you have always been this thin, your weight is probably okay. But don't let yourself get any thinner. If you have dieted and exercised to get this thin, then this isn't a healthy weight for you. Do not try to lose any more weight. Allow yourself to gain some weight back by following *Canada's Guidelines for Healthy Eating*.

#### BMI between 20 and 25 (lines cross in the dotted area)

Congratulations! Keep up the good work. Your challenge is to maintain this healthy weight for life. To do this, focus on healthy eating and regular physical activity.

#### BMI 25 to 27 (lines cross just above the dotted area)

Time for action! You aren't overweight yet... but you're headed in that direction. Think of yourself as borderline right now. What should you do? Don't starve yourself. Focus on becoming more physically active and establishing a healthy eating pattern as described in this cookbook.

#### BMI over 27 (lines cross above the dotted line)

You are overweight and it's probably no surprise to you. You are at greater risk for a variety of health problems including heart disease, diabetes, arthritis and cancer. Return to Guideline # 4 page 8 for some advice on how to lose weight by becoming more physically active and following a lower-calorie healthy eating pattern.

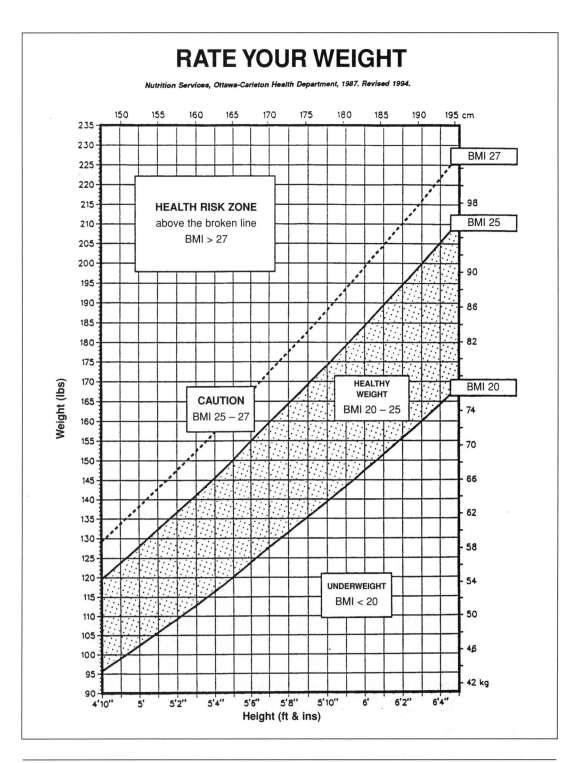

Developed by the Ottawa-Carleton Health Department, 1987. Revised 1994. Printed with permission. Nutrition Services, Ottawa-Carleton Health Department.

# APPENDIX B: Fat and Calorie Content of Meat, Fish and Poultry

| Type and/or cut (Portion: 3 1/2 oz (100g)) | Grams fat | Calories |
|---|---|---|
| **Beef (TRIMMED—*1/4", removed after cooking)** | | |
| Cross rib roast,* lean only, braised | 11 | 251 |
| Prime rib roast, lean only, roasted | 11 | 220 |
| Rump roast, lean only, roasted | 8 | 199 |
| Brisket,* lean only, braised | 13 | 242 |
| Flank steak, lean + fat, braised | 10 | 237 |
| T-bone steak, lean only, broiled | 9 | 198 |
| Round steak, inside, lean only, broiled | 4 | 163 |
| Sirloin steak,* lean only, broiled | 7 | 186 |
| Tenderloin,* broiled | 9 | 199 |
| Ground beef, extra lean, pan fried | 10 | 220 |
| Ground beef, lean, broiled, well done | 15 | 252 |
| Ground beef, regular, broiled, well done | 22 | 304 |
| Veal, loin roast, lean only | 7 | 175 |
| | | |
| **Pork (TRIMMED)** | | |
| Ham, roasted, lean only | 6 | 157 |
| Pork loin chop, lean only, broiled | 8 | 202 |
| Pork loin roast, lean only | 9 | 199 |
| Pork loin back ribs, broiled, lean only | 15 | 258 |
| Spareribs, back, lean + fat, roasted | 30 | 370 |
| Spareribs, side, lean + fat | 22 | 317 |
| Bacon, back, grilled | 8 | 185 |
| Bacon, side | 49 | 576 |
| Bacon, back, 4 slices (93g), fried crisp | 8 | 172 |
| Bacon, side, 4 slices (25g), fried crisp | 12 | 144 |
| | | |
| **Lamb (New Zealand) (TRIMMED)** | | |
| Lamb shoulder, lean only, braised | 16 | 285 |
| Lamb leg, roasted, lean only | 7 | 181 |
| Lamb loin chop, broiled, lean only | 8 | 199 |

**Poultry**

| | | |
|---|---|---|
| Chicken wing with skin, roasted | 19 | 290 |
| Chicken breast without skin, roasted | 2 | 159 |
| Chicken, dark meat without skin, roasted | 10 | 205 |
| Chicken, ground, lean (less than 17% fat by weight) | 12.4 | 204 |
| Turkey, breast without skin, roasted | 3 | 146 |
| Turkey, dark meat without skin, roasted | 7 | 173 |
| Duck, without skin, roasted | 11 | 201 |
| Goose, without skin, roasted | 13 | 238 |

**Processed Meats**

| | | |
|---|---|---|
| Beef wiener (1), hot dog (37g) | 8 | 103 |
| Beef & Pork wiener (1), hot dog (37g) | 7 | 106 |
| Chicken wiener (1), (37g) | 7 | 92 |
| Bologna, pork, 2 slices (60g) | 12 | 148 |
| Salami, beef, 2 slices (60g) | 12 | 134 |
| Sausage (1), pork (68g) | 14 | 182 |

**Fish, cooked with no added fat, skinless**

| | | |
|---|---|---|
| Cod | 1 | 105 |
| Haddock | 1 | 112 |
| Halibut | 3 | 140 |
| Mackerel* | 18 | 262 |
| Orange Roughy | 1 | 89 |
| Salmon, fresh, Atlantic, farmed* | 12 | 206 |
| Salmon, fresh, Atlantic, wild* | 8 | 182 |
| Salmon, pink, canned* | 7 | 136 |
| Salmon, sockeye, canned* | 10 | 163 |
| Shrimp, boiled | 1 | 99 |
| Sole fillets | 2 | 117 |
| Trout, rainbow, farmed | 7 | 169 |
| Tuna, light in water, canned | 1 | 116 |
| Tuna, light, in oil, canned, drained | 8 | 198 |

*high in Omega 3 Fatty Acids

# APPENDIX C

*Dishes that are a Very High Source or a
High Source of Dietary Fiber*

**VERY HIGH SOURCES OF FIBER (MORE THAN 6 G
OF DIETARY FIBER PER SERVING)**

**Soups**
Bean and Vegetable Soup
Easy Tomato-Bean Chowder

**Salads**
Bermuda Bean Salad
Spinach Supper Salad
White Kidney Bean Salad

**Meat**
Stuffed Peppers with Tomato Basil Sauce
Tex-Mex Chili

**Vegetarian and Grain Dishes**
Bulgur Wheat, Tofu and Sweet Peppers
Deep-Dish Vegetable Pizza
Fettuccine with Fresh Tomatoes and Basil
Moroccan Vegetable Couscous
Pasta with Broccoli, Mushrooms,
Cauliflower in Basil-Cream Sauce
Tuscan White Kidney Beans and Tomato

**Vegetables**
Parsnip Purée

**Muffins, Breads, Cakes and Cookies**
Whole-Wheat Pizza Dough

**HIGH SOURCES OF FIBER (MORE THAN 4 AND
LESS THAN 6 G OF DIETARY FIBER)**

**Soups**
Italian Vegetable Soup with Pesto
Split Pea Soup

**Salads**
Artichoke Tomato Salad
Bulgur Salad with Peas and Onions
Mediterranean Lentil Salad
Melon and Bean Salad
Tabbouleh

**Meat**
Beef and Vegetable Stew
Chinese Pork and Vegetables

**Fish and Seafood**
Linguine with Shrimp and Tomato
Scallops and Shrimp in Thai Lemon Cream
Sole Poached with Tomatoes, Artichokes
and Mushrooms

**Vegetarian and Grain Dishes**
Barley and Parsley Pilaf
Bulgur Pilaf with Fresh Basil, Mushrooms
and Tomatoes
Creamy Penne with Tomatoes
Winter Vegetable Stew

**Vegetables**
Orange Sherried Sweet Potatoes

**Muffins, Breads, Cakes and Cookies**
Banana Apricot Bran Muffins
Refrigerator Applesauce-Spice Bran
Muffins

**Desserts**
Blackberries with Orange Cream Sauce
Cinnamon Applesauce
Pear Crisp with Ginger

**Breakfast**
Breakfast Bran-and-Fruit Mix
Honey Granola
Swiss Fruit Muesli

# References and Resources

*Canada's Food Guide to Healthy Eating*. Health Canada. Health Promotion Directorate, 1992.

Harvard Report on Cancer Prevention:Volume 1: "Causes of Human Cancers. Cancer Causes and Control." Volume 7 Supplement November 1996.

Thune, I., and A.S. Furberg. "Physical activity and cancer risk: dose-response and cancer, all sites and site-specific." *Medicine & Science in Sports & Exercise*: 530-550, 2001.

World Cancer Research Fund. *Food, Nutrition and the Prevention of Cancer: a global perspective*. American Institute for Cancer Research, Washington, 1997.

## IF YOU HAVE CANCER

The foods that you eat play an important role in your experience with cancer. Being well nourished can help give you energy, strength and stamina before, during and after treatment, and contribute to your sense of well-being.

The Canadian Cancer Society publishes resources that can help people with cancer find answers to common nutrition questions.

### ADDITIONAL RESOURCE MATERIALS (AVAILABLE FROM YOUR UNIT OFFICE)
- Nutrition Guide for People with Cancer
- Good Nutrition: A Resource for Families of Children with Cancer
- Chemotherapy and You: A Guide to Self-Help during Treatment
- Radiation Therapy and You: A Guide to Self-Help during Treatment

The Canadian Cancer Society is a national, community-based organization of volunteers whose mission is the eradication of cancer and the enhancement of the quality of life of people living with cancer.

The Society achieves its mission by funding research, advocating for healthy public policy, promoting healthy lifestyles, providing comprehensive cancer information and supporting people living with cancer.

When you want to know more about cancer or services in your community, call the Canadian Cancer Society at 1 888 939-3333 or visit www.cancer.ca.

# Canadian Cancer Society Division Offices

**British Columbia/Yukon Division**
Canadian Cancer Society
565 West 10th Avenue
Vancouver, BC
V5Z 4J4
(604) 872-4400

**Alberta and Northwest Territories Division**
Canadian Cancer Society
# 200, 2424, 4th. Street S.W.
Calgary, AB
T2S 2T4
(403) 228-4487

**Saskatchewan Division**
Canadian Cancer Society
1910 McIntyre Street
Regina, SK
S4P 2R3
(306) 757-4260

**Manitoba Division**
Canadian Cancer Society
193 Sherbrook Street
Winnipeg, MB
R3C 2B7
(204) 774-7483

**Ontario Division**
Canadian Cancer Society
1639 Yonge Street
Toronto, ON
M4T 2W6
(416) 488-5400

**Québec Division**
Canadian Cancer Society
5151, boul. l'Assomption
Montréal, QC
H1T 4A9
(514) 255-5151

**New Brunswick Division**
Canadian Cancer Society
P.O. Box 2089, 133 Prince William Street
Saint John, NB
E2L 3T5
(506) 634-6272

**Nova Scotia Division**
Canadian Cancer Society
Suite 1, 5826 South Street
Halifax, NS
B3H 1S6
(902) 423-6183

**Newfoundland and Labrador Division**
Canadian Cancer Society
P.O. Box 8921
Crosbie Building, 2nd Floor
Crosbie Place, Crosbie Road
St. John's, NF
A1B 3R9
(709) 753-6520

**Prince Edward Island Division**
Canadian Cancer Society
Suite 1, 1 Rochford Street
Charlottetown, PEI
C1A 9L2
(902) 566-4007

# Index